CONQUE

FROM STEPPE TO EMPIRE

THE RISE AND FALL OF
GENGHIS KHAN, ATTILA THE HUN,
ALEXANDER THE GREAT, AND NAPOLEON BONAPARTE

BOOK 1
GENGHIS KHAN: THE RISE OF A CONQUEROR
BOOK 2
ATTILA THE HUN: FROM BARBARIAN TO LEGEND
BOOK 3
ALEXANDER THE GREAT: FROM MACEDONIA TO THE INDUS
BOOK 4
NAPOLEON BONAPARTE: FROM REVOLUTION TO EMPIRE

BY A.J. KINGSTON

Published by A. J. Kingston
Library of Congress Cataloging-in-Publication Data
ISBN 978-1-83938-319-9
Cover design by Rizzo

Disclaimer

The contents of this book are based on extensive research and the best available historical sources. However, the author and publisher make no claims, promises, or guarantees about the accuracy, completeness, or adequacy of the information contained herein. The information in this book is provided on an "as is" basis, and the author and publisher disclaim any and all liability for any errors, omissions, or inaccuracies in the information or for any actions taken in reliance on such information.

The opinions and views expressed in this book are those of the author and do not necessarily reflect the official policy or position of any organization or individual mentioned in this book. Any reference to specific people, places, or events is intended only to provide historical context and is not intended to defame or malign any group, individual, or entity.

The information in this book is intended for educational and entertainment purposes only. It is not intended to be a substitute for professional advice or judgment. Readers are encouraged to conduct their own research and to seek professional advice where appropriate.

Every effort has been made to obtain necessary permissions and acknowledgments for all images and other copyrighted material used in this book. Any errors or omissions in this regard are unintentional, and the author and publisher will correct them in future editions.

Join Our Productivity Group and Access your Bonus

If you're passionate about history books and want to connect with others who share your love of the subject, joining our Facebook group (search for "History Books by A.J.Kingston") can be a great way to do so. By joining a group dedicated to history books, you'll have the opportunity to connect with like-minded individuals, share your thoughts and ideas, and even discover new books that you might not have come across otherwise. You can also access your FREE BONUS once you joined our Facebook group called "History Books by A.J.Kingston".

One of the biggest advantages of joining our Facebook group is the sense of community it provides. You'll be able to interact with other history book enthusiasts, ask questions, and share your own knowledge and expertise. This can be especially valuable if you're a student or someone who is just starting to explore the world of history books.

If you love audiobooks, then joining our YouTube channel that offers free audiobooks on a weekly basis can be a great way to stay entertained and engaged. By subscribing to our channel, you'll have access to a range of audiobooks across different genres, all for free. Not only this is a great opportunity to enjoy some new audiobooks, but it's also a chance to discover new authors and titles that you might not have come across otherwise.

Lastly, don't forget to follow us on Facebook and YouTube by searching for A.J. Kingston.

Introduction

Welcome to Conquerors: From Steppe to Empire, a thrilling bundle of books that will take you on a journey through the lives of some of the world's greatest conquerors. In this collection, you will delve into the stories of four legendary figures who rose to power from humble beginnings, each with their own unique set of circumstances that propelled them to the heights of empire.

The first book, Genghis Khan: The Rise of a Conqueror, explores the remarkable story of the boy who would become one of the most feared and respected leaders in history. From his humble beginnings in the harsh wilderness of the Mongolian steppe to his eventual conquest of much of Asia, Genghis Khan's story is one of resilience, determination, and unrelenting ambition.

In Attila the Hun: From Barbarian to Legend, readers will discover the true story of the man who terrorized the Roman Empire. While history has painted Attila as a savage barbarian, this book reveals a more nuanced portrait of a leader who was both feared and respected by his enemies, and whose legacy still lives on today.

Alexander the Great: From Macedonia to the Indus is a gripping account of the young king who conquered much of the known world before his untimely death at the age of 33. From his early military campaigns to his legendary march into India, Alexander's story is one of unbridled ambition, strategic brilliance, and enduring legacy.

Finally, Napoleon Bonaparte: From Revolution to Empire tells the story of one of history's most enigmatic and ambitious leaders. From his early days as a Corsican soldier to his rise to power in post-revolutionary France, Napoleon's story is one of political intrigue, military conquests, and ultimate defeat.

Together, these four books offer a fascinating glimpse into the lives of some of history's greatest conquerors. From their humble beginnings to their eventual rise to power, each of these leaders changed the course of history in their own unique way. So, join us on this journey through time, and discover the remarkable stories of Genghis Khan, Attila the Hun, Alexander the Great, and Napoleon Bonaparte.

BOOK 1

GENGHIS KHAN
THE RISE OF A CONQUEROR

BY A.J. KINGSTON

Chapter 1 Early Life and Struggles

Genghis Khan, the founder and first emperor of the Mongol Empire, was born in the early thirteenth century on the vast grasslands of the Eurasian steppes. Little is known of his early years, but it is believed that he was born in the year 1162, to a noble family that was part of the Borjigin tribe. His father, Yesugei, was a chief of the tribe, and his mother, Hoelun, was a member of another prominent Mongol clan.

Genghis Khan's birth and early childhood occurred during a tumultuous period in the history of the steppes. The Mongols were a nomadic people, constantly on the move in search of grazing lands for their herds of sheep, horses, and cattle. They were also a people divided, with various tribes and clans competing for resources and power. In this context, Genghis Khan's family was relatively powerful and influential, but they were not immune to the dangers of the steppes.

According to legend, when Genghis Khan was only nine years old, his father was poisoned by the Tatars, a rival tribe. This event had a profound impact on the young boy, who was forced to flee with his mother and siblings to avoid retribution from the Tatars. They lived a life of hardship and struggle, constantly on the move and fighting for survival. It was during this time that Genghis Khan began to develop the skills that would make him a great leader and conqueror.

Despite the difficulties of his early years, Genghis Khan was blessed with a strong and resilient constitution, honed by the harsh realities of life on the steppes. He was known for his physical prowess and his ability to endure hardship, which would serve him well in his later military campaigns. He was also known for his intelligence and cunning, which he learned from his mother, a woman of great resourcefulness and determination.

As a child, Genghis Khan had little formal education, but he learned important skills from his family and community. He was taught to ride horses, hunt, and fight from a young age, and he quickly became proficient in these areas. He also learned the value of loyalty and discipline, as these were essential traits for survival on the steppes.

Despite his lack of formal education, Genghis Khan was a quick learner and had a keen mind for strategy and tactics. He was able to observe the movements of enemy forces and devise clever plans to outmaneuver them. He also had a gift for inspiring loyalty and courage in his followers, which would be essential to his success as a conqueror.

In summary, Genghis Khan's birth and childhood were marked by the challenges and hardships of life on the steppes. He was born into a powerful family, but one that was also vulnerable to the dangers of the nomadic lifestyle. Despite the difficulties he faced, Genghis Khan developed important skills and traits that would serve him well in his later life. His physical prowess, intelligence, and cunning, combined with his keen mind for strategy and tactics, would make him one of the most successful conquerors in world history.

The murder of Genghis Khan's father, Yesugei, was a turning point in the young nomad's life. Yesugei was a respected chief of the Borjigin clan, and his death left a power vacuum that would have profound consequences for his family and tribe.

According to legend, Yesugei was poisoned by members of a rival tribe while on a journey to arrange a marriage for his son. The motive for the murder is not entirely clear, but it may have been an act of revenge or a bid to eliminate a powerful rival. Whatever the reason, the murder of Yesugei was a traumatic event for Genghis Khan and his family, and it set the stage for a period of instability and uncertainty.

In the aftermath of his father's death, Genghis Khan and his family were forced to flee their traditional lands and seek refuge with other Mongol clans. This was a difficult and dangerous time for the young nomad, who was now a potential target for his father's enemies. He was also responsible for protecting his mother and siblings, a daunting task for a boy of his age.

Despite these challenges, Genghis Khan quickly established himself as a leader among his people. He was brave, resourceful, and determined, and he had a deep sense of loyalty to his family and tribe. He began to make strategic alliances with other Mongol clans, forging strong bonds of friendship and cooperation that would serve him well in the years to come.

However, Genghis Khan's early leadership was not without its setbacks. He suffered several defeats in battles against rival tribes, and he was even captured and enslaved by a group of Tartars at one point. These early losses were a humbling experience for Genghis Khan, but they also taught him important lessons about strategy, tactics, and the realities of life on the steppes.

Despite these setbacks, Genghis Khan was undeterred. He continued to build his power and influence, slowly but surely emerging as a major figure in Mongol society. He married and had children, and he began to establish his own clan within the Borjigin tribe. He also continued to forge alliances with other clans, working to build a network of support that would help him to achieve his goals.

The murder of his father and the early losses that Genghis Khan suffered were defining moments in his life. They tested his courage, resilience, and determination, and they set him on a path of leadership and conquest that would change the course of history. Genghis Khan would go on to become one of the greatest conquerors the world has ever seen, but he never forgot the lessons he learned in his early years on the steppes. They were the foundation upon which he built his empire, and they were the source of his strength and determination in the face of adversity.

Genghis Khan's early life was marked by hardship and danger, including a period of captivity and slavery that would shape his character and his approach to leadership.

According to legend, Genghis Khan was captured by a rival tribe when he was a young man, and he spent several years in slavery before he was able to escape. This experience was a traumatic one for Genghis Khan, who was forced to endure harsh conditions and brutal treatment at the hands of his captors.

During his captivity, Genghis Khan was forced to perform menial tasks and endure physical abuse. He was often hungry and cold, and he had little hope of escape. However, despite these hardships, Genghis Khan refused to give up. He remained determined and resourceful, using his wits and his strength to survive and eventually escape.

Genghis Khan's experiences as a slave taught him important lessons about perseverance, resilience, and the importance of self-reliance. He learned to adapt to difficult circumstances and to rely on his own skills and abilities to overcome adversity. These were qualities that would serve him well in his later life, as he faced even greater challenges and obstacles on his path to conquest and leadership.

In addition to his experiences as a slave, Genghis Khan also suffered other periods of captivity and confinement during his early years. He was imprisoned by a rival clan at one point, and he was even held captive by his own uncle for a time. These experiences were no doubt difficult for Genghis Khan, but they also helped to shape his character and his approach to leadership.

As a result of these experiences, Genghis Khan developed a deep sense of empathy and compassion for those who were suffering or oppressed. He understood firsthand the pain and suffering of captivity and slavery, and he was determined to create a society that was more just and equitable. This was a radical idea in a world where slavery and oppression were the norm, but Genghis Khan was a visionary leader who believed in the power of people to work together for the common good.

In summary, Genghis Khan's experiences as a captive and slave were defining moments in his life. They tested his character and his resilience, and they helped to shape his approach to leadership and his vision for a more just and equitable society. Despite the hardships he faced, Genghis Khan emerged from these experiences with a deep sense of empathy and compassion for his fellow humans, and a determination to create a better world. These were the qualities that would make him one of the most successful conquerors in history, and a leader whose legacy endures to this day.

The formation of Genghis Khan's personal army was a crucial step in his rise to power, and it marked the beginning of his conquests on the steppes of Central Asia.

Genghis Khan recognized that he needed a well-trained and disciplined force if he was to achieve his goals of unifying the Mongol tribes and expanding his territory. He began by recruiting men from his own clan and from other allied tribes, selecting only the strongest and most skilled warriors to serve in his personal army.

Under Genghis Khan's leadership, this army became a formidable force, renowned for its skill and discipline. Genghis Khan was a brilliant tactician and strategist, and he quickly established himself as a master of both offensive and defensive warfare.

His early military conquests were equally impressive. He led successful campaigns against rival tribes, capturing territories and expanding his sphere of influence. He was especially skilled at siege warfare, and he was able to defeat much larger armies through his innovative use of tactics and strategy.

One of Genghis Khan's most notable early conquests was the city of Yinchuan, which he captured in 1227. This was a major victory for the young conqueror, and it demonstrated the strength and effectiveness of his army. He went on to conquer other major cities and territories, including the Jin Dynasty in northern China and parts of Central Asia.

Throughout his early conquests, Genghis Khan was careful to establish a strong administration and governance system to ensure the stability and prosperity of the territories he conquered. He instituted laws and regulations to protect the rights and freedoms of his people, and he established a system of taxation and commerce that encouraged trade and economic growth.

Despite his early successes, Genghis Khan faced many challenges and setbacks on his path to conquest and unification. He suffered defeats and setbacks at the hands of rival tribes, and he faced resistance from those who were opposed to his vision of a unified Mongol state.

However, Genghis Khan was undeterred. He continued to build his army and his network of alliances, and he remained committed to his vision of a strong, unified Mongol state. He was a charismatic leader, inspiring loyalty and devotion in his followers, and he had a deep understanding of the politics and culture of the steppes.

In summary, the formation of Genghis Khan's personal army and his early military conquests were crucial steps in his rise to power. He recognized the importance of a well-trained and disciplined force, and he was able to leverage his skills as a tactician and strategist to achieve impressive victories on the battlefield. These early conquests established him as a major figure on the steppes, and they set the stage for his later conquests and the eventual creation of the Mongol Empire. Genghis Khan was a visionary leader who was able to inspire loyalty and devotion in his followers, and his legacy endures to this day as one of the greatest conquerors in history.

Chapter 2: Uniting the Mongol Tribes

Genghis Khan's vision of unifying the Mongol tribes was a driving force behind his early military conquests and his later campaigns of expansion. He recognized the importance of creating a unified Mongol state, and he developed a series of plans and strategies to achieve this goal.

One of Genghis Khan's early plans was to establish a network of alliances with other Mongol tribes. He recognized that he could not achieve his goals through military conquest alone, and he knew that he needed the support of other tribes if he was to create a unified Mongol state. He began by forging alliances with neighboring tribes, offering them protection and support in exchange for their loyalty and assistance in his military campaigns.

Genghis Khan was also a master of diplomacy, and he was able to negotiate treaties and agreements with other leaders and rulers. He recognized that he needed to build relationships with other powerful figures in order to achieve his goals, and he worked tirelessly to establish himself as a respected and influential leader.

Another key strategy employed by Genghis Khan was the creation of a unified legal and administrative system. He recognized that a unified Mongol state required a strong system of governance, and he set about establishing a series of laws and regulations to govern the behavior of his people. He also created a system of taxation and commerce, which helped to encourage economic growth and stability throughout the territories he conquered.

One of the most important aspects of Genghis Khan's vision of unification was his emphasis on religious tolerance and freedom. He recognized that different tribes and cultures had different beliefs and practices, and he was committed to creating a society that respected and celebrated these differences. He was especially tolerant of religious minorities, allowing them to practice their faith without fear of persecution or discrimination.

Perhaps most importantly, Genghis Khan's vision of unification was fueled by his commitment to creating a more just and equitable society. He recognized the importance of creating a society that was based on merit and skill, rather than on birth or social status. He encouraged education and the development of skills and talents, and he rewarded those who demonstrated excellence and dedication.

In summary, Genghis Khan's vision of unification was a powerful driving force behind his early military conquests and his later campaigns of expansion. He recognized the importance of creating a unified Mongol state, and he developed a series of plans and strategies to achieve this goal. He was a master of diplomacy, a skilled military tactician, and a visionary leader who was committed to creating a more just and equitable society. His legacy endures to this day, as one of the greatest conquerors and leaders in history.

Genghis Khan's diplomatic efforts were a crucial element in his strategy to unite the Mongol tribes and create a powerful, unified state. He recognized that he could not achieve his goals through military conquest alone, and he understood the importance of building relationships with other leaders and rulers in the region.

One of Genghis Khan's early diplomatic efforts was to send envoys to neighboring tribes, offering them protection and support in exchange for their loyalty and assistance in his military campaigns. He was able to build a network of alliances with other tribes, which provided him with crucial military and logistical support as he sought to expand his territory and influence.

In addition to his efforts to build alliances with neighboring tribes, Genghis Khan also established relationships with other powerful figures in the region. He was a master of diplomacy, and he was able to negotiate treaties and agreements with other leaders and rulers. He understood the importance of building relationships with other powerful figures in order to achieve his goals, and he worked tirelessly to establish himself as a respected and influential leader.

One of Genghis Khan's most notable diplomatic achievements was his relationship with the Khwarazmian Empire, a powerful state that controlled much of Central Asia. In the early 13th century, tensions between the Mongols and the Khwarazmians had been building for some time, and the two sides were on the brink of war.

However, Genghis Khan recognized the importance of avoiding conflict, and he sent a series of envoys to the Khwarazmian emperor, requesting that the two sides negotiate a peace settlement. Despite initial resistance, the Khwarazmian emperor eventually agreed to the peace settlement, and the two sides were able to avoid a costly and destructive war.

Genghis Khan's diplomatic efforts were not limited to his relationships with other leaders and rulers. He also recognized the importance of building relationships with the people he conquered, and he worked tirelessly to establish himself as a respected and admired figure among his subjects.

One of the ways in which he did this was by demonstrating a deep respect for the cultures and beliefs of the people he conquered. He was tolerant of religious minorities, allowing them to practice their faith without fear of persecution or discrimination. He was also known for his generosity and his willingness to share the spoils of war with his subjects.

In summary, Genghis Khan's diplomatic efforts were a crucial element in his strategy to unite the Mongol tribes and create a powerful, unified state. He recognized the importance of building alliances with other tribes and leaders, and he worked tirelessly to establish himself as a respected and influential figure in the region. His diplomatic achievements were marked by his masterful negotiating skills, his deep respect for the cultures and beliefs of others, and his commitment to building relationships with the people he conquered. His legacy endures to this day as one of the greatest conquerors and leaders in history.

Genghis Khan's military campaigns were a defining feature of his reign, and they played a key role in his efforts to unite the Mongol tribes and create a powerful, unified state. From the early years of his reign, Genghis Khan was a master of military strategy and tactics, and he was able to consistently defeat larger, more established armies through a combination of superior tactics, discipline, and innovation.

One of Genghis Khan's earliest military conquests was his campaign against the Tatar tribe in 1202. The Tatars had been a thorn in the side of the Mongol tribes for many years, and their defeat was an important step in Genghis Khan's efforts to unite the tribes under his leadership.

Genghis Khan was able to achieve victory in this campaign by employing a number of innovative tactics. He made use of the terrain to his advantage, using hills and valleys to conceal his movements and launch surprise attacks on the Tatars. He also made use of his knowledge of the Tatars' weaknesses and vulnerabilities, using psychological warfare and deception to sow confusion and disarray among their ranks.

Genghis Khan's military successes continued throughout his reign, and he was able to conquer and subjugate many other tribes in the region. One of his most notable conquests was the defeat of the Jin Dynasty in northern China in the early 13th century. The Jin had been a powerful empire for centuries, but they were unable to withstand the military might of the Mongols, who used their superior tactics and military technology to achieve victory.

In addition to his military campaigns in China, Genghis Khan also waged war against other neighboring states and empires, including the Khwarazmian Empire in Central Asia and the Kievan Rus' in Eastern Europe. These campaigns were marked by Genghis Khan's incredible tactical acumen, as well as his ability to inspire loyalty and discipline among his troops.

One of the key factors in Genghis Khan's military success was his ability to adapt to changing circumstances and respond quickly to new threats and challenges. He was known for his ability to improvise and innovate on the battlefield, constantly developing new tactics and strategies to overcome his enemies.

Another factor in Genghis Khan's military success was his ability to inspire loyalty and discipline among his troops. He was a strict but fair leader, and he demanded the highest standards of discipline and professionalism from his soldiers. He also treated his troops with respect and generosity, sharing the spoils of war with them and providing for their needs.

In summary, Genghis Khan's military conquests were a defining feature of his reign, and they played a crucial role in his efforts to unite the Mongol tribes and create a powerful, unified state. His success on the battlefield was due to his superior tactics and military technology, as well as his ability to adapt to changing circumstances and inspire loyalty and discipline among his troops. His military legacy endures to this day as a testament to his incredible strategic and tactical skills, and his reputation as one of the greatest military commanders in history remains firmly established.

The unification of the Mongol tribes under the leadership of Genghis Khan was a remarkable achievement that transformed the region and had far-reaching consequences for world history. This unification process was made possible by a combination of Genghis Khan's visionary leadership and his strategic and tactical brilliance.

One of the key factors in Genghis Khan's success as a leader was his ability to inspire loyalty and unity among the tribes. He was able to do this by appealing to their shared cultural and linguistic heritage and emphasizing the importance of cooperation and mutual support. He also demonstrated his leadership qualities through his personal example, always leading from the front and taking the greatest risks in battle.

Another important factor in Genghis Khan's success as a leader was his strategic vision. He recognized that the only way to unite the Mongol tribes was through military conquest, and he set about developing a comprehensive strategy for achieving this goal. This strategy involved a combination of military campaigns, diplomatic efforts, and administrative reforms, all designed to strengthen his position and undermine his rivals.

Genghis Khan's military campaigns were the most visible aspect of his strategy, and they played a crucial role in his efforts to conquer and subjugate the other tribes. However, he also recognized the importance of diplomacy and negotiation, and he was willing to make alliances and engage in negotiations when it served his interests.

In addition to his military and diplomatic efforts, Genghis Khan also instituted a number of administrative reforms that helped to strengthen his position and create a unified Mongol state. He established a system of laws and regulations that applied to all members of the empire, regardless of their tribal affiliation, and he worked to improve the infrastructure and governance of the region.

One of the most important aspects of Genghis Khan's leadership was his ability to adapt and innovate in response to changing circumstances. He was always looking for new ways to strengthen his position and overcome his enemies, and he was willing to take risks and try new approaches when necessary.

Perhaps the most impressive aspect of Genghis Khan's leadership was his ability to maintain his position and influence over such a vast and diverse empire. He recognized the importance of keeping his allies close and his enemies closer, and he was always vigilant for signs of disloyalty or dissent. He also made a point of involving members of other tribes in the governance of the empire, giving them a stake in its success and ensuring their loyalty.

In summary, Genghis Khan's role in the unification process was pivotal, and his leadership and strategic brilliance were critical factors in the success of this remarkable achievement. His ability to inspire loyalty and unity among the tribes, his strategic vision, his diplomatic skills, and his administrative reforms all played important roles in the creation of a unified Mongol state. His legacy as a leader and strategist endures to this day, and his example serves as an inspiration to leaders and strategists around the world.

Chapter 3: Conquests in China and Central Asia

The formation of the Mongol Empire was a remarkable achievement that transformed the political and cultural landscape of the region. This process was led by the legendary Genghis Khan, whose vision and leadership were critical to the success of this remarkable endeavor. However, the formation of the Mongol Empire was not without its challenges, and Genghis Khan faced many obstacles in his efforts to unite the Mongol tribes.

Genghis Khan's early successes in uniting the Mongol tribes came as a result of his military prowess and strategic vision. He recognized that the only way to unite the disparate tribes was through military conquest, and he set about developing a comprehensive strategy for achieving this goal. This strategy involved a combination of military campaigns, diplomatic efforts, and administrative reforms, all designed to strengthen his position and undermine his rivals.

One of Genghis Khan's earliest military conquests was the defeat of the Tangut Empire, a powerful regional power that controlled much of modern-day China. This conquest demonstrated Genghis Khan's military prowess and signaled to the other tribes that he was a leader to be reckoned with.

Another key component of Genghis Khan's strategy was his ability to form alliances and negotiate treaties with other tribes. He recognized the importance of maintaining a delicate balance of power and was willing to make alliances and engage in negotiations when it served his interests. One of his most important alliances was with the Khwarazmian Empire, which helped him to expand his territory and strengthen his position.

Despite his successes, Genghis Khan faced many challenges in his efforts to unite the Mongol tribes. One of the biggest challenges was the resistance of rival tribes and the internal divisions within his own tribe. Genghis Khan was able to overcome these challenges through a combination of military force, diplomacy, and administrative reforms.

One of the most important administrative reforms instituted by Genghis Khan was the creation of a system of laws and regulations that applied to all members of the empire, regardless of their tribal affiliation. This helped to create a sense of unity and shared purpose among the diverse tribes and helped to minimize internal conflicts.

Another challenge that Genghis Khan faced was the need to maintain the loyalty of his followers and allies. He recognized the importance of keeping his allies close and his enemies closer, and he was always vigilant for signs of disloyalty or dissent. He also made a point of involving members of other tribes in the governance of the empire, giving them a stake in its success and ensuring their loyalty.

In addition to his military and administrative achievements, Genghis Khan also had a significant impact on the cultural and intellectual development of the region. He was a patron of the arts and sciences, and he helped to promote the exchange of ideas and knowledge among the diverse tribes of the region. This cultural exchange helped to lay the foundation for a shared Mongol identity that transcended tribal affiliations and helped to unite the region.

In summary, the formation of the Mongol Empire was a remarkable achievement that transformed the political and cultural landscape of the region. Genghis Khan's vision, leadership, and strategic brilliance were critical to the success of this endeavor, and his legacy as a leader and strategist endures to this day. Despite the many challenges he faced, Genghis Khan was able to overcome internal divisions, form alliances with other tribes, and establish a unified Mongol state that would endure for centuries to come.

The campaigns against the Khwarezmian Empire were among the most important and far-reaching military expeditions undertaken by Genghis Khan during his reign as the leader of the Mongol Empire. The Khwarezmian Empire was a powerful state that controlled much of Central Asia and the Middle East, and its defeat represented a significant milestone in the expansion of Mongol power and influence.

Genghis Khan's decision to invade the Khwarezmian Empire was motivated by a number of factors, including the empire's strategic location, its wealth and resources, and its status as a rival power. The invasion was also fueled by a desire for revenge, as the Khwarezmian Empire had previously humiliated and insulted Mongol envoys, prompting Genghis Khan to vow revenge.

The campaign against the Khwarezmian Empire was a massive undertaking that involved a large and highly organized military force. Genghis Khan led his army into the empire in 1219, and the campaign quickly became a brutal and bloody conflict. The Mongol army was able to gain the upper hand early on, thanks in part to its superior military tactics and the advanced weapons and equipment it possessed.

One of the key battles of the campaign was the Siege of Otrar, a city that was strategically important to the Khwarezmian Empire. The Mongol army was able to breach the city's defenses and capture the governor, who was executed in retaliation for the killing of Mongol envoys. This brutal act set the tone for the rest of the campaign and signaled to the Khwarezmian Empire that the Mongols were not to be trifled with.

Despite their early successes, the Mongols faced a number of challenges as they advanced deeper into the Khwarezmian Empire. The harsh desert terrain and extreme weather conditions made it difficult to maintain supply lines and keep troops fed and hydrated. The Mongols also faced stiff resistance from the Khwarezmian army, which employed a range of tactics designed to slow the Mongol advance.

Despite these challenges, the Mongols were able to press on and eventually defeated the Khwarezmian army in a decisive battle near the city of Samarkand. This victory marked the end of the Khwarezmian Empire and established the Mongols as the dominant power in the region.

The campaign against the Khwarezmian Empire had a number of significant consequences for the region and for the Mongol Empire more broadly. One of the most important outcomes was the acquisition of vast new territories and resources, including gold, silver, and precious stones. The campaign also helped to consolidate Mongol power in Central Asia and paved the way for further expansion into the Middle East.

The campaign against the Khwarezmian Empire also had important cultural and social consequences. The Mongol army encountered a number of different cultures and religions during their campaign, including Islam, Buddhism, and Zoroastrianism. These encounters helped to shape the Mongol worldview and influenced the development of Mongol culture and identity.

In summary, the campaign against the Khwarezmian Empire was one of the most important military campaigns of Genghis Khan's reign, and it had significant consequences for the region and for the Mongol Empire more broadly. The campaign was marked by brutal battles and fierce resistance, but it ultimately resulted in a decisive victory for the Mongols and established their dominance over Central Asia and the Middle East. The campaign also had important cultural and social consequences, helping to shape the development of Mongol identity and influence the course of world history.

The Battle of the Indus River was a pivotal moment in Genghis Khan's campaign of conquest in Asia. The battle marked the first time that the Mongol Empire had attempted to invade India, and it demonstrated both the incredible military might of the Mongol army and the fierce resistance that they faced from the Indian forces.

Genghis Khan had long been interested in expanding his empire into India, which was known for its wealth, resources, and strategic location.

He had already conquered much of Central Asia and the Middle East, and he believed that India would be a valuable addition to his growing empire.

In 1221, Genghis Khan led a massive army across the Indus River and into northern India. The Indian forces were caught off guard by the Mongol invasion and were initially unable to mount an effective defense. The Mongols were able to advance quickly and capture several key cities, including Lahore and Multan.

However, the Mongols soon faced a significant challenge in the form of the Indian ruler Jalal ad-Din Mingburnu, who had rallied a large army to defend against the invasion. The two forces clashed in a massive battle on the banks of the Indus River, which would come to be known as the Battle of the Indus River.

The battle was a brutal and protracted affair, with both sides suffering heavy losses. The Mongols were able to deploy their advanced military tactics and weapons to great effect, but they faced stiff resistance from the Indian forces, who were determined to defend their homeland.

Despite the fierce fighting, the Mongols were eventually able to emerge victorious, thanks in part to the leadership and strategic acumen of Genghis Khan. The Indian forces were driven back, and the Mongols were able to establish a foothold in northern India.

The Battle of the Indus River had significant consequences for both the Mongol Empire and the Indian subcontinent. For the Mongols, the victory demonstrated their military prowess and marked the beginning of their expansion into India. It also helped to secure their position in Central Asia and the Middle East, which were critical regions for the Mongol Empire.

For India, the battle had more negative consequences. The invasion by the Mongols and the subsequent defeat of the Indian forces contributed to the decline of the Delhi Sultanate, which had previously been the dominant power in the region. The battle also paved the way for further invasions by the Mongols and other foreign powers, leading to a period of instability and turmoil in northern India.

Despite the negative consequences for India, the Battle of the Indus River remains a significant moment in the history of the Mongol Empire. It demonstrated the incredible military might of the Mongol army and helped to secure their position as one of the most powerful empires in the world. The battle also had important geopolitical consequences, shaping the course of world history for centuries to come.

The conquest of Jin China was one of the most significant military campaigns of Genghis Khan's career. The Jin dynasty, which controlled much of northern China, was a major power in the region and posed a significant threat to the Mongol Empire. However, under the leadership of Genghis Khan, the Mongols were able to mount a successful invasion and eventually conquer the Jin dynasty.

The conquest of Jin China began in the early 1200s, when Genghis Khan began to send his armies into the region. The Mongols were able to make significant gains, capturing several key cities and defeating the Jin army in a series of battles. However, the Jin dynasty was a powerful and well-organized state, and they were able to mount a strong defense against the Mongol invasion.

Despite the challenges they faced, the Mongols were able to persevere and gradually chip away at the Jin dynasty's power. They were able to win the support of many of the local people, who saw the Mongols as a more just and equitable ruler than the Jin dynasty. They also developed new military tactics and weapons, such as the use of gunpowder and the siege engine known as the trebuchet.

One of the most significant battles of the campaign was the siege of Zhongdu, the capital city of the Jin dynasty. The city was heavily fortified and well-defended, and the Mongols faced significant challenges in attempting to breach its walls. However, they were eventually able to succeed, thanks in part to the use of the trebuchet and other advanced military technologies.

The fall of Zhongdu was a major turning point in the campaign, as it allowed the Mongols to gain control of much of northern China. The Jin dynasty was weakened and unable to mount an effective defense against the Mongol invasion. The Mongols were able to consolidate their power and eventually establish their own government in the region, known as the Yuan dynasty.

The conquest of Jin China was a major accomplishment for Genghis Khan and the Mongol Empire. It helped to secure their position as one of the most powerful empires in the world and gave them control over a significant portion of Asia. The conquest also had significant cultural and economic consequences, as the Mongols brought new ideas, technologies, and trade routes to the region.

However, the conquest of Jin China was not without its costs. The Mongol invasion led to significant loss of life and destruction, particularly in the major cities and population centers of the region. The Mongols also faced significant challenges in governing the region, as they were viewed as foreign conquerors by many of the local people.

Despite these challenges, the conquest of Jin China remains a significant moment in the history of the Mongol Empire. It demonstrated the incredible military power and strategic acumen of Genghis Khan and his armies, and helped to shape the course of world history for centuries to come.

The fall of the Western Xia Dynasty was a significant moment in the early career of Genghis Khan and the Mongol Empire. The Western Xia Dynasty was a powerful state located in northwest China, and it had long been a thorn in the side of the Mongols. Under the leadership of Genghis Khan, the Mongols launched a major invasion of the Western Xia, eventually bringing the dynasty to its knees and establishing the Mongol Empire as a major force in the region.

The invasion of the Western Xia began in the early 1200s, when Genghis Khan began to send his armies into the region. The Western Xia was a powerful state with a well-trained army and a sophisticated system of fortifications, making it a formidable opponent for the Mongols. However, the Mongols were able to make significant gains, capturing several key cities and defeating the Western Xia army in a series of battles.

One of the most significant battles of the campaign was the siege of Yinchuan, the capital city of the Western Xia. The city was heavily fortified and well-defended, but the Mongols were able to breach its walls and capture the city after a long and bloody siege. The fall of Yinchuan was a major turning point in the campaign, as it allowed the Mongols to gain control of much of the Western Xia's territory.

The fall of the Western Xia was not just a military victory for the Mongols, but also a cultural and economic one. The Western Xia Dynasty had long been a center of art, culture, and learning, and the Mongols were able to seize many of its treasures and bring them back to their own empire. The Mongols also opened up new trade routes and brought new technologies and ideas to the region, transforming the economy and society of northwest China.

Despite the Mongols' success in the campaign, the invasion of the Western Xia was not without its costs. The Mongols faced significant challenges in governing the region, as they were viewed as foreign conquerors by many of the local people. They also faced significant opposition from the remaining Western Xia forces, who continued to mount resistance against the Mongol invaders.

However, the fall of the Western Xia Dynasty was a major accomplishment for Genghis Khan and the Mongol Empire. It helped to cement their position as one of the most powerful empires in the world and gave them control over a significant portion of Asia. The invasion also had significant cultural and economic consequences, as the Mongols brought new ideas, technologies, and trade routes to the region.

The fall of the Western Xia Dynasty was a key moment in the early career of Genghis Khan and the Mongol Empire. It demonstrated their incredible military power and strategic acumen, and helped to shape the course of world history for centuries to come. The conquest of the Western Xia paved the way for further Mongol invasions of China and the establishment of the Yuan dynasty, and it remains an important moment in the history of the Mongol Empire.

Genghis Khan's conquest of China and Central Asia was not just a military campaign, but also a psychological one. The Mongols used a variety of tactics to intimidate and demoralize their enemies, ranging from brutal acts of violence to sophisticated forms of propaganda. This strategy of psychological warfare played a crucial role in the Mongols' success in the region, and helped to establish the Mongol Empire as one of the most powerful empires in history.

One of the most effective forms of psychological warfare employed by the Mongols was their reputation for brutality. The Mongols were known for their merciless treatment of their enemies, often executing prisoners of war en masse and leaving their bodies on display as a warning to others. This tactic of mass intimidation was highly effective, as it discouraged potential challengers from rising up against the Mongols and helped to secure their control over vast territories.

Another key tactic of psychological warfare employed by the Mongols was their use of propaganda. The Mongols were skilled at crafting narratives that painted them as invincible and divinely appointed rulers, and disseminating these narratives through a variety of channels. They used emissaries to spread tales of their military prowess and generosity to potential allies, and sent letters to potential adversaries warning them of the dire consequences of opposing the Mongols.

The Mongols were also skilled at exploiting cultural and religious divisions in the regions they conquered. They often played different factions against one another, and used their own religious beliefs (which were highly syncretic) to appeal to local populations. The Mongols were known to incorporate elements of local religions and customs into their own practices, which helped them to gain the support of many conquered peoples.

Perhaps one of the most effective tactics employed by the Mongols was their use of terror. The Mongols were known to engage in highly symbolic acts of violence, such as slaughtering entire populations of cities and leaving behind pyramids of skulls as a warning to others. These acts of terror were highly effective in cowing their enemies and creating a climate of fear that helped to ensure their dominance.

The Mongols were also highly skilled at adapting their tactics to different environments. In the steppes of Central Asia, they relied heavily on cavalry warfare and hit-and-run tactics to wear down their enemies. In China, they adapted their tactics to the highly urbanized environment, using siege warfare and infiltration to gain control of cities.

Ultimately, the Mongols' success in China and Central Asia was due in no small part to their mastery of psychological warfare. By using a combination of brutality, propaganda, cultural adaptation, and terror, they were able to intimidate and subdue their enemies, creating a vast empire that spanned much of Asia. Their legacy as masters of psychological warfare has been felt in the centuries since, and has influenced military strategy and tactics to this day.

Chapter 4: Expansion into Eastern Europe and Russia

In the early 13th century, the Mongol Empire under the leadership of Genghis Khan set its sights on the Khwarazmian Empire, a powerful Islamic state that controlled much of Central Asia. Genghis Khan viewed the Khwarazmian Empire as a threat to his own ambitions of expanding Mongol control over the region, and launched a series of devastating campaigns that would ultimately result in the destruction of the Khwarazmian Empire.

The invasion of the Khwarazmian Empire was marked by some of the most brutal warfare of the medieval period. The Mongols utilized a combination of psychological warfare and military strategy to subdue their opponents. They were known for their use of terror tactics, including the massacre of entire cities and the brutal execution of prisoners of war. These tactics helped to create a climate of fear that enabled the Mongols to gain control over much of Central Asia.

The Mongols also relied on their superior military technology and tactics to overwhelm their opponents. They were known for their skilled use of cavalry, which enabled them to move quickly across the steppes and engage in hit-and-run attacks on enemy forces. They also employed siege warfare tactics, including the use of trebuchets and other siege engines, to breach the fortifications of enemy cities.

The Khwarazmian Empire was unable to withstand the onslaught of the Mongol forces, and was ultimately destroyed. The consequences of this invasion would be felt far beyond the borders of the Khwarazmian Empire, however. The Mongol Empire continued to expand, and soon came into conflict with the Western European powers.

The Mongol invasion of the Khwarazmian Empire had a profound impact on the balance of power in Europe. The Mongols had demonstrated their military superiority on the battlefield, and their conquests had brought them into contact with the Islamic world. The fall of the Khwarazmian Empire had also disrupted trade routes and destabilized the region, which had significant economic consequences for Europe.

In response to the growing threat of the Mongols, European powers began to take steps to defend themselves. They formed alliances with one another, built fortifications, and developed new military technologies. These efforts would prove critical in the centuries to come, as Europe would soon find itself in direct conflict with the Mongol Empire.

The Mongol invasion of the Khwarazmian Empire also had cultural and intellectual consequences. The Mongols were known for their tolerance of different religions and their willingness to incorporate elements of local cultures into their own practices. This cultural syncretism had a profound impact on the Islamic world, and helped to shape the development of Islamic culture and thought in the centuries to come.

Overall, the invasion of the Khwarazmian Empire was a turning point in world history. It marked the beginning of the Mongol Empire's expansion into Central Asia, and had far-reaching consequences for the balance of power in Europe and the Islamic world. The Mongols' use of brutal tactics and psychological warfare would have a lasting impact on military strategy and tactics, while their cultural syncretism would shape the development of Islamic civilization. The legacy of the Mongol Empire continues to be felt to this day, and remains a subject of fascination for historians and scholars around the world.

The Battle of the Kalka River in 1223 marked one of Genghis Khan's most notable military campaigns, as he led his armies against the Kievan Rus, a confederation of Eastern Slavic tribes in what is now modern-day Ukraine. While much of the historical record of the battle has been lost, what remains offers a glimpse into Genghis Khan's military strategies and the nature of warfare during the Mongol Empire.

According to surviving accounts, Genghis Khan's forces were vastly outnumbered, with estimates ranging from 40,000 to 100,000 Kievan Rus soldiers and only around 20,000 Mongol troops. Despite these odds, Genghis Khan remained confident in his military tactics and the discipline of his troops. He split his forces into several smaller units, allowing for greater flexibility and mobility on the battlefield.

As the two armies clashed, Genghis Khan's forces unleashed a barrage of arrows upon the Kievan Rus soldiers, causing significant casualties and confusion among their ranks. The Mongols then charged forward, taking advantage of the disarray and cutting down enemy soldiers with their swords and spears.

The Kievan Rus, however, were not without their own strategies. They employed a tactic known as the "wheeling attack," in which they circled around the Mongol troops, attempting to break their formation and isolate individual units. The Kievan Rus also had the advantage of heavy cavalry, which could charge into the Mongol ranks and cause significant damage.

Despite these challenges, Genghis Khan's military prowess proved decisive. He ordered his archers to target the horses of the Kievan Rus cavalry, effectively neutralizing their most powerful weapon. The

Mongols then closed in with their own cavalry, surrounding and cutting down the remaining enemy soldiers.

The battle was a significant victory for Genghis Khan and marked the expansion of Mongol territory into Eastern Europe. The Kievan Rus, weakened by their defeat, were unable to mount an effective resistance to further Mongol invasions, and the region would remain under Mongol rule for several decades.

The Battle of the Kalka River also highlights the effectiveness of Genghis Khan's military strategies, which relied heavily on discipline, mobility, and surprise. His forces were able to overcome significant disadvantages in numbers and technology through their superior tactics and ability to adapt to changing circumstances on the battlefield.

Furthermore, the battle underscores the brutal nature of warfare during the Mongol Empire. Accounts suggest that the Kievan Rus soldiers suffered immense casualties, with some estimates placing the death toll in the tens of thousands. The Mongols, for their part, showed little mercy to their enemies, slaughtering those who surrendered and sparing only a handful of prisoners.

Overall, the Battle of the Kalka River stands as a testament to Genghis Khan's military prowess and the power of the Mongol Empire. It also serves as a reminder of the brutality of war and the devastating consequences that can arise from conflicts between different peoples and cultures.

The conquests of Genghis Khan were not limited to Asia and Europe, but also extended to the Russian territories. Among the major Russian cities that Genghis Khan targeted was Volohai, which was situated on the banks of the Volga River. This city was a major center of trade and commerce in the region, and its conquest was of immense significance to the Mongol Empire.

The Mongol conquest of Volohai was part of a larger campaign that aimed to establish Mongol dominance over the entire region. The city was a strategic target due to its location on the Volga River, which was an important artery for trade and transportation in the region. The conquest of Volohai would allow the Mongols to control the trade routes of the Volga and consolidate their control over the surrounding areas.

The siege of Volohai began in the year 1223, when a Mongol army led by Subutai and Jebe arrived at the gates of the city. The defenders of the city were ill-prepared to face the Mongol army, and their resistance was quickly overcome. The Mongols breached the city walls and entered the city, engaging in fierce hand-to-hand combat with the defenders.

Despite their initial success, the Mongols faced a stubborn resistance from the defenders, who fought with great valor and determination. The defenders of the city were well-equipped with weapons and armor, and their fortifications were well-maintained. The Mongols faced a tough challenge in overcoming the defenders and capturing the city.

The siege of Volohai lasted for several weeks, during which time the Mongols employed a variety of tactics to weaken the defenses of the city. They launched several assaults on the city walls, using siege engines and catapults to breach the defenses. They also resorted to psychological warfare, using loud music and drums to keep the defenders awake and disoriented.

The Mongols eventually succeeded in breaking through the defenses of the city, using battering rams to breach the gates and walls. Once inside the city, they engaged in brutal hand-to-hand combat with the defenders, who fought with great bravery but were eventually overwhelmed by the sheer force of the Mongol assault.

The Mongol conquest of Volohai was a significant achievement for the Mongol Empire, as it allowed them to consolidate their control over the Russian territories and expand their trade networks. The conquest of Volohai was also a major setback for the Russian princes, who had hoped to resist the Mongol invasion and maintain their independence.

The conquest of Volohai was followed by a series of other campaigns against the Russian territories, including the conquest of Kiev and the sack of Moscow. These campaigns cemented Mongol control over the region and established the Mongol Empire as a dominant power in Eurasia.

In summary, the conquest of Volohai was a significant achievement for Genghis Khan and the Mongol Empire. The siege of the city was a testament to the military prowess and strategic acumen of the Mongol commanders, who overcame a determined defense to capture the city. The conquest of Volohai also marked the beginning of a new chapter in the history of the Mongol Empire, as they expanded their control over the Russian territories and consolidated their position as a major power in Eurasia.

In the early 13th century, Genghis Khan had succeeded in uniting the various nomadic tribes of Mongolia under his rule, creating a formidable military force. With the unification of his people complete, he looked beyond the borders of his homeland, seeking new territories to conquer and expand his growing empire. Genghis Khan's sights soon fell on the fertile lands of Eastern Europe, which had long been the target of invading nomads.

The conquest of Eastern Europe was a crucial part of Genghis Khan's strategy for expanding his empire. His armies had already swept through China, Central Asia, and the Middle East, bringing vast territories under Mongol control. Now, he turned his attention to the west, setting his sights on the fertile lands of Hungary and Poland.

The Mongol conquest of Hungary and Poland began in the early 1240s. Genghis Khan had dispatched his armies to the west under the command of his trusted generals, Subutai and Batu Khan. The Mongol army was one of the most formidable fighting forces the world had ever seen. They were skilled horsemen, adept at using their bows and arrows while riding at full gallop, and were able to cover vast distances quickly.

The Mongol army marched across the steppes of Central Asia, crossing the Caspian Sea and entering the Caucasus Mountains. They then swept across the plains of Eastern Europe, laying waste to everything in their path. The Mongols attacked and captured cities such as Kiev, Chernihiv, and Pereiaslav, as well as numerous smaller towns and villages.

The Mongol invasion of Hungary and Poland was characterized by swift and brutal military campaigns. The Mongols would attack with overwhelming force, often catching their enemies off guard. They would then sack and burn cities, kill and enslave the population, and move on to the next target.

One of the key battles in the Mongol invasion of Hungary and Poland was the Battle of Mohi, fought in April 1241. The Mongols faced a combined army of Hungarians, Poles, and other European forces. The Mongol army was vastly outnumbered, but their superior tactics and training allowed them to emerge victorious.

After the Battle of Mohi, the Mongols continued their westward march, capturing more cities and territories. By 1242, they had reached the Adriatic Sea, effectively controlling a vast swath of Eastern Europe.

Genghis Khan's invasion of Hungary and Poland had far-reaching consequences for Europe. The Mongol conquest had disrupted trade routes and devastated the economies of the region. The Mongol invasion had also weakened the power of the Holy Roman Empire, which had been the dominant political force in Europe at the time. It paved the way for the rise of new powers such as Poland and Lithuania, who would eventually emerge as major players in Eastern Europe.

In summary, Genghis Khan's expansion into Eastern Europe marked a significant chapter in the history of the Mongol Empire. The swift and brutal campaigns of the Mongol armies left a lasting impression on the people of the region, and their impact would be felt for centuries to come. The Mongol conquest of Hungary and Poland also played a key role in shaping the political and economic landscape of Europe, setting the stage for the rise of new powers and the decline of old ones.

In the early 13th century, Genghis Khan had already conquered and united the Mongol tribes, expanded his empire into Central Asia and China, and had even set his sights on Europe. His military conquests had brought him to the borders of the Holy Roman Empire, and in 1241, Genghis Khan led a massive army of Mongol warriors into the heart of Europe.

The Mongol army numbered in the hundreds of thousands, and was led by Genghis Khan's sons, Batu and Subutai. They swept through Eastern Europe, sacking cities and laying waste to entire regions. The Europeans were caught off guard by the ferocity of the Mongol attack, and were unable to mount an effective defense.

The Mongol army first entered Hungary, where they defeated the Hungarian king, Béla IV, in a series of battles. They then moved on to Poland, where they encountered the combined forces of the Polish and German armies. The Mongols were vastly outnumbered, but they made up for this disadvantage with their superior tactics and weaponry.

The Battle of Liegnitz, also known as the Battle of Legnica, was fought on April 9, 1241, between the Mongol army and the forces of the Polish and German armies. The Polish-German army numbered around 30,000 soldiers, while the Mongols had an estimated 100,000 warriors.

The Mongols began the battle with a feigned retreat, drawing the Polish-German army into a trap. They then unleashed a massive attack, using their superior archery skills to rain down arrows on the enemy forces. The Polish-German army was decimated, and their leaders were either killed or captured.

One of the most notable casualties of the Battle of Liegnitz was the Duke of Silesia, Henry II the Pious. He was captured by the Mongols and later executed, along with many other high-ranking officials. The defeat was a major blow to the European powers, and the Mongols continued their campaign of conquest, eventually reaching as far west as the Adriatic Sea.

The Battle of Liegnitz was a turning point in European history, and is often considered to be the last great battle of the medieval period. It marked the end of the Mongol invasion of Europe, and the beginning of a new era of European military tactics and strategies. The Mongols had shown that they were a formidable force, capable of taking on even the mightiest armies of Europe.

Despite their defeat at Liegnitz, the Mongol legacy continued to have a profound impact on Europe. Their military tactics and strategies were studied and imitated by European armies, and many of their innovations, such as the stirrup and the composite bow, were adopted by European warriors. The Mongol conquests also paved the way for the rise of the Ottoman Empire, which would go on to conquer much of the Balkans and Eastern Europe in the centuries that followed.

In summary, the Battle of Liegnitz was a significant event in European history, marking the end of the Mongol invasion of Europe and the beginning of a new era of military tactics and strategies. The defeat of the European armies by the Mongols was a wake-up call, and led to a renewed focus on military training and innovation. The legacy of the Mongols continued to have an impact on Europe for centuries to come, shaping the course of history and leaving a lasting mark on the continent.

Chapter 5: The Creation of a Military Empire

In the annals of military history, few armies have been as feared and respected as the Mongol Horde. Under the leadership of Genghis Khan, the Mongol army swept across the Eurasian steppe, conquering countless tribes and kingdoms and leaving a trail of devastation in its wake. One of the key reasons for the Mongols' success was their military organization, which allowed them to move quickly and efficiently across vast distances and to project power far beyond their own borders.

At the heart of the Mongol army was the cavalry, which formed the core of Genghis Khan's fighting force. The Mongols were renowned for their horsemanship, and their horses were specially bred for speed, agility, and endurance. Mongol warriors were expert riders and archers, capable of firing arrows accurately and rapidly while riding at full gallop. They were also skilled at close-quarters combat, using swords, lances, and other weapons to deadly effect.

But the Mongols' success on the battlefield was not just due to their individual skills as warriors. Equally important was the organization and discipline of their army. Under Genghis Khan, the Mongols developed a sophisticated system of military hierarchy and command. At the top was the Khan himself, who held absolute authority over the army and was responsible for its overall strategy and direction.

Beneath the Khan were a series of commanders, each of whom was responsible for a specific unit or division of the army. These commanders were chosen not based on social status or family connections, but on their merit as warriors and leaders. They were expected to lead by example, displaying courage, discipline, and loyalty to the Khan at all times.

Below the commanders were the ordinary warriors, who made up the bulk of the Mongol army. These soldiers were organized into groups of ten, each led by a senior warrior known as a "tumen". The tumen was responsible for the discipline and training of his group, and was expected to maintain a high level of readiness at all times. Each tumen was in turn part of a larger unit known as a "kharachin", which consisted of ten tumens.

This system of organization allowed the Mongols to move quickly and decisively on the battlefield. Each unit was trained to operate independently, allowing the army to split into smaller groups and attack from multiple directions. At the same time, each unit was closely coordinated with the others, ensuring that the army could act as a cohesive whole when necessary.

Another key aspect of the Mongol army was its use of intelligence and espionage. Genghis Khan recognized the importance of information in warfare, and he established a network of spies and scouts who could gather intelligence on enemy positions, movements, and weaknesses. This information was then used to plan attacks and to exploit weaknesses in the enemy's defenses.

Overall, the Mongol army was a highly effective and formidable force, thanks to its combination of superior horsemanship, expert archery and close combat skills, and sophisticated organization and discipline. Under the leadership of Genghis Khan, it conquered vast territories and established one of the largest and most powerful empires in history.

In the early thirteenth century, Genghis Khan led the Mongol Empire to one of the most remarkable series of conquests in world history. This empire was built on a foundation of military prowess, discipline, and innovation that allowed the Mongols to conquer and control vast swathes of territory across Asia and Europe. The Mongol military was a formidable force that relied heavily on the power and mobility of its cavalry, but it was also distinguished by a strict code of conduct that governed the behavior of its soldiers both in and out of battle.

At the heart of the Mongol military was the cavalry. The Mongols were renowned for their skill on horseback and their ability to move quickly and decisively across the open steppe terrain. They were adept at riding and shooting from horseback, and their ponies were hardy, fast, and capable of enduring long periods of hardship. The Mongols typically traveled light, with few possessions and no wagons or carts. This allowed them to move quickly and easily across the vast expanses of land they were conquering.

The Mongol army was organized into units of 10, 100, 1,000, and 10,000 soldiers, with each unit under the command of a leader who was responsible for ensuring that his troops were properly trained, equipped, and disciplined. The Mongols were a highly disciplined force, with strict rules that governed every aspect of military life. For example, soldiers were required to wear specific colors and patterns on their clothing and were not allowed to deviate from these designs. They were also required to carry specific weapons, such as the composite bow and the saber, and were trained in a variety of fighting techniques, including archery, hand-to-hand combat, and siege warfare.

One of the key factors that contributed to the success of the Mongol military was their code of conduct, which was known as the yasa. The yasa was a set of laws that governed the behavior of soldiers both in and out of battle. These laws were strict and were designed to maintain discipline and order within the army. For example, soldiers were not allowed to steal from civilians, were required to respect the property and dignity of civilians, and were forbidden from killing women, children, or the elderly. Violations of the yasa were punished severely, often with death.

In addition to the yasa, the Mongols also had a set of military ethics that governed the behavior of soldiers in battle. These ethics were based on the idea of honor and were designed to encourage soldiers to fight bravely and with dignity. For example, soldiers were encouraged to be loyal to their leaders and to fight with courage and determination. They were also expected to show mercy to defeated enemies who surrendered peacefully.

Another important aspect of the Mongol military was their use of intelligence gathering and espionage. The Mongols were skilled at gathering information about their enemies, using spies and scouts to gather intelligence about enemy movements, troop strengths, and weaknesses. They were also skilled at psychological warfare, using tactics such as deception, intimidation, and terror to demoralize and defeat their enemies.

The Mongol military was not without its weaknesses, however. The Mongols were not particularly skilled at siege warfare, and often relied on brute force to conquer fortified cities and towns. They were also vulnerable to guerrilla warfare and ambushes, as their reliance on open terrain and cavalry made them vulnerable to surprise attacks.

Despite these weaknesses, the Mongol military was a formidable force that played a significant role in shaping the history of the thirteenth century. Their success was due in large part to their skill on horseback, their discipline and organization, and their strict code of conduct that governed every aspect of military life.

The Mongols under Genghis Khan were known for their unparalleled military tactics and strategy. They were able to conquer vast territories and defeat powerful armies, leaving a lasting impact on the history of warfare. Next, we will explore the methods and innovations that made the Mongols so successful in battle.

One of the key factors that contributed to the Mongols' success was their use of cavalry. The Mongols were skilled horsemen and their horses were specially bred for speed, endurance, and maneuverability. They could cover long distances quickly, making it possible for them to launch surprise attacks and then retreat before their enemies could mount a counter-attack.

In addition to their speed and mobility, the Mongol cavalry was also well-organized and disciplined. They were divided into units of ten, with each unit led by a commander responsible for the training and discipline of his men. This allowed the Mongols to coordinate their movements and execute complex maneuvers with precision.

Another key factor in the Mongols' success was their use of intelligence and espionage. Genghis Khan established a network of spies and informants throughout his empire, which allowed him to gather valuable intelligence on his enemies' strengths and weaknesses. This information was used to plan military campaigns and develop strategies that would exploit the weaknesses of the enemy.

The Mongols also employed psychological tactics in their warfare. They would often use fear to their advantage, using tactics such as beheading captured enemies and stacking their heads in pyramids to intimidate their foes. They also used propaganda to sow dissent and confusion among their enemies, spreading rumors and misinformation to undermine morale and weaken resistance.

In terms of weaponry, the Mongols were skilled with a variety of weapons, including the bow and arrow, the sword, and the lance. Their bows were particularly effective, as they were designed to be used from horseback and could shoot arrows with great force and accuracy over long distances.

One of the most innovative aspects of Mongol warfare was their use of tactics such as the feigned retreat. The Mongols would often lure their enemies into chasing them, only to turn and attack when their pursuers were in disarray. This tactic allowed the Mongols to exploit their enemies' lack of discipline and cohesion, and to inflict devastating losses on their forces.

Finally, the Mongols were able to maintain a highly centralized command structure, which allowed for efficient communication and rapid decision-making. This was achieved through the use of a complex system of messengers, who were able to relay information quickly and accurately across vast distances.

In summary, the Mongols' success in warfare can be attributed to a variety of factors, including their use of cavalry, intelligence and espionage, psychological tactics, effective weaponry, innovative tactics, and centralized command structure. These factors allowed the Mongols to conquer vast territories and establish one of the largest empires in history. Their legacy lives on, not only in the conquered lands but also in the development of military strategy and tactics that continue to influence modern warfare.

The Mongol Empire is often remembered for its great military power and unmatched conquests. One of the key factors in their success was their use of advanced technology and weaponry, which allowed them to dominate their enemies on the battlefield.

The Mongols were skilled horsemen and archers, and their bows were of a superior design compared to those used by their adversaries. The Mongol bow was made of multiple layers of horn, wood, and sinew, and was able to shoot an arrow up to 300 yards with deadly accuracy. They were also known for their use of the composite bow, which was made from a combination of materials, including bone, wood, and sinew. These bows were light, powerful, and could be used while on horseback, giving the Mongols a distinct advantage in warfare.

In addition to their superior weaponry, the Mongols were also skilled in the use of siege engines and gunpowder. They were the first to use gunpowder in warfare, and they developed a variety of weapons that used this explosive material, including bombs, grenades, and rockets. They also used trebuchets and other siege engines to lay siege to cities and fortresses, which allowed them to capture strategic locations and expand their territory.

The Mongols also had a highly effective military strategy that involved a combination of speed, deception, and surprise. They were known for their use of feigned retreats, in which they would appear to be fleeing the battlefield, only to suddenly turn around and attack their pursuers. This tactic allowed them to draw their enemies into an ambush, where they could then surround and defeat them.

The Mongols were also skilled at using their cavalry to strike quickly and effectively. They would use their horses to encircle their enemies, making it difficult for them to escape, while at the same time raining down arrows from a safe distance. The Mongols were able to move quickly across the open steppes, and their horses were able to cover vast distances without tiring, giving them a significant advantage over their slower-moving opponents.

Another key factor in the Mongols' success was their ability to adapt to different terrains and environments. They were able to navigate through the mountains and deserts of Central Asia, and they were equally skilled at fighting in the flat plains of Eastern Europe. This adaptability allowed them to conquer a wide range of territories, from China and Korea to Persia and Russia.

Overall, the Mongols' use of advanced technology and innovative military tactics helped them to create one of the most successful empires in history. Their legacy lives on, not just in the territory they conquered, but in the way that they changed the nature of warfare forever.

The rise of the Mongol Empire was a testament to the power of communication. The vast distances of the empire were covered by a system of messenger stations known as the Yam, which enabled the rapid transmission of information across the empire. This system, coupled with the Mongol's military might and innovative tactics, allowed them to conquer vast territories and build one of the largest empires in history.

The Yam was a series of stations that were strategically placed along the empire's main routes, with each station staffed by messengers who were tasked with transmitting messages from one station to the next. These messengers were highly trained and could cover vast distances in a short amount of time, thanks to the use of fast horses and the knowledge of the local terrain.

The importance of the Yam cannot be overstated. It allowed Genghis Khan and his successors to maintain control over their vast empire, to communicate orders to their generals, and to receive information about the movements of their enemies. The Mongols were able to respond quickly to any threat, thanks to their highly effective communication network.

The Yam was not the only communication tool used by the Mongols. They also employed a system of spies and informants, who were tasked with gathering intelligence about the movements of their enemies. These spies were highly trained and could infiltrate enemy camps and cities, gathering valuable information that could be used to plan military campaigns.

The Mongols were also adept at using visual communication. They used signal fires and smoke signals to convey messages across long distances, and they employed flags and banners to identify their troops on the battlefield.

But perhaps the most important communication tool used by the Mongols was their ability to speak multiple languages. As they conquered new territories, they absorbed the local populations, and many Mongols became fluent in the languages of the people they conquered. This allowed them to communicate effectively with their subjects and to understand their cultures and customs.

The Mongols were also known for their use of propaganda. They would often exaggerate their victories and minimize their losses, in order to intimidate their enemies and maintain the loyalty of their subjects. They would also make a show of their military might, marching their troops through conquered cities and displaying their wealth and power.

In addition to their communication skills, the Mongols were also renowned for their military tactics and strategies. They were skilled horsemen and archers, and they could fire arrows accurately while riding at full gallop. They would often use feigned retreats and other deception tactics to lure their enemies into traps, and they were known for their ability to adapt to changing circumstances on the battlefield.

The Mongols also developed innovative siege tactics, using a variety of weapons and tactics to breach city walls and fortifications. They would often use large siege engines, such as trebuchets and battering rams, to break down walls and gates, and they would also dig tunnels and use sappers to undermine fortifications from beneath.

The importance of technology in Mongol conquests cannot be ignored. They developed advanced weaponry, such as the composite bow and the stirrup, which allowed their horsemen to fire arrows more accurately while riding. They also developed tactics for using gunpowder, which they obtained from the Chinese, and they were known for their use of flamethrowers and other incendiary weapons.

In summary, the success of the Mongols was due in large part to their ability to communicate effectively and their innovative military tactics and strategies. The Yam, their system of messenger stations, was a crucial tool in their conquests, allowing them to transmit information quickly and efficiently across their vast empire. The Mongols' ability to speak multiple languages and understand the customs of their conquered subjects also played a key role in their success.

Chapter 6: Administration and Governance of the Mongol Empire

The Mongol Empire was the largest land empire in history, stretching from Eastern Europe to China, and encompassing much of Central Asia and the Middle East. The sheer size and complexity of this vast empire were made possible by a well-structured and organized administration that ensured its efficient operation. The structure of the Mongol Empire was based on a sophisticated system of provinces, divisions, and ranks that helped to maintain the empire's unity and strength.

At the top of the hierarchy was the Great Khan, who was the supreme ruler of the Mongol Empire. Under him were several lesser khans, who were responsible for the administration of various provinces. The provinces were divided into several smaller administrative units, each of which was overseen by a governor appointed by the Great Khan. The governors were responsible for the collection of taxes, the maintenance of law and order, and the provision of military support to the central administration.

The Mongol Empire was divided into several divisions, each of which was headed by a prince or a member of the imperial family. These divisions were created to manage the vast territorial expanse of the empire and to ensure its effective governance. The divisions were also responsible for the defense of the empire's borders and for the administration of justice in their respective territories.

The Mongol Empire was further divided into smaller military units known as tumens. A tumen consisted of ten thousand cavalry soldiers, who were divided into units of one thousand and one hundred. The tumens were the basic building blocks of the Mongol military, and they played a crucial role in the empire's expansion and consolidation. The Mongol army was renowned for its cavalry, which was unparalleled in its speed, mobility, and ferocity.

The Mongol Empire was a highly centralized state, and its governance was based on a system of meritocracy. The Great Khan and the khans appointed officials based on their merit and competence, rather than their family connections or social status. This merit-based system ensured that the most capable and talented individuals were appointed to positions of power and responsibility.

The Mongol Empire was a multicultural and multiethnic empire, and it was marked by a remarkable degree of tolerance and pluralism. The Mongols respected the cultures and religions of the peoples they conquered and allowed them to continue practicing their own customs and beliefs. The Mongols were also receptive to foreign ideas and innovations, and they actively encouraged the exchange of knowledge and ideas among the various regions of the empire.

In summary, the structure of the Mongol Empire was a testament to the vision and foresight of its leaders. The empire's well-organized administration ensured its smooth functioning and efficient operation, while its military strength and technological innovations made it a formidable force on the battlefield. The Mongol Empire's legacy is a reminder of the power of effective governance and the importance of unity and diversity in building a strong and lasting state.

In the vast expanse of the Mongol Empire, a set of laws and codes governed the behavior of its subjects. This system, known as the Yassa, was put in place by the empire's founder, Genghis Khan, and was designed to create a cohesive and organized society.

The Yassa was not a written document, but rather a set of oral traditions and customs that were passed down through generations of Mongol leaders. It covered a wide range of topics, from property rights to criminal justice, and was enforced through a system of appointed officials and local leaders.

One of the key principles of the Yassa was the idea of unity and loyalty to the empire. Subjects were expected to put aside their personal interests and loyalties in favor of the greater good of the empire. This was particularly important in matters of war, where the Mongols were known for their fierce loyalty to their commanders and their willingness to sacrifice themselves for the greater cause.

Another important principle of the Yassa was the concept of justice. Crimes such as theft and murder were punished severely, often with death, and there was little tolerance for disobedience or insubordination. However, the system was also designed to be fair and impartial, and all subjects, regardless of their status or position, were subject to the same laws and penalties.

In addition to these principles, the Yassa also covered a wide range of social and economic issues. It regulated the ownership of property, established rules for trade and commerce, and even set guidelines for the care of animals. The code was constantly evolving and adapting to new situations and challenges, reflecting the pragmatic and flexible nature of Mongol society.

Despite its many strengths, the Yassa was not without its flaws. It could be harsh and unforgiving, and its strict rules and regulations could stifle creativity and innovation. Additionally, its focus on loyalty and unity could lead to the suppression of dissent and individuality.

Despite these limitations, the Yassa was a key factor in the success of the Mongol Empire. It helped to create a strong and unified society, capable of conquering vast territories and sustaining itself through difficult times. Even today, the Yassa remains an important part of Mongol culture and heritage, a testament to the enduring legacy of Genghis Khan and his vision for a united and powerful empire.

In the vast and sprawling Mongol Empire, the role of the Khan was paramount. The Khan was the leader of the Mongol people, the commander-in-chief of their armies, and the ruler of their vast lands. Without the Khan, the Mongol Empire could not have existed, much less flourished as it did.

The position of the Khan was not necessarily hereditary, although it often became so in practice. Instead, it was determined by a combination of factors, including personal charisma, military prowess, and political acumen. The Khan had to be able to command the respect and loyalty of his followers, both within the Mongol nation and beyond its borders.

The Khan was also responsible for maintaining order and justice within the empire. The Yassa, a code of laws and customs that governed Mongol society and behavior, was often attributed to Genghis Khan himself, and subsequent Khans built on this framework to ensure that their subjects behaved in a manner that was conducive to the empire's success.

The Khan was not an absolute ruler, however. He had to take into account the opinions and desires of his advisors and subordinates, particularly the members of the Great Council, which acted as a kind of parliament or advisory body. The Khan also had to be mindful of the needs and aspirations of the various ethnic groups and tribes that made up the empire, and to ensure that they were treated fairly and with respect.

One of the most important functions of the Khan was to maintain the military strength and readiness of the empire. The Mongol armies were renowned for their mobility, discipline, and sheer ferocity, and the Khan had to ensure that they were always prepared for battle. This required a massive logistical effort, including the provision of food, weapons, and other supplies, as well as the recruitment and training of soldiers.

The Khan was also responsible for conducting diplomacy and maintaining relationships with other nations and empires. This was particularly important for the Mongols, who relied on the cooperation and goodwill of their neighbors to maintain their borders and secure their trade routes. The Khan had to be adept at negotiating alliances and treaties, as well as at dealing with potential threats and enemies.

Throughout the history of the Mongol Empire, the role of the Khan was one of paramount importance. It was the Khan who set the tone and direction of the empire, who maintained its military and political strength, and who ensured that justice and order were maintained within its borders. Without the Khan, the Mongol Empire would not have been the powerful and influential force that it was, and the course of world history might have been very different indeed.

In the vast expanse of the Mongol Empire, the role of women was both complex and significant. While patriarchal traditions were deeply ingrained in Mongol society, women played important roles in the governance of the empire, especially during times of war and conflict.

Women were often instrumental in the formation of alliances between tribes and clans, and were frequently called upon to negotiate treaties and agreements. In fact, it was not uncommon for women to hold positions of significant authority within the empire. One example of this was Sorkhaqtani Beki, the wife of Tolui and mother of Kublai Khan. Sorkhaqtani played an important role in Mongol politics, acting as a mediator and peacekeeper during times of conflict and helping to stabilize the empire after the death of Genghis Khan.

In addition to political power, women also played a vital role in the economy of the empire. As nomadic pastoralists, the Mongols relied heavily on the labor of women in the care of animals and the production of goods. Women were responsible for the processing of animal products such as wool and milk, as well as the production of clothing and other textiles. Women were also involved in trade, and many were skilled merchants who conducted business across the vast expanse of the empire.

Despite their importance to the Mongol economy and political structure, women still faced significant social and cultural barriers. They were expected to be submissive to men and were often treated as property rather than individuals. However, there were exceptions to this rule, and some women were able to gain significant power and influence.

One notable example of a powerful woman in Mongol society was Khutulun, the daughter of Kaidu, a powerful leader of the Mongol empire in the late 13th century. Khutulun was a skilled warrior and wrestler, and she famously declared that she would only marry a man who could defeat her in a wrestling match. Many men attempted to win her hand, but none succeeded, and Khutulun went on to lead a successful military career, commanding armies and fighting in battles alongside her male counterparts.

In addition to their military and economic contributions, women also played a significant role in the religious practices of the Mongol Empire. Shamanism was the predominant religion among the Mongols, and women were often the ones who performed the rituals and ceremonies associated with this faith. In some cases, women even served as shamans, interpreting dreams and communicating with spirits to gain insight and guidance.

Overall, the role of women in Mongol society was complex and multifaceted. While they were often marginalized and relegated to secondary roles, women also held positions of power and influence within the empire. They played an important role in the economy, politics, and culture of the Mongol Empire, and their contributions helped to shape the course of history in significant ways.

The Mongol Empire was not only a military superpower but also an economic powerhouse. The Empire, which spanned from Asia to Europe, was home to a diverse range of peoples and cultures, and it was the Mongols who managed to unify and rule over them all. The key to their success was their economic policies, which allowed for efficient trade and commerce across vast distances.

The Mongols relied heavily on trade as a means of generating wealth and supporting their empire. They established a vast network of trade routes that connected China to Europe, the Middle East, and the Indian subcontinent. This network, known as the Silk Road, was one of the most important trade routes in history and played a significant role in the Mongol Empire's economic success.

The Mongols also imposed a tax system that was designed to support their military campaigns and to maintain the Empire's infrastructure. These taxes were collected from the peoples of the conquered territories, and the money was used to support the Mongol army and to fund public works such as roads, bridges, and irrigation systems. The tax system was efficient and effective, and it allowed the Mongols to maintain their vast empire with relatively little resistance.

In addition to trade and taxes, agriculture played an important role in the Mongol economy. The Empire's vast grasslands were home to millions of horses and sheep, which provided food, transportation, and raw materials for the Mongol people. Agriculture, however, was not the main focus of the Mongols, and they did not develop advanced farming techniques or irrigation systems like some other civilizations.

The Mongol Empire also had a unique system of paper money, known as chao, which was widely used in China during the Yuan Dynasty. The use of paper money was revolutionary for its time, and it allowed for more efficient trade and commerce across vast distances.

The Mongol Empire's economic policies were not without their flaws, however. The Empire's reliance on trade and the Silk Road made it vulnerable to disruptions in the flow of goods and people. The Mongols also faced challenges in managing their vast empire, and corruption and mismanagement were common problems.

Despite these challenges, the Mongol Empire's economic policies were remarkably successful. The Empire's vast wealth allowed for the construction of monumental works of architecture, such as the capital city of Karakorum, and supported a vibrant and diverse culture that included artists, writers, and scholars.

In summary, the Mongol Empire's economic policies were crucial to its success as a military and political power. The Empire's focus on trade, taxes, and the efficient use of resources allowed it to maintain its vast territory and support its people. While there were challenges and shortcomings in the Mongol economy, its overall success is a testament to the innovative and effective policies put in place by the Mongol leadership.

Chapter 7: The Role of Religion in Mongol Society

Shamanism, at its core, is a belief in the supernatural ability of individuals to communicate with the spiritual realm. In Mongol culture, shamans were considered to be the mediators between the living and the spirits, the keepers of ancient knowledge, and the healers of the sick. Shamans had a significant role in Mongol society, especially in their religious practices, which were deeply rooted in the belief in the existence of spirits, both good and evil.

Animism, on the other hand, is a belief in the existence of spirits in every animate and inanimate object. The Mongols, being a nomadic people, held the belief that the spirits of their ancestors watched over them, and that they were responsible for ensuring the well-being of their families, livestock, and land. They also believed in the spirits of the natural world, including the sun, moon, and stars, as well as spirits of specific locations, such as mountains, rivers, and sacred groves.

The shamanic and animistic beliefs of the Mongols were closely intertwined and integrated into their daily lives, including their military campaigns. Genghis Khan himself was known to have consulted with shamans and relied on their advice during his conquests. For example, before embarking on a battle, the Mongol soldiers would perform rituals and make offerings to the spirits, seeking their protection and guidance.

The Mongols also believed in the power of amulets and talismans, which they believed could protect them from harm and bring them good fortune. These items were often made from natural materials, such as animal bones, teeth, and horns, as well as feathers, leather, and precious metals. The Mongols would wear these amulets and talismans around their necks or carry them in pouches, believing that they provided spiritual protection in times of need.

Another significant aspect of Mongol religious practice was ancestor worship. The Mongols believed that their ancestors continued to play an important role in their lives, and they would offer prayers and sacrifices to them, seeking their guidance and protection. The Mongols also believed that their ancestors could influence the spirits of nature, and that by invoking their ancestors' help, they could achieve success in their endeavors.

The role of religion in the Mongol Empire was not limited to spiritual practices. The Yassa, the legal code that governed Mongol society and behavior, also contained provisions related to religion. For example, the Yassa prohibited the killing of livestock during religious festivals, and it required all Mongols to honor their ancestors and participate in ancestor worship.

In summary, the traditional beliefs of the Mongol people during the time of Genghis Khan were rooted in shamanism and animism. These beliefs were closely intertwined with their daily lives, including their military campaigns, and were integrated into their culture and society. The Mongols believed in the power of spirits, amulets, and talismans, as well as ancestor worship. Religion played a significant role in the Mongol Empire, not only in their spiritual practices but also in their legal code and societal behavior.

The Mongol Empire is often remembered for its military conquests and rapid expansion across the Eurasian continent. However, the Mongols also possessed a unique cultural and religious identity that played an important role in the governance of their vast empire. In this chapter, we will explore the religious practices and beliefs of the Mongols, as well as their attitudes towards other religions and the concept of tolerance and syncretism.

The traditional beliefs of the Mongol people were rooted in shamanism and animism, which were the dominant religious practices of the nomadic peoples of Central Asia. Shamanism is a spiritual practice in which shamans, or spiritual leaders, communicate with the spirit world and perform rituals to heal, protect, and guide their communities. Animism is the belief that all objects, including animals, plants, and natural phenomena, have spirits and should be respected and honored.

The Mongols believed in a complex pantheon of gods and spirits, including Tengri, the supreme god of the sky, and Ulgen, the god of light and creation. They also revered ancestors and ancestral spirits, believing that they could intercede on behalf of the living and provide guidance and protection.

As the Mongol Empire expanded, it encountered many different religions and belief systems, including Islam, Christianity, Buddhism, and Taoism. The Mongols were generally tolerant of other religions, although they sometimes used religious differences as a pretext for warfare. Genghis Khan himself was known to be tolerant of other faiths, and he appointed leaders of different religions to high positions in his court.

The Mongols were particularly interested in Buddhism, which they encountered in their campaigns against the Khwarezmian Empire and the Jin Dynasty. Many Mongols, including some of the khans themselves, converted to Buddhism, which they saw as a way to gain enlightenment and connect with the divine. Under the Mongols, Buddhism spread throughout Central Asia and into China, where it had a profound influence on the culture and society.

In addition to Buddhism, the Mongols also had interactions with Islam and Christianity. While they did not adopt these religions themselves, they were generally respectful of their followers and allowed them to practice their faiths freely. Some Mongols even converted to Islam, including Berke Khan, who established the Golden Horde in the western part of the empire.

One of the most remarkable aspects of Mongol religious beliefs was their willingness to syncretize different practices and beliefs. Rather than rejecting other religions outright, the Mongols sought to incorporate elements of other faiths into their own. For example, they incorporated Buddhist and Taoist elements into their shamanistic beliefs, and they also adopted Islamic and Christian concepts of monotheism and divine justice.

The Mongols also had a unique concept of religious tolerance, which was based on the idea that all religions were equally valid paths to the divine. They believed that different religions were simply different ways of understanding the same spiritual truths, and that no one religion held a monopoly on the truth. This attitude of tolerance and acceptance allowed the Mongols to govern their diverse empire with relative ease and prevented religious conflicts from tearing the empire apart.

In summary, the Mongol Empire was a complex and diverse society that was shaped by its religious beliefs and practices. While the Mongols were primarily shamanistic and animistic, they were also open to other religions and adopted elements of Buddhism, Islam, and Christianity. Their unique concept of tolerance and syncretism allowed them to govern their empire with relative ease and created a legacy of religious diversity and acceptance that still resonates today.

In the early days of the Mongol Empire, the traditional beliefs of shamanism and animism dominated Mongol religious practices. These beliefs centered around a spiritual connection with nature and the belief that spirits existed in all things. The Mongol people believed that these spirits could be harnessed through the use of shamanistic practices such as divination, rituals, and offerings.

However, as the Mongol Empire expanded and encountered new cultures and religions, the attitudes towards religion began to shift. The Mongol leaders recognized the importance of religious tolerance and adopted a policy of syncretism, the blending of different religious beliefs and practices.

One of the religions that had a significant impact on the Mongol Empire was Buddhism. Buddhism was introduced to the Mongol Empire during the reign of Genghis Khan, when he met with the Buddhist monk Haiyun. Haiyun impressed Genghis Khan with his wisdom and knowledge, and the Mongol leader became interested in the teachings of Buddhism. He encouraged his followers to learn about Buddhism and even granted tax exemptions to Buddhist monasteries.

Under the reign of Genghis Khan's grandson, Kublai Khan, Buddhism became the dominant religion in the Mongol Empire. Kublai Khan was a devout Buddhist and patronized Buddhist temples and monasteries. He also invited Tibetan monks to come to his court and teach him about Buddhism. It was during Kublai Khan's reign that Buddhism began to spread throughout the Mongol Empire and became a significant influence in Mongol culture.

Taoism was another religion that had an impact on the Mongol Empire. Taoism was introduced to the Mongols through contact with the Chinese, who had a long history of Taoist beliefs and practices. The Mongols were impressed by the philosophical and mystical teachings of Taoism and adopted many of its practices into their own religious beliefs. One of the most significant Taoist practices that the Mongols adopted was the use of feng shui, a system of geomancy that is believed to bring harmony and balance to the environment. The Mongols believed that by following the principles of feng shui, they could bring prosperity and success to their empire.

The Mongols also practiced a form of syncretism known as tengrism, which blended elements of shamanism, animism, and other religions into a unique belief system. Tengrism was centered around the worship of Tengri, the Mongol sky god, who was believed to control the fate of the empire. Tengri was considered to be the most powerful spirit in the Mongol pantheon and was worshiped through offerings and rituals.

Despite the adoption of Buddhism, Taoism, and tengrism, the Mongol Empire remained tolerant of other religions. Christians, Muslims, and Jews were all allowed to practice their religions within the empire, and many Mongol leaders even patronized these religions.

The religious tolerance and syncretism of the Mongol Empire had a significant impact on world history. It allowed for the exchange of ideas and beliefs between different cultures and contributed to the spread of Buddhism and other religions throughout Asia. The Mongols also played a role in the transmission of technology, ideas, and culture between Europe and Asia, which had a lasting impact on the development of both regions.

Islam and Christianity are two of the world's major religions and have played a significant role in shaping the history of the world. During the 13th century, the Mongol Empire emerged as one of the most powerful empires in the world, covering a vast area that included much of Asia and Europe. The Mongols, being a polytheistic people, were open to religious diversity and tolerance, and as they conquered new territories, they encountered and adopted different religions, including Islam and Christianity.

Islam was one of the major religions that the Mongols encountered during their conquests. Islam originated in Arabia in the 7th century, and by the time of the Mongol Empire, it had spread throughout much of the Middle East and Central Asia. Many of the territories that the Mongols conquered, such as Persia and the Khwarezmian Empire, were predominantly Muslim. As the Mongols extended their rule over these territories, they encountered and interacted with Muslim scholars and religious leaders.

The Mongols' initial approach to Islam was one of tolerance and respect. In fact, some Mongol leaders, including Genghis Khan himself, were said to have shown an interest in learning about the religion. They also employed Muslims in important administrative and military positions. For example, many of the scribes who wrote official documents for the Mongol Empire were Muslims. Additionally, the Mongols allowed Muslim judges to continue to use the Sharia law, which is based on the Quran, in areas where they ruled.

However, despite the Mongols' initial tolerance towards Islam, conflicts between the two religions eventually arose. In the mid-13th century, the Mongols launched a campaign against the Muslim Khwarezmian Empire, which ended in the total destruction of the empire. This brutal campaign caused great resentment among many Muslims towards the Mongols, and this resentment was further fueled by the Mongols' adoption of Buddhism and other religions, which were seen as pagan by many Muslims.

Christianity, on the other hand, was a religion that the Mongols encountered to a lesser extent. Christianity originated in the Middle East in the 1st century and had spread throughout much of Europe by the time of the Mongol Empire. Although the Mongols did not conquer any major Christian territories, they did encounter Christians during their campaigns in Europe.

The Mongols' attitude towards Christianity was also one of tolerance and respect. Some Mongol leaders, such as Hulagu Khan, who led the conquest of the Middle East, were even said to have shown an interest in

Christianity. Additionally, the Mongols employed Christian scribes and advisers, and allowed Christian communities to practice their religion freely.

However, like with Islam, conflicts eventually arose between the Mongols and Christians. In the mid-13th century, the Mongols launched a campaign against the Christian Kingdom of Georgia, which resulted in the destruction of many Christian churches and the forced conversion of many Georgian Christians to Islam. This caused great resentment among many Christians towards the Mongols.

In summary, the Mongols' encounters with Islam and Christianity played a significant role in shaping their history and the history of the world. Despite initial tolerance and respect towards both religions, conflicts eventually arose between the Mongols and these religions, leading to resentment and hostility. However, the Mongols' openness to religious diversity and tolerance had a lasting impact on the territories they conquered, and helped pave the way for the spread of different religions throughout the world.

It is not uncommon for historians to examine the impact of religious institutions on political affairs, and the Mongol Empire is no exception. Religious leaders in the empire played an essential role in shaping Mongol society and governance. Next, we will explore the role of religious leaders in the Mongol Empire, including the power and influence of lamas, imams, and priests.

Firstly, it is essential to recognize that the Mongol Empire was not a theocracy, meaning that religious leaders did not have a direct hand in the governance of the empire. However, religion and religious leaders still played a crucial role in the lives of Mongol citizens. Genghis Khan himself had a tolerant attitude towards religion and allowed the free practice of various faiths within the empire. This policy was continued by his successors, and the empire became a melting pot of religious diversity.

One of the most influential religious leaders in the Mongol Empire was the Tibetan Buddhist lama, Pakpa. Pakpa was the spiritual advisor to Kublai Khan, one of the most significant Mongol rulers. Kublai Khan was not initially a follower of Buddhism, but after meeting Pakpa, he became a devoted practitioner. Pakpa's influence over Kublai Khan was significant, and he was instrumental in shaping the emperor's policies towards religion.

Pakpa was also responsible for introducing Tibetan Buddhism to the Mongol Empire. This new form of Buddhism quickly gained popularity among the Mongol nobility and eventually became the dominant religion of the Yuan Dynasty. Tibetan Buddhism's popularity in the empire was due in large part to its unique blend of shamanism and Mahayana Buddhism, which resonated with the Mongol worldview.

In addition to Buddhism, Islam also played an important role in the Mongol Empire. Many Mongols converted to Islam during their conquest of Persia and the Middle East. One of the most significant Muslim leaders in the empire was Rashid al-Din, a Persian physician and advisor to the Ilkhanate court. Rashid al-Din was an influential figure in the Mongol Empire and played an important role in the governance of the Ilkhanate. He was also responsible for promoting religious tolerance in the empire, which helped to maintain stability and prevent conflict between different religious groups.

Christianity also had a presence in the Mongol Empire, although to a lesser extent than Buddhism and Islam. The Nestorian Church, a sect of Christianity that originated in Persia, had been present in the region for centuries before the arrival of the Mongols. The church was able to survive under Mongol rule and even thrived in some areas. The Mongol rulers were tolerant of the Nestorian Church and even employed Nestorian Christians in administrative positions within the empire.

While the role of religious leaders in the Mongol Empire was not direct, their influence on society and governance cannot be understated. The religious leaders provided guidance and support to the rulers and helped to shape policies that were inclusive and tolerant of different faiths. The Mongol Empire was a unique example of religious diversity and tolerance in a pre-modern society.

In summary, the role of religious leaders in the Mongol Empire was significant, even if they did not hold direct power. The influence of religious leaders, such as lamas, imams, and priests, played a crucial role in shaping Mongol society and governance. Their contribution to the empire's religious diversity and tolerance helped to maintain stability and prevent conflict between different religious groups.

Chapter 8: The Legacy of Genghis Khan

In the early 13th century, Genghis Khan embarked on a campaign to unite the nomadic tribes of the Mongol steppes and build an empire that would be unlike any other in history. Through his unparalleled military prowess and strategic vision, he succeeded in creating an empire that spanned from the Danube River in Europe to the Pacific Ocean in Asia. At its height, the Mongol Empire covered more than 24 million square kilometers, making it the largest contiguous empire in history.

Genghis Khan's early campaigns in Central Asia and China laid the foundation for the expansion of his empire. By 1215, he had conquered the Khwarezmian Empire in present-day Iran, Turkmenistan, and Uzbekistan. This victory gave the Mongols access to trade routes that stretched all the way to the Mediterranean Sea, providing them with a vast network of economic resources. Genghis Khan also launched a series of successful campaigns against the Western Xia Dynasty in China, which resulted in the annexation of their territory.

As the Mongol Empire grew, Genghis Khan continued to focus on expanding his territories in China. In 1219, he launched a massive campaign against the Khwarezmian Empire, which at the time controlled much of Central Asia. The campaign was a success, and the Mongols were able to conquer much of the region, including cities such as Samarkand and Bukhara. The fall of these cities had significant consequences for the Islamic world, as they were centers of learning and commerce that had been vital to the development of the Silk Road.

Genghis Khan's campaign in the Middle East also had far-reaching effects in Europe. The Mongols' defeat of the Khwarezmian Empire disrupted the balance of power in the region and opened the way for the Mongols to invade Eastern Europe. In 1237, Genghis Khan's grandson, Batu Khan, led a massive invasion of Russia and Eastern Europe. The Mongols conquered cities such as Kiev and Moscow and went on to establish the Golden Horde, a Mongol state that lasted for centuries.

Genghis Khan's empire was not only vast in size but also diverse in terms of its ethnic and cultural makeup. The Mongols were a minority in their own empire, and Genghis Khan recognized the importance of incorporating other groups into his administration. He employed a system of meritocracy, where positions of power were given to those who had proven themselves in battle or in other areas of expertise, regardless of their ethnicity.

To govern such a vast empire, Genghis Khan developed a sophisticated system of administration that relied on the principle of decentralization. Local leaders were given a high degree of autonomy, allowing them to govern their regions in a way that was most effective for their particular needs. This system of governance helped to ensure that the diverse needs of the different regions of the empire were met, while also allowing for a degree of central control.

Despite the size and complexity of the Mongol Empire, Genghis Khan was able to maintain a sense of unity among his subjects. He instituted a common legal code, known as the Yassa, which helped to standardize laws and regulations throughout the empire. The Yassa also promoted justice and equality, as it recognized the rights of all people, regardless of their social status or ethnicity.

The Mongol Empire also had a profound impact on the development of world history. The Mongols facilitated the spread of ideas and goods across Eurasia, helping to bring different cultures into contact with one another. They also helped to create a new system of international relations, which relied on diplomacy and trade rather than conquest and subjugation.

The Mongol Empire, under the leadership of Genghis Khan, was one of the largest empires in world history. It extended from the Pacific Ocean to the Caspian Sea, and from Siberia to the Himalayas. At its height, the empire encompassed over 12 million square miles and had a population of over 100 million people. Yet despite its vast size and diverse population, the Mongol Empire was characterized by a period of relative peace and stability, known as the Pax Mongolica.

The Pax Mongolica, which lasted from the 13th to the 14th century, was a time of economic, cultural, and technological exchange between East and West. The Mongols themselves were not interested in imposing their own culture or religion on the conquered peoples. Instead, they adopted a policy of religious tolerance and cultural assimilation, allowing the people they conquered to retain their own customs, languages, and beliefs. This policy was central to the stability and success of the empire.

The Mongols also established a network of trade routes, known as the Silk Road, which connected the East and the West. This allowed for the exchange of goods, ideas, and technologies, which contributed to the economic growth and prosperity of the empire. The Mongols themselves were skilled traders and merchants, and they were able to capitalize on the trade routes they established to expand their own wealth and power. One of the key factors that contributed to the Pax Mongolica was the Mongols' military prowess. The Mongol army was highly organized and disciplined, and they were able to conquer vast territories with relative ease. This military might made other nations hesitant to challenge Mongol rule, as they knew that they would likely be defeated. The Mongols also established a system of government that was highly efficient and effective, allowing them to maintain control over their vast empire with minimal effort.

Another factor that contributed to the Pax Mongolica was the Mongols' use of technology. They were skilled in the use of siege weapons, such as catapults and trebuchets, which allowed them to conquer heavily fortified cities. They were also skilled in the use of firearms, which gave them an advantage over their enemies in battle.

The Mongols were also known for their strong legal system, which was based on the Yassa, a set of laws and codes that governed Mongol society. The Yassa was designed to ensure justice and fairness, and it was enforced rigorously throughout the empire. This helped to maintain law and order, and contributed to the overall stability of the empire.

Finally, the Pax Mongolica was facilitated by the Mongols' ability to communicate effectively over long distances. They developed a sophisticated system of messaging and intelligence gathering, which allowed them to maintain control over their vast empire. This system included a network of relay stations, where riders would stop to rest and exchange messages. This allowed messages to be transmitted quickly and efficiently, which was essential for maintaining control over such a vast territory.

In summary, the Pax Mongolica was a period of relative peace and stability that characterized Mongol rule in the 13th and 14th centuries. This stability was facilitated by a number of factors, including the Mongols' policy of religious tolerance and cultural assimilation, their military prowess, their use of technology, their strong legal system, and their sophisticated system of communication. The legacy of the Pax Mongolica can still be seen in the modern world, as it contributed to the growth and development of many of the countries that were part of the Mongol Empire.

In the vast and diverse lands conquered by the Mongol Empire, the exchange of goods and ideas between different peoples flourished like never before. The Mongols, though feared for their military prowess, were also skilled diplomats and shrewd merchants. They were able to establish trade routes and foster cultural exchange that spanned thousands of miles.

One of the most important consequences of the Mongol conquests was the opening up of new trade routes. The Mongols established a vast network of roads, bridges, and caravan stations that linked the various regions of the empire. This facilitated the exchange of goods and ideas between China, the Middle East, Central Asia, and Europe. For example, Chinese silks and porcelain were transported westwards to the Middle East, while European textiles and metals were transported eastwards to China.

The Mongol Empire was also a melting pot of different cultures and religions. Under the Mongol rule, people of different ethnicities and religions coexisted peacefully. The Mongols themselves were shamanists, but they also respected the religions of their subjects, including Buddhism, Christianity, Islam, and Taoism. In fact, some Mongol rulers became patrons of these religions and supported the construction of religious institutions.

One of the most important cultural exchanges during the Mongol Empire was the transmission of knowledge and technologies. In China, for instance, the Mongols promoted the study of mathematics, astronomy, and medicine, which had already been advanced during the Tang and Song dynasties. They also introduced new technologies, such as gunpowder and papermaking, to the West.

In the Middle East, the Mongols fostered the translation of Greek and Persian works into Arabic. The famous Arabic historian, Ibn al-Athir, wrote extensively about the Mongols, and the Persian poet Rumi, whose works are still popular today, wrote some of his most famous poems during the Mongol era.

Another important cultural exchange during the Mongol Empire was the movement of artists and artisans. The Mongols had a great appreciation for art and architecture, and they brought many skilled artisans to their capital city of Karakorum. These artisans came from all over the empire, and they brought with them their own regional styles and techniques. For example, Persian artists brought the use of geometric patterns and calligraphy to Mongol art, while Chinese artists introduced landscape painting.

The Mongol Empire also had an impact on the development of international law. Genghis Khan and his successors were known for their respect for the law, and they were careful to codify and enforce laws that would apply to all of their subjects. They established courts and tribunals that were independent of local rulers, and they were committed to ensuring that justice was served for all.

Finally, the Mongol Empire played a significant role in the history of human migration. As the Mongols conquered new territories, they often resettled entire communities of people. This led to the movement of peoples across vast distances, and it had a profound impact on the ethnic and linguistic composition of various regions.

In summary, the Mongol Empire was not just a military conquest, but a cultural exchange of epic proportions. It facilitated the exchange of goods, ideas, and technologies between different regions of the world, and it had a profound impact on the development of international law and the movement of peoples. The Pax Mongolica was a time of peace and stability that allowed for this exchange to take place, and its legacy can still be felt today in the diverse cultural landscape of the world.

The Mongol Empire, under the leadership of Genghis Khan and his successors, was one of the most powerful and influential empires in world history. Their invasions and conquests of vast territories across Eurasia in the 13th and 14th centuries had a significant impact on the political, economic, and cultural landscape of the region. The legacy of the Mongols can still be felt today, and their story is one of both triumph and tragedy.

Genghis Khan was the driving force behind the creation of the Mongol Empire. Born in 1162 on the grassy steppes of Central Asia, he was the son of a minor tribal chieftain. As a young man, he was captured by a rival tribe and sold into slavery, an experience that would shape his personality and leadership style for the rest of his life. After escaping from captivity, he began to rise through the ranks of his own tribe, demonstrating a gift for military strategy and leadership that would eventually make him one of the most successful conquerors in history.

Genghis Khan's initial conquests were aimed at unifying the various tribes of the Mongolian steppes under his leadership. He used a combination of diplomacy and military force to win the loyalty of other tribal leaders, and he was skilled at recognizing and rewarding talent within his own ranks. He also introduced a number of innovations to the traditional Mongol military, such as the use of horse archers and a highly mobile army that could quickly move across large distances.

With the Mongol tribes united, Genghis Khan set his sights on expanding his empire beyond the steppes. His first target was the Khwarezmian Empire, a powerful state that controlled much of Central Asia. In 1219, Genghis Khan launched a massive invasion of Khwarezmia, using his army's mobility and surprise to defeat the Khwarezmian forces and capture the capital city of Samarkand.

The conquest of Khwarezmia marked the beginning of a new phase in Mongol expansion. Over the next few decades, Genghis Khan and his successors would launch a series of campaigns across Asia and Europe, conquering vast territories and establishing a powerful and far-reaching empire.

One of the most significant of these campaigns was the invasion of China. In 1211, Genghis Khan led his army across the Gobi Desert and into the Jin Empire, a state that controlled much of northern China. The Mongols were initially repelled by the Jin forces, but they regrouped and returned with a vengeance, using their superior mobility and tactics to defeat the Jin army in a series of battles.

With the Jin Empire under their control, the Mongols turned their attention to the Southern Song Dynasty, another Chinese state that controlled the southern part of the country. The conquest of the Song Dynasty was a long and difficult process, requiring years of siege warfare and guerilla tactics. But by 1279, the Mongols had finally defeated the Song forces and established their control over all of China.

The Mongol Empire also expanded westward, into Central Asia, the Middle East, and Europe. They conquered the Khwarazmian Empire, Persia, and much of the Islamic world, as well as parts of Russia and Eastern Europe. They even made it as far as Hungary before being turned back by a coalition of European armies.

The Mongol Empire was not just a military power, however. It was also a cultural and economic force, facilitating the exchange of goods, ideas, and technologies across the vast territories it controlled. The famous Silk Road, a network of trade routes connecting China to Europe, flourished under Mongol rule, and many new innovations and discoveries were made during this time.

Genghis Khan, the founder of the Mongol Empire, is a towering figure in the history of Mongolia. Even today, his legacy looms large over the country, with his name being synonymous with strength, unity, and courage. Next, I will explore the influence of Genghis Khan on modern Mongolia, examining the ways in which his legacy has shaped the country's culture, politics, and national identity.

Genghis Khan was born in 1162, in what is now the northern part of Mongolia. He grew up as a nomadic herder, learning to ride horses and hunt from a young age. As he grew older, he became increasingly interested in military strategy and warfare, eventually emerging as a skilled leader and tactician. In 1206, he was elected as the Khan, or ruler, of the Mongol tribes, and he set about consolidating his power and building a vast empire that would stretch from China to Eastern Europe.

Today, Genghis Khan is widely regarded as a hero in Mongolia, with his image appearing on everything from banknotes to vodka bottles. His influence can be seen in many aspects of modern Mongolian life, from the country's politics to its cultural traditions. One of the most visible manifestations of his legacy is the giant statue of Genghis Khan that stands outside Ulaanbaatar, the capital city. The statue, which stands over 40 meters tall, is a symbol of the country's pride in its history and heritage.

Genghis Khan's legacy can also be seen in the way that Mongolian politics are structured. The country has a parliamentary system, with a president who serves as the head of state and a prime minister who serves as the head of government. However, the president has relatively limited powers, and the prime minister is the one who wields most of the executive power. This system is reminiscent of the traditional Mongolian system of government, which was based on a council of elders who advised the Khan.

In addition to politics, Genghis Khan's influence can be seen in Mongolian culture and traditions. For example, the country's traditional wrestling competitions are a direct descendant of the wrestling contests that were popular among the Mongol warriors. Similarly, the Mongolian diet is still heavily influenced by the nomadic lifestyle of the country's ancestors, with meat and dairy products forming the core of many dishes.

Another way in which Genghis Khan's legacy is felt in modern Mongolia is through the country's military traditions. The Mongolian Armed Forces have a reputation for toughness and resilience, and this is largely attributed to the influence of Genghis Khan. The military's use of horseback riding and archery is also seen as a nod to the tactics and strategies employed by the Mongol warriors of the past.

Perhaps the most important aspect of Genghis Khan's legacy, however, is his role in shaping Mongolia's national identity. Even today, over 800 years after his death, Genghis Khan is seen as a symbol of Mongolian strength, unity, and pride. His story is taught in schools across the country, and his image is revered in countless statues, monuments, and works of art. For many Mongolians, Genghis Khan is not just a historical figure, but a source of inspiration and pride.

In summary, Genghis Khan's influence on modern Mongolia is profound and far-reaching. His legacy can be seen in everything from the country's politics to its cultural traditions, and his story continues to inspire and inform Mongolian society today. Although he lived over 800 years ago, Genghis Khan remains a towering figure in Mongolian history, and his influence on the country and its people will continue to be felt for generations to come.

Chapter 9: Myths and Misconceptions about Genghis Khan

Genghis Khan, the founder and first emperor of the Mongol Empire, is one of the most feared and revered figures in world history. His name conjures up images of brutality, violence, and destruction. He is remembered as a fierce conqueror who built one of the largest and most powerful empires in human history through sheer force of will and an unrelenting thirst for power. However, much of what we know about Genghis Khan is based on myths and legends, and it is important to separate fact from fiction in order to understand the true nature of this remarkable figure.

One of the most persistent myths about Genghis Khan is that he was a bloodthirsty conqueror who delighted in killing and pillaging. However, this image is largely the product of Western propaganda and misinterpretation. In reality, Genghis Khan was a military genius who understood the value of strategic planning, organization, and discipline. He recognized the importance of minimizing casualties and preserving the lives of his soldiers whenever possible. In fact, he was known to be a surprisingly merciful and lenient ruler, often forgiving his enemies and allowing them to live in peace under Mongol rule.

Another myth that surrounds Genghis Khan is that he was a barbarian who had no respect for culture or learning. This image is also misleading, as Genghis Khan was a highly intelligent and cultured man who valued knowledge and education. He encouraged his subjects to learn and develop their skills, and he was known to be an avid reader and patron of the arts. He understood the importance of diplomacy and negotiation, and he was able to forge alliances with neighboring tribes and kingdoms by using his wit and intelligence.

Despite his reputation as a ruthless conqueror, Genghis Khan was also a visionary leader who understood the importance of creating a strong and stable empire. He implemented a number of reforms that helped to consolidate Mongol power and ensure the long-term stability of the empire. He established a system of governance that allowed local rulers to maintain a degree of autonomy while still remaining loyal to the Mongol throne. He also encouraged trade and commerce, which helped to create a thriving economy that benefitted both the Mongol elite and the common people.

It is important to note, however, that Genghis Khan was not without his flaws. He was a product of his time, and his actions were shaped by the harsh realities of life on the steppes. He was a fierce warrior who believed in the value of strength and power, and he was willing to do whatever it took to achieve his goals. He could be brutal and ruthless when he needed to be, and he did not hesitate to use violence and intimidation to achieve his objectives.

In summary, Genghis Khan is a complex and multifaceted figure who defies easy categorization. While he was certainly a powerful and effective conqueror, he was also a visionary leader who understood the importance of stability, diplomacy, and cultural exchange. His reputation as a bloodthirsty conqueror is largely the result of Western propaganda and exaggeration, and it is important to recognize the many nuances and complexities of his life and legacy. As we continue to study the life and times of Genghis Khan, we will no doubt gain a deeper understanding of this remarkable figure and the impact that he had on the course of world history.

The figure of Genghis Khan has long been shrouded in myth and mystery. Some portray him as a ruthless and bloodthirsty conqueror, while others see him as a visionary leader who transformed his people and created a great empire. However, one of the most common misconceptions about Genghis Khan is that he was a barbarian, a savage and uncivilized warlord who led his people to victory through brute force and intimidation. Next, we will explore this misconception and attempt to understand the true nature of Genghis Khan's character.

To begin with, it is important to understand the context in which Genghis Khan lived. He was born in the early 13th century on the steppes of Central Asia, a region that was home to a variety of nomadic tribes. These tribes were known for their warrior culture, and violence was often a part of daily life. However, this does not mean that they were uncivilized. They had their own languages, customs, and beliefs, and they had a highly organized and sophisticated society.

Genghis Khan himself was raised in a family of nomads, and from a young age, he was trained in the art of war. However, he was also taught the importance of diplomacy, negotiation, and respect for other cultures. He was not simply a brute force, but a highly skilled and intelligent leader who was able to unite his people and create a powerful empire.

One of the reasons why Genghis Khan is often portrayed as a barbarian is because of his military tactics. He was known for his ruthless campaigns of conquest, and his armies were feared for their speed and efficiency. However, it is important to remember that war was a way of life for the nomads of Central Asia. They were constantly fighting for resources and territory, and Genghis Khan was simply following in this tradition.

Moreover, Genghis Khan was not indiscriminate in his use of violence. He had a clear strategy for his conquests, and he was careful to avoid unnecessary bloodshed. He was also known for his policy of amnesty, whereby he would spare the lives of those who surrendered peacefully. This was a highly unusual policy for the time, and it demonstrated Genghis Khan's desire to minimize the human cost of his conquests.

Another reason why Genghis Khan is often portrayed as a barbarian is because of his treatment of prisoners of war. It is true that he did not have the same concept of human rights that we do today, and he was not averse to using prisoners as slaves or hostages. However, it is important to remember that this was a common practice at the time, and that Genghis Khan was actually more lenient than many other rulers of his day. He also had a system of tribute, whereby he would allow conquered peoples to continue practicing their own religions and cultures, as long as they paid tribute to the Mongol Empire.

In fact, Genghis Khan was a great patron of the arts and sciences, and he was known for his support of religious tolerance and intellectual inquiry. He was particularly interested in the traditions of Buddhism, Taoism, and Islam, and he was known for his respect for the beliefs of others. He was also a great admirer of Chinese culture, and he worked to incorporate many aspects of Chinese civilization into his own society.

In summary, the idea of Genghis Khan as a barbarian is a misconception that is based on a narrow and stereotypical view of the nomadic tribes of Central Asia. While he was certainly a formidable warrior and a skilled military strategist, he was also a highly intelligent and sophisticated leader who was able to create a great empire through diplomacy, negotiation, and respect for other cultures.

Amidst the vast steppes of Central Asia, the name Genghis Khan evokes a sense of awe and fear. His empire spanned across much of Asia and Eastern Europe, and his conquests were known for their brutality and swiftness. However, the perception of Genghis Khan as a destroyer of cultures is largely a misinterpretation of history.

It is true that the Mongol Empire under Genghis Khan's rule was one of the most expansive and powerful empires in history, and that his military campaigns were often brutal and devastating. But to call him a destroyer of cultures ignores the complexities and nuances of his rule.

First and foremost, it must be noted that Genghis Khan was not simply a conqueror, but also a shrewd statesman and strategist. He recognized the importance of governance and administration, and implemented a sophisticated system of laws, taxation, and organization to keep his empire running smoothly.

Furthermore, Genghis Khan was not just interested in conquering territory and expanding his power, but also in learning from the cultures he encountered. He actively sought out scholars and experts from conquered regions, and invited them to his court to share their knowledge and expertise.

Under Genghis Khan's rule, the Mongol Empire became a melting pot of cultures, with ideas and technologies flowing freely between regions. The Silk Road trade routes flourished, connecting East and West and facilitating the exchange of goods and ideas. Genghis Khan's policy of religious tolerance also allowed for the coexistence of different faiths within his empire, with Muslims, Buddhists, and Christians all living and practicing their religions under Mongol rule.

It is important to note that while Genghis Khan's conquests were undoubtedly violent, they were not solely responsible for the destruction of cultures. Many of the civilizations he conquered were already in decline, weakened by internal conflicts and external pressures. In fact, the Mongol Empire often provided a measure of stability and protection to conquered territories, especially in comparison to the constant warfare and upheaval that preceded their arrival.

Ultimately, the image of Genghis Khan as a destroyer of cultures is a simplistic and inaccurate portrayal of a complex historical figure. While his rule was marked by conquest and expansion, it was also characterized by a curiosity and openness to new ideas and cultures. The Mongol Empire under Genghis Khan's rule was a dynamic and multicultural society, shaped by the exchange of ideas and the blending of different cultures.

Genghis Khan is often portrayed as a ruthless and bloodthirsty conqueror who single-handedly built an empire through sheer military might. This portrayal, however, is both inaccurate and simplistic. While Genghis Khan was certainly a skilled military leader, the truth is that the Mongol Empire was built through a combination of factors, including superior technology, efficient organization, and effective diplomacy.

One of the most persistent myths about Genghis Khan is that he was a one-man army, capable of defeating entire armies on his own. In reality, Genghis Khan was not a superhuman warrior, but a talented strategist who relied on his military commanders and the loyalty of his troops. He recognized the importance of training and discipline, and he invested heavily in his army's equipment and organization. His tactics were often based on surprise and deception, and he was skilled at exploiting his enemies' weaknesses.

Another myth about Genghis Khan is that he was a bloodthirsty conqueror who enjoyed killing and plundering. This image is largely a product of biased Western accounts of the Mongol Empire. In reality, Genghis Khan was a pragmatic leader who recognized the importance of keeping his subjects alive and productive. He was known for his tolerance of other religions and cultures, and he often incorporated conquered peoples into his own army and administration.

Genghis Khan's military prowess was not the only factor that led to his success. He was also a skilled diplomat, who understood the importance of alliances and negotiations. He frequently used marriage alliances to cement relationships with other tribes, and he was known for his generosity towards his allies. This approach helped him to expand his power base and to consolidate his rule over the vast territories he conquered.

Another key to Genghis Khan's success was his use of technology. The Mongols were adept at adapting and improving upon the technologies of their conquered peoples, including the stirrup, the composite bow, and the siege engine. They were also skilled at building and maintaining a vast network of roads and trade routes, which helped to facilitate communication and commerce throughout the empire.

Perhaps the most enduring legacy of Genghis Khan is the system of governance he established. Under his rule, the Mongols developed a sophisticated system of administration, with a hierarchy of officials responsible for everything from tax collection to military recruitment. The empire was divided into provinces, each of which was ruled by a governor appointed by Genghis Khan. This system of government helped to ensure stability and efficiency throughout the empire, and it provided a blueprint for future rulers seeking to build and maintain large, diverse empires.

In summary, while Genghis Khan was certainly a skilled military leader, his success was due to a combination of factors, including superior technology, efficient organization, and effective diplomacy. He was not a bloodthirsty conqueror, but a pragmatic leader who recognized the importance of maintaining the loyalty and productivity of his subjects. His legacy is one of innovation and sophistication, and his empire provided a model for future rulers seeking to build and maintain large, diverse states.

The name of Genghis Khan has become synonymous with a variety of negative traits: brutality, bloodlust, savagery, and destruction. However, this portrayal of the great Mongol leader as a universal villain is a gross oversimplification of a complex figure who played a significant role in shaping the world as we know it today. Next, I will examine the various ways in which Genghis Khan has been misunderstood and misinterpreted throughout history.

To begin with, it is important to understand that Genghis Khan was a product of his times. He was born in a world where war and conquest were the norm, where different tribes and nations fought for power and territory. In this context, Genghis Khan was not an anomaly, but rather a product of a violent and unstable era. It is unfair to judge him by modern standards, as the values and morals of his time were vastly different from our own.

Another common misconception about Genghis Khan is that he was a bloodthirsty conqueror who reveled in the destruction of cultures and civilizations. While it is true that the Mongol invasions resulted in the loss of countless lives and the destruction of many cities, it is important to remember that the Mongols were not alone in their violent conquests. Every major civilization of the time engaged in warfare and conquest, and many were just as ruthless as the Mongols. In fact, Genghis Khan was known to be surprisingly tolerant of different religions and cultures, and often employed skilled artisans and craftsmen from conquered territories to enhance the cultural richness of his empire.

Furthermore, Genghis Khan's legacy extends beyond his military conquests. He was a great innovator and reformer, introducing new laws and policies that helped to modernize and improve the lives of his subjects. He created a merit-based system of government, where individuals were promoted based on their abilities rather than their social status or family connections. He also established a system of universal taxation and the use of paper money, which helped to facilitate trade and commerce within his vast empire.

Genghis Khan's military prowess is also often exaggerated. While it is true that he was a skilled military strategist, he did not achieve his victories through brute force alone. He was a master of psychological warfare, using tactics such as deception, intimidation, and surprise to gain the upper hand in battle. He also recognized the importance of discipline and organization within his army, and implemented strict rules and regulations to ensure that his soldiers were well-trained and prepared for battle.

Another important aspect of Genghis Khan's leadership was his commitment to the welfare of his people. He recognized the importance of infrastructure and public works, and invested heavily in the construction of roads, bridges, and other infrastructure projects throughout his empire. He also implemented policies to promote agriculture and other industries, which helped to ensure a stable food supply and a thriving economy.

In summary, the image of Genghis Khan as a ruthless and bloodthirsty conqueror is a distorted one, and does not accurately reflect the complexities of his life and legacy. While he was certainly a military leader who engaged in conquest and warfare, he was also a visionary leader who implemented innovative policies and reforms, and was committed to the welfare of his people. To fully understand the impact of Genghis Khan on world history, it is important to view him in the context of his times, and to recognize the many positive contributions he made to the development of his empire and the world at large.

Chapter 10: Genghis Khan's Impact on World History

In the history of East Asia, no event had as great an impact as the Mongol conquest of China. The rise of the Mongol Empire, under the leadership of Genghis Khan, transformed the geopolitical landscape of the region and ushered in a new era of cultural and commercial exchange between China and the rest of the world. The Mongol conquest of China had far-reaching implications not just for the Chinese, but for the neighboring countries as well.

The Mongol conquest of China was a long and arduous process that spanned several decades. It began in 1205, when Genghis Khan led his army across the Gobi Desert and invaded the Jin Dynasty, which ruled northern China at the time. Although the Jin Dynasty was able to repel Genghis Khan's initial incursions, the Mongols were persistent, and they continued to launch raids into northern China throughout the 1210s and 1220s.

In 1234, the Mongols finally succeeded in conquering the Jin Dynasty, after a lengthy siege of the capital city of Kaifeng. With the Jin Dynasty defeated, the Mongols turned their attention to the Southern Song Dynasty, which ruled southern China. The Southern Song was a more formidable foe than the Jin, but the Mongols were determined to conquer all of China, and they launched a massive invasion in 1279. After a protracted campaign, the Southern Song was finally defeated, and the Mongols established the Yuan Dynasty, which ruled China from 1279 to 1368.

The Mongol conquest of China had a profound impact on the country's culture, politics, and economy. One of the most significant changes was the adoption of Mongol culture by the ruling class. The Mongols were known for their love of hunting, their military prowess, and their nomadic lifestyle, and these values were adopted by the Chinese elites. The Chinese also adopted the Mongol language, which became the language of the imperial court.

The Mongol conquest also brought about significant changes in the Chinese economy. The Mongols established a system of taxation and administration that allowed for the efficient collection of tribute from the Chinese people. They also promoted international trade, which helped to bring wealth and prosperity to China. The Mongols were responsible for building the Grand Canal, which connected the Yellow River in the north to the Yangtze River in the south. This canal allowed for the easy transportation of goods between the two regions, and it helped to facilitate economic growth.

The Mongol conquest of China also had a significant impact on the rest of East Asia. The Mongols established the Pax Mongolica, a period of peace and stability that lasted for much of the 13th and 14th centuries. During this time, the Mongols encouraged cultural and commercial exchange between China and other countries in the region. They promoted the spread of Buddhism and Daoism, and they allowed for the free movement of people and goods across their vast empire.

The Mongol conquest of China also had a significant impact on Japan and Korea. The Mongols attempted to invade Japan twice, in 1274 and 1281, but both attempts were thwarted by the Japanese. The invasions, however, had a profound impact on Japanese culture and politics. They contributed to the rise of the samurai class, and they helped to create a sense of national identity among the Japanese.

In Korea, the Mongol conquest had a more lasting impact. The Mongols ruled Korea from 1231 to 1356, and during this time they introduced a number of cultural and political innovations. They established a system of government that was modeled on the Chinese imperial system, and they introduced Buddhism and Confucianism to the Korean people.

The Mongol invasion of Russia was a pivotal moment in Eastern European history, leaving an indelible mark on the region's political, economic, and social landscape. The impact of Mongol rule on Russia would reverberate for centuries, shaping the country's development and influencing its relations with neighboring states.

The invasion of Russia began in the early 13th century, as the Mongol armies under the command of Batu Khan swept across the steppes of Central Asia and into the lands of the Kievan Rus. The Rus were a confederation of Slavic tribes who had formed a loose federation in the 9th century and had developed a sophisticated and cosmopolitan culture centered around the city of Kiev.

The Mongol invasion of Russia was a catastrophic event for the Rus, who were caught off guard by the speed and ferocity of the Mongol assault. The Rus armies were unable to mount a successful defense against the Mongols, who used their superior mobility, tactics, and weaponry to devastating effect.

As the Mongols advanced deeper into Russia, they laid waste to countless towns and cities, killing, plundering, and enslaving the local population. The Mongols were known for their brutality and their willingness to use terror tactics to cow their opponents, and their invasion of Russia was no exception.

Despite the devastation wrought by the Mongol invasion, the Kievan Rus was not completely destroyed. Many of the surviving Rus princes pledged allegiance to the Mongol Empire, and were allowed to retain their positions of power in exchange for tribute and military service. The Mongols established a vassal state in Russia known as the Golden Horde, with its capital at Sarai on the Volga River.

Under Mongol rule, Russia underwent a period of profound transformation. The Mongols brought with them a highly centralized political system, with power concentrated in the hands of the Khan and his appointed governors. This system replaced the decentralized, tribal-based governance that had characterized the Rus confederation.

The Mongols also introduced new technologies and economic systems to Russia. They were skilled horsemen and archers, and their cavalry tactics proved highly effective in Russian warfare. The Mongols also developed a sophisticated system of trade and commerce, which they used to extract wealth from their vassals and to maintain the loyalty of the Rus princes.

Despite the changes wrought by Mongol rule, Russia remained an important center of culture and learning throughout the period of Mongol domination. The Orthodox Church continued to flourish, and Russian art, literature, and music continued to evolve and develop.

Over time, the influence of the Mongols in Russia began to wane. As the power of the Mongol Empire declined, the Golden Horde began to splinter into smaller, more localized khanates. The Rus princes took advantage of this fragmentation to assert their independence, and by the 15th century, the Golden Horde had lost much of its power and influence.

Despite the decline of Mongol rule in Russia, the legacy of the Mongol invasion remained. The centralized political system introduced by the Mongols would endure, and would influence Russian politics for centuries to come. The impact of Mongol rule on the Russian economy and society was equally profound, and would shape the course of Russian development for centuries.

In summary, the Mongol invasion of Russia was a turning point in the history of Eastern Europe. The devastation wrought by the Mongols was significant, but the lasting impact of Mongol rule was even greater. The Mongols transformed the political, economic, and social landscape of Russia, leaving behind a legacy that would endure for centuries.

The rise of the Mongol Empire in the 13th century marked one of the most significant events in world history. The empire was established by Genghis Khan and his descendants, who conquered vast territories across Asia and Eastern Europe, including parts of China, Russia, and the

Islamic world. The impact of Mongol rule on these regions was profound and long-lasting, and it was particularly notable in the Islamic world.

The Mongol invasions of the Islamic world began in the early 13th century when Genghis Khan led his armies into Khwarezmia, a region in what is now Iran and Uzbekistan. The Khwarezmian Empire was no match for the Mongols, and it fell to Genghis Khan's armies in 1221. The Mongols then turned their attention to the rest of the Islamic world, invading the Abbasid Caliphate in Baghdad in 1258 and conquering the Ayyubid dynasty in Egypt in 1260.

The Mongol conquest of the Islamic world was characterized by brutal warfare and the destruction of many cities, including Baghdad, which was sacked by the Mongols in 1258. The Mongols were notorious for their ruthlessness in battle and their treatment of civilians, often massacring entire populations in conquered cities. The historian Ibn Khaldun wrote that the Mongols "left nothing but ruins and the corpses of men and animals behind them."

Despite the devastation wrought by the Mongols, their rule had significant and lasting effects on the Islamic world. The Mongols' military success was due in part to their adoption of new military technologies and tactics, including the use of firearms and the incorporation of foreign soldiers into their armies. This had a profound impact on the Islamic world, which had been slow to adopt new technologies and had relied on traditional forms of warfare.

The Mongols also brought new political and economic structures to the Islamic world. Under Mongol rule, the Islamic world was organized into a series of provinces, each governed by a Mongol prince or a local ruler appointed by the Mongols. This system of administration helped to integrate the Islamic world into the larger Mongol Empire and facilitated trade and commerce between different regions.

Despite their reputation for brutality, the Mongols were relatively tolerant of different religions and cultures. This was particularly notable in the Islamic world, where the Mongols allowed the practice of Islam to continue and even patronized Islamic scholars and artists. The Mongol rulers also patronized other religions, such as Christianity and Buddhism, and allowed them to flourish in the regions they conquered.

The Mongol Empire also had a significant impact on the development of Islamic art and architecture. Under Mongol rule, a new style of architecture emerged that combined traditional Islamic forms with Mongol elements. This style was characterized by the use of bright colors, intricate ornamentation, and the incorporation of Mongol motifs such as lotus blossoms and dragons.

The impact of the Mongol Empire on the Islamic world was not limited to military conquest and cultural exchange. The Mongols also had a profound impact on the political and social structures of the regions they conquered. In many cases, the Mongol rulers supplanted the traditional ruling classes with their own appointees, who often had little connection to the local population. This led to a degree of resentment and alienation among the conquered populations, which in some cases led to rebellions and uprisings against Mongol rule.

Despite these challenges, the Mongol Empire left an indelible mark on the Islamic world. The integration of different regions into a larger empire facilitated trade and commerce, leading to the growth of cities and the development of new technologies. The Mongols also helped to spread Islamic culture and scholarship to new regions, and their legacy can still be seen in the art and architecture of many Islamic countries.

In the midst of the 13th century, the Mongol Empire under the leadership of Genghis Khan had spread across much of the Eurasian continent, dominating regions from China to Russia. This vast empire included a diverse range of cultures, religions, and political systems, but none were more impacted by Mongol rule than the Christian states of Europe engaged in the Crusades.

The Crusades, launched by Christian Europe in the 11th century with the aim of reclaiming Jerusalem and the Holy Land from Muslim control, had already experienced significant setbacks by the time the Mongol Empire emerged as a major player in the region. The Fourth Crusade, for example, had famously ended in the sacking of Constantinople and the establishment of a Latin Empire in the Byzantine territories. The Seventh Crusade, led by King Louis IX of France, was in progress when the Mongols first made their appearance in the region.

The Mongol Empire, under the leadership of Genghis Khan's successors, was a formidable force that posed a significant threat to the Christian states of Europe engaged in the Crusades. Mongol armies had already conquered much of Asia and Eastern Europe, and their advance into the Middle East meant that they were now on the doorstep of the Holy Land. It is not surprising, then, that the arrival of the Mongols caused great concern among the Christian powers of Europe.

Despite their fears, however, the Mongols did not initially target the Crusader states. In fact, they were initially more interested in consolidating their power in the Islamic world, where they faced significant resistance from the Khwarezmian Empire, the Seljuk Turks, and other Muslim states. The Mongol Empire under Genghis Khan's successors continued to expand, however, and by the mid-13th century, they had conquered much of the Middle East, including Baghdad and Aleppo.

The Mongols' expansion into the Islamic world had significant consequences for the Crusader states. The Crusaders had previously relied on alliances with Muslim states such as the Fatimids and the Seljuks to secure their position in the region. However, the Mongol conquests disrupted these alliances, as many Muslim states came under Mongol control or were forced to align themselves with the Mongol Empire. This left the Crusader states isolated and vulnerable.

Despite this, the Crusaders did not initially view the Mongols as a significant threat. In fact, there were even some Christian states, such as the Armenian Kingdom of Cilicia, that allied themselves with the Mongols in the hope of securing their own positions in the region. However, this changed in 1260 when the Mongols, under the leadership of Hulagu Khan, launched an invasion of the Mamluk Sultanate of Egypt.

The Battle of Ain Jalut, fought between the Mongols and the Mamluks in September 1260, was a decisive turning point in the Mongol's relationship with the Crusader states. The Mamluks, led by Sultan Qutuz, were able to defeat the Mongols and force them to retreat from the region. This marked the first time that the Mongols had suffered a significant military defeat in the Islamic world.

The Battle of Ain Jalut had important implications for the Crusader states. The Mongols had been seen as a potential ally against the Muslims, but their defeat at Ain Jalut made it clear that they were not invincible. This gave renewed hope to the Crusaders, who began to see the Mongols as a potential threat to their own interests in the region.

It is difficult to overstate the impact of Genghis Khan and the Mongol Empire on world history. From their humble beginnings as a collection of nomadic tribes on the vast steppes of Central Asia, the Mongols under Genghis Khan's leadership went on to conquer vast swaths of territory, extending from Eastern Europe to the Middle East and East Asia. The Mongol Empire, at its height, was the largest contiguous empire in history, and its impact on world history continues to be felt to this day.

One of the most significant legacies of Genghis Khan and the Mongol Empire was their impact on the spread of ideas, technologies, and cultures. The Mongols were masterful at assimilating new ideas and technologies from the societies they conquered and incorporating them into their own way of life. This led to a cultural exchange unlike any other in history, as ideas and technologies from Europe, the Middle East, and East Asia spread throughout the Mongol Empire and beyond.

The Mongols were also known for their military prowess and tactics. Genghis Khan himself was a brilliant strategist, and the Mongol army was known for its speed, mobility, and adaptability. The Mongols were skilled horsemen, and they used their cavalry to devastating effect in battles against their enemies. The Mongols also developed new technologies, such as the compound bow and the trebuchet, which gave them a distinct advantage over their opponents.

Another significant legacy of Genghis Khan and the Mongol Empire was their impact on the global economy. The Mongols established a vast trade network that connected Europe, the Middle East, and East Asia, and their control of this network allowed them to exert tremendous economic power. The Mongols were also known for their tolerance of different religions and cultures, which facilitated trade and cultural exchange throughout their empire.

However, the Mongols were also known for their brutality and ruthlessness, and their conquests led to the deaths of millions of people. The Mongols were known for their tactics of terror and psychological warfare, such as the use of mass executions and the destruction of entire cities. The impact of Mongol conquests on the societies they conquered was often devastating, and it took many years for these societies to recover.

Despite these negatives, the impact of Genghis Khan and the Mongol Empire on world history cannot be denied. The Mongols helped to establish a new era of globalization, connecting disparate regions of the world through trade, cultural exchange, and technological innovation. The legacy of Genghis Khan and the Mongol Empire is still felt to this day in the cultures and societies of Central Asia, East Asia, and the Middle East, and their impact on world history will continue to be studied and debated for centuries to come.

BOOK 2

ATTILA THE HUN
FROM BARBARIAN TO LEGEND

BY A.J. KINGSTON

Chapter 1: Early Life and Rise to Power

The Huns are a people who loom large in the historical imagination, largely because of their reputation as fierce and warlike invaders. But who were the Huns, and where did they come from?

The Huns were a nomadic people who lived on the Central Asian steppes, a vast grassland that stretches from Hungary in the west to China in the east. They were part of a larger group of people known as the Xiongnu, who inhabited the region around the third century BCE.

The Huns were a warrior people, skilled in horsemanship and archery. They were known for their fearsome military tactics, which involved lightning-fast raids on enemy settlements and the use of terror tactics to demoralize their opponents.

The origins of the Huns are shrouded in mystery, but it is believed that they were originally a confederation of tribes who lived in the region now known as Mongolia. They may have been related to other Central Asian nomads, such as the Scythians and the Sarmatians.

The Huns began to move westward in the fourth century CE, possibly due to pressure from other tribes or changes in the climate that made it harder to sustain a nomadic lifestyle. They first encountered the Roman Empire in the mid-fourth century, when they raided across the Danube River into what is now modern-day Bulgaria.

Over the next few decades, the Huns continued to raid and plunder across Europe, striking fear into the hearts of those who encountered them. They defeated the armies of the Eastern Roman Empire in several battles, and their leader, Attila, became known as the "Scourge of God" for his devastating military campaigns.

Despite their fearsome reputation, the Huns were not solely focused on warfare. They were skilled horsemen and herders, and they traded goods such as furs, leather, and horses with other tribes and nations. They also had their own religion, which is believed to have been a form of shamanism that involved worshiping the spirits of nature and the ancestors.

The Huns were not a homogeneous people, but rather a loose confederation of tribes that were united by a common language, culture, and way of life. They were not organized into a centralized state, but instead operated as a federation of independent groups that were loosely bound together by ties of kinship and mutual self-interest.

Despite this lack of centralization, the Huns were a formidable force on the battlefield. They were skilled archers and horsemen, and they had a flexible and adaptive military strategy that allowed them to respond quickly to changing circumstances.

Today, the legacy of the Huns lives on in the many stories and legends that have been told about them over the centuries. They remain a symbol of the power of the nomadic tribes that once roamed the steppes of Central Asia, and of the complex and interconnected history of the peoples of Eurasia.

The life of Attila, the Hun leader who terrorized the Roman Empire in the 5th century AD, is shrouded in mystery and legend. According to the sources, Attila was born around 406 AD, into a royal family that belonged to the Hunnic confederation. His father was Mundzuk, a chieftain who ruled over the Huns and other tribes of the Central Asian steppes. Attila's uncle Ruga was also a prominent figure among the Huns, and served as a mentor to his nephew.

Attila's childhood was spent on the steppes, where the Huns were a nomadic people who lived by hunting, fishing, and herding. Attila grew up with a love for horses and a strong attachment to his people and their way of life. The Huns were known for their fierce fighting spirit, their horsemanship, and their skill with the bow and arrow. From an early age, Attila was trained in the arts of war and hunting, and learned to ride and shoot with great proficiency.

Attila's youth was marked by political turmoil and shifting alliances among the Hunnic tribes. The Huns were a confederation of various tribes and clans, each with their own leaders and interests. Attila's father Mundzuk was a powerful figure, but he faced challenges from rival clans and factions within the Huns. Attila's uncle Ruga was one such rival, who at one point forced Mundzuk to flee from the Huns and seek refuge among other tribes.

Attila's youth was also marked by contact with the Roman Empire, which had long been a neighbor and occasional adversary of the Huns. The Romans viewed the Huns as a barbarian threat to their frontiers, and often resorted to diplomacy and military force to keep them in check. Attila himself was said to have been a hostage at the Roman court, sent there as a pledge of peace by his father Mundzuk.

Attila's experiences in Rome had a profound impact on him, and may have shaped his views of the Romans and their civilization. According to some sources, Attila was impressed by the wealth and luxury of the Roman court, and may have envied their power and sophistication. However, other sources suggest that Attila was appalled by the decadence and corruption of Roman society, and saw them as weak and effeminate.

After returning from Rome, Attila became increasingly involved in Hunnic politics and military affairs. He served as a military commander under his uncle Ruga, and led raids against neighboring tribes and Roman settlements. Attila quickly gained a reputation as a fierce warrior and a cunning strategist, and was admired by his followers for his bravery and leadership.

As Attila grew older, he began to assert his independence from his uncle Ruga and other Hunnic leaders. He formed alliances with other tribes and clans, and established himself as a powerful figure among the Huns. Attila also became increasingly hostile towards the Romans, seeing them as a constant threat to Hunnic independence and power.

In summary, Attila's childhood and youth were shaped by the turbulent politics and nomadic culture of the Hunnic tribes, as well as by his encounters with the Roman Empire. His experiences in Rome may have given him a glimpse of the power and riches that could be gained by conquering the Romans, while his upbringing among the Huns instilled in him a deep loyalty to his people and a love for the nomadic way of life.

In the annals of history, few names have stirred up as much terror and awe as Attila the Hun. Born in the early 5th century CE, Attila was the most renowned king of the Huns, a fierce nomadic people that originated in Central Asia. Although much of his early life remains shrouded in mystery and legend, it is known that Attila rose to power after the death of his uncle Rugila, who had been the leader of the Huns.

Rugila's death sparked a power struggle within the Hunnic confederation, with various chieftains vying for control. Attila and his elder brother Bleda emerged as the frontrunners, and in 434 CE they were jointly elected to succeed their uncle as the new rulers of the Huns.

Although Attila was the younger of the two brothers, he quickly established himself as the dominant force in the partnership. He was a charismatic and ambitious leader, with a talent for inspiring his warriors to great feats of bravery and ferocity. Under his command, the Huns launched a series of devastating raids against their neighbors, including the Goths, the Thracians, and the Eastern Roman Empire.

Attila's early campaigns were marked by his aggressive and expansionist policies. He was determined to extend the reach of the Hunnic empire, and he used his formidable military prowess to subdue and conquer neighboring tribes. He was also known for his cunning diplomacy, often using threats or the promise of alliance to force weaker kingdoms to submit to his authority.

Attila's success on the battlefield brought him great wealth and power. He became one of the wealthiest men in the world, with vast herds of horses, cattle, and sheep, as well as a treasure trove of gold and silver. His court was a glittering spectacle of luxury and excess, with feasting, drinking, and music that lasted for days on end.

But Attila's rise to power was not without its challenges. He faced opposition from both within and outside the Hunnic confederation, and he had to fight to maintain his position as the undisputed leader of the Huns. In particular, his relationship with his brother Bleda was fraught with tension and conflict, as the two brothers jostled for control of the empire.

Ultimately, Attila emerged victorious, and by the mid-5th century CE he had consolidated his position as the most powerful king of the Huns. He had also established himself as one of the greatest military commanders of his time, with a reputation for ruthlessness and brutality that struck fear into the hearts of his enemies.

Although Attila's legacy is largely one of destruction and violence, there is no denying the impact that he had on the history of the world. His conquests and campaigns shaped the political and social landscape of Europe and Asia for centuries to come, and his name remains a byword for savagery and ferocity even today.

Attila, the King of the Huns, was a military genius who conquered vast territories through his brilliant campaigns and tactics. He was born into a royal family in the early 5th century, and from an early age, showed a natural talent for leadership and warfare.

Attila began his military career by fighting alongside his uncle, King Rugila, in campaigns against the Eastern Roman Empire. When Rugila died in 434 AD, Attila became the sole ruler of the Huns, and he immediately set his sights on expanding his territory.

Attila's early conquests were focused on the Roman Empire, and he quickly established himself as a formidable opponent. He invaded the Balkans in 441 AD, and his army of mounted archers wreaked havoc on the Roman legions. Attila also targeted the Eastern Roman Empire, launching several campaigns in the 440s and 450s AD.

Attila's military strategy was based on mobility, speed, and surprise. He relied heavily on his cavalry, which was composed of skilled horsemen and archers. Attila's cavalry was able to move quickly and strike with deadly force, making it difficult for his enemies to defend themselves. Attila also used psychological warfare to his advantage, spreading fear and panic among his enemies through his reputation as a ruthless and merciless conqueror.

Attila's most famous campaign was his invasion of the Western Roman Empire in 451 AD. Attila led an army of Huns, Goths, and other tribes across the Rhine River into Gaul, with the intention of sacking Rome itself. The Roman general Aetius, however, was able to gather a coalition of Roman and barbarian forces to confront Attila's army.

The two armies met at the Battle of the Catalaunian Plains, where Attila's army was defeated. Despite the defeat, Attila was able to withdraw his army and launch a new invasion of Italy the following year. This invasion was also unsuccessful, and Attila was forced to retreat.

Attila's military campaigns were not limited to the Roman Empire. He also waged war against the Sassanian Empire in the east, and against the Germanic tribes in the north. Attila's campaigns against the Germanic tribes were particularly brutal, and he earned a reputation as a ruthless and bloodthirsty conqueror.

Attila's military genius was not just in his tactics and strategy, but also in his ability to inspire loyalty and devotion among his soldiers. He was known for his personal courage and bravery, and his soldiers were willing to follow him to the ends of the earth. Attila was also skilled in diplomacy, and he was able to forge alliances with other tribes and rulers to further his military objectives.

Attila's military prowess was a major factor in the decline of the Roman Empire, and his legacy continues to be felt in modern Europe. He is often portrayed as a brutal and savage conqueror, but his military genius and leadership cannot be denied. Attila's campaigns and tactics have been studied by military leaders throughout history, and his legacy continues to inspire awe and respect.

In the waning days of the Western Roman Empire, a young and ambitious warrior emerged on the steppes of Central Asia. This man would come to be known as Attila, the Scourge of God, and would lead a fearsome confederation of nomadic tribes on a campaign of conquest and destruction that would shake the foundations of Europe.

Attila was born in the early 5th century CE, the son of a chieftain named Mundzuk. Little is known about his early life, but it is believed that he was raised on the harsh and unforgiving steppes of modern-day Hungary and Romania. As a young man, he served as a warrior in his father's tribe, honing his skills as a horseman and archer and learning the art of war.

When Mundzuk died in 434 CE, Attila and his elder brother Bleda inherited the leadership of the tribe. Together, they set out to expand their territory and establish themselves as the dominant power on the steppes. Their early campaigns were marked by a fierce and ruthless style of warfare, characterized by lightning-fast cavalry charges, surprise attacks, and devastating raids on enemy settlements.

Attila and Bleda quickly gained a reputation as fearsome warriors and skilled tacticians, and soon they were able to unite a confederation of tribes under their banner. With this powerful army at their disposal, they began to turn their sights towards the Roman Empire.

In 441 CE, Attila and Bleda launched a devastating raid across the Danube River, penetrating deep into Roman territory and sacking the city of Margus. The Romans were taken aback by the ferocity and speed of the Hunnic attack, and they quickly sued for peace.

The terms of the peace agreement were favorable to the Huns, who were granted a large tribute of gold and silver in exchange for their promise not to attack Roman territory again. This tribute made Attila and Bleda among the richest men in the world, and they used their newfound wealth to strengthen their position and prepare for further conquests.

Over the next several years, the Huns continued to raid and pillage Roman territory with increasing frequency, launching devastating attacks on cities and towns throughout the Balkans and Italy. Attila and Bleda's military strategy was based on a combination of speed, surprise, and overwhelming force, and they were able to overwhelm even the most well-defended cities with ease.

In 445 CE, Bleda died under mysterious circumstances, leaving Attila as the sole leader of the Huns. With his brother's death, Attila's power and influence only grew, and he set his sights on even greater conquests.

In 447 CE, Attila launched a massive assault on the Eastern Roman Empire, crossing the Danube with a massive army and laying siege to the city of Constantinople. The siege was ultimately unsuccessful, but it demonstrated the Huns' growing power and the threat that they posed to the Roman Empire.

Over the next several years, Attila continued to expand his empire, conquering much of Eastern Europe and establishing himself as the most powerful ruler on the continent. His military prowess and strategic genius made him a legend in his own time, and his name would become synonymous with terror and destruction for centuries to come.

However, Attila's success was short-lived. In 453 CE, he died suddenly while on a military campaign in the east, leaving his empire in disarray and his legacy in doubt. Despite his many victories and conquests, Attila was ultimately unable to build a lasting dynasty or establish a stable political system, and his empire quickly crumbled in the years following his death.

Chapter 2: Attila's Military Tactics and Strategies

Attila, the infamous king of the Huns, was known for his skillful use of cavalry in his military campaigns. Cavalry was the backbone of the Hunnic army, and Attila recognized its potential and made it the centerpiece of his tactics and strategy.

The Hunnic cavalry consisted primarily of mounted archers who were expert horsemen and skilled at shooting arrows from horseback. These warriors could fire their arrows while riding at full gallop, making them a formidable force on the battlefield. They were also highly mobile and could move quickly over rough terrain, making them difficult to catch and even harder to defeat.

Attila recognized the potential of his cavalry and used it to devastating effect in his military campaigns. He used his cavalry to encircle and trap enemy forces, firing arrows from all sides and causing chaos and confusion. This allowed his infantry to advance and finish off the disorganized and demoralized enemy troops.

Attila also used his cavalry to raid and plunder enemy villages and towns, striking fast and disappearing before the enemy could react. This tactic not only brought wealth and resources to the Hunnic Empire but also spread fear and terror among their enemies.

Another important aspect of Attila's cavalry was its mobility. The Huns were a nomadic people who were accustomed to living and fighting on horseback. They were used to traveling long distances quickly and could cover vast stretches of land in a short time. Attila used this to his advantage by launching surprise attacks on his enemies, catching them off guard and inflicting heavy losses before they could mount a defense.

Attila's cavalry was also highly adaptable, able to adjust to changing conditions on the battlefield. They could switch from a ranged attack to a close-combat charge at a moment's notice, depending on the situation. They were also able to fight in difficult terrain, such as mountains and forests, where other armies would struggle.

Despite the effectiveness of his cavalry, Attila was not entirely reliant on it. He also used his infantry to great effect, particularly in siege warfare. His infantry was known for its toughness and endurance, and could withstand long sieges while waiting for reinforcements.

Attila's use of cavalry was not without its challenges, however. His warriors were skilled horsemen, but they were not heavily armored and were vulnerable to enemy missile fire. Attila compensated for this by using tactics such as feigned retreats, where his cavalry would draw the enemy into an ambush or lead them into unfavorable terrain.

In addition to their battlefield prowess, Attila's cavalry was also instrumental in his efforts to maintain control over his vast empire. He used his cavalry to patrol the borders of the Hunnic Empire, preventing invasion by neighboring tribes and kingdoms. He also used his cavalry to suppress rebellion and maintain order within the empire.

In summary, Attila's use of cavalry was a key factor in his military successes and his domination of Europe in the 5th century. He recognized the potential of mounted archers and fast-moving horsemen and used them to devastating effect in his military campaigns. His cavalry was highly mobile, adaptable, and skilled in both ranged and close-combat, making them a formidable force on the battlefield. Despite their vulnerabilities, Attila's cavalry played a crucial role in maintaining control over his empire and preventing invasion by neighboring powers.

Attila the Hun, the notorious leader of the Huns, was renowned for his military prowess and feared for his reputation for brutality and violence. His strategy of "scare" was a tactic of psychological warfare that helped him in many of his military campaigns.

Attila was a master of using fear to his advantage. He knew that his reputation for brutality and violence would strike fear into the hearts of his enemies and make them less likely to resist. Attila understood that fear could be just as effective as force in winning battles, and he used it to great effect in many of his campaigns.

One of Attila's most famous campaigns was his invasion of the Eastern Roman Empire in the mid-fifth century. Attila and his army swept through the Balkans and approached the walls of Constantinople. The Roman emperor Theodosius II was terrified by the approach of the Huns, and he sent a delegation to negotiate with Attila.

Attila used his reputation to intimidate the Roman delegation. He told them that he was the "Scourge of God," and that he had been sent by the Almighty to punish the Romans for their sins. The delegation returned to Constantinople with the message that Attila was unstoppable, and that the city should surrender to him.

Theodosius was so terrified by Attila's reputation that he decided to pay him a tribute of 2,100 pounds of gold and an annual payment of 700 pounds of gold in exchange for peace. This tribute was a significant amount of money, but it was a small price to pay to avoid the wrath of the Huns.

Attila's reputation as a ruthless and brutal leader helped him to win many battles without actually having to fight. His enemies were often so scared of him that they surrendered without a fight, which saved Attila and his army from a bloody battle. Attila's reputation also helped him to secure alliances with other tribes, as many of them saw him as a powerful and unstoppable leader who could help them to achieve their goals.

However, Attila's reputation for brutality and violence was not always accurate. Many historians believe that the stories of his cruelty were exaggerated by his enemies, who wanted to discredit him and make him seem more terrifying than he actually was. Attila was a shrewd politician and military strategist, and he knew that he did not need to resort to brutality to win battles.

In fact, Attila was often merciful to his defeated enemies. He would spare the lives of those who surrendered to him, and he would sometimes even allow them to keep their land and possessions. Attila understood that it was often more beneficial to him to have peaceful relations with his defeated enemies, rather than to destroy them.

In summary, Attila the Hun's reputation for brutality and violence was a tactic of psychological warfare that helped him to win many battles without having to fight. His enemies were often so scared of him that they surrendered without a fight, which saved Attila and his army from a bloody battle. However, his reputation was not always accurate, and Attila was often merciful to his defeated enemies. Despite his reputation, Attila was a shrewd politician and military strategist who understood the value of peaceful relations with his enemies.

The art of siege warfare has always been a crucial component of military strategy, and Attila the Hun was a master of this tactic. His campaigns across Europe were marked by numerous successful sieges that allowed him to capture and hold key cities and territories. The key to Attila's success in siege warfare was his ability to adapt and innovate his tactics, using new technologies and strategies to overcome the defenses of his enemies.

Attila's armies were highly mobile and skilled in maneuver warfare, and this made them well-suited to conducting sieges. They could quickly encircle and isolate enemy fortifications, cutting off supply lines and preventing reinforcements from arriving. Attila's soldiers were also highly disciplined and well-trained, able to maintain the siege for weeks or even months if necessary, and could withstand enemy counterattacks with relative ease.

One of Attila's most famous sieges was that of the Roman city of Aquileia in northern Italy. Aquileia was a major commercial and strategic center, and its capture would have been a significant blow to the Western

Roman Empire. Attila's army encircled the city and launched a massive assault on its walls, using battering rams, siege towers, and other siege engines to breach the defenses. The Roman defenders fought valiantly, but they were ultimately overwhelmed by the Hunnic onslaught, and the city fell to Attila's forces.

Attila's success in siege warfare was due in part to his ability to innovate and adapt new tactics and technologies. He used a wide range of siege engines, including catapults, trebuchets, and siege towers, and his soldiers were skilled in the use of ladders and grappling hooks to scale walls and gain entry to fortified positions. Attila also recognized the importance of using psychological tactics to weaken the resolve of his enemies, and he would often launch surprise attacks or make exaggerated claims about the size and strength of his army to sow fear and confusion among his opponents.

Despite his success in siege warfare, Attila was not invincible, and he suffered some notable defeats when attempting to capture fortified positions. One such defeat occurred at the Roman city of Orleans in central France. Attila's army was unable to breach the walls of the city, and he was forced to withdraw after suffering heavy losses. Similarly, at the Battle of the Catalaunian Plains in 451 AD, Attila's army was unable to capture the Roman city of Troyes despite a lengthy siege.

Nevertheless, Attila's skill in siege warfare allowed him to capture and hold numerous key territories across Europe, including much of the Balkans, Italy, and parts of modern-day Germany and France. His reputation as a fearsome warrior and master strategist was cemented by his success on the battlefield, and his legacy as one of history's greatest conquerors endures to this day.

In summary, Attila's success in siege warfare was due to his ability to innovate and adapt his tactics to overcome the defenses of his enemies. His armies were highly mobile and skilled in maneuver warfare, and they could quickly isolate and encircle enemy fortifications. Attila's use of new technologies and psychological tactics also played a key role in his success, allowing him to overcome even the most well-defended positions. While he was not invincible, his skill in siege warfare allowed him to capture and hold numerous territories, and cemented his legacy as one of history's greatest conquerors.

In the annals of military history, few figures loom as large as Attila the Hun. His name is synonymous with barbarism, savagery, and bloodshed, and his campaigns across Europe in the 5th century AD left a trail of destruction in their wake. But beyond the lurid tales of massacre and mayhem lies a strategic genius, a military innovator who redefined the art of warfare and left a lasting legacy on the battlefield.

One of the key elements of Attila's success was his emphasis on mobility. Unlike many of his contemporaries, who relied on heavy infantry and fortified positions, Attila's army was based on fast-moving cavalry and light infantry. This allowed him to cover vast distances quickly and outmaneuver his enemies, who were often bogged down in siege warfare or slow-moving infantry battles.

Attila's cavalry was composed of two main groups: the mounted archers and the heavy cavalry. The mounted archers, armed with composite bows and deadly accuracy, were the backbone of Attila's army. They could shoot arrows while on the move, and their speed and agility made them virtually impossible to catch or outrun. The heavy cavalry, meanwhile, served as a shock force, charging into battle with lances and swords to break the enemy lines and create chaos.

But Attila's mobility extended beyond just his cavalry. He was a master of logistics, able to move his entire army, including non-combatants and supplies, over long distances with remarkable speed and efficiency. His ability to live off the land, combined with his skill in foraging and plundering, meant that his army could march for days or even weeks without needing to return to a supply depot or base.

This mobility allowed Attila to strike deep into enemy territory, bypassing fortified positions and attacking vulnerable towns and cities. He would often launch surprise attacks, catching his enemies off-guard and forcing them to react hastily. This put his opponents at a disadvantage, as they were unable to mount a coordinated response and were forced to fight on unfamiliar ground.

Attila's reliance on mobility also meant that he could easily retreat from battle if necessary. Rather than risking his army in a protracted and costly engagement, he would often withdraw and regroup, using his speed and maneuverability to avoid being trapped or surrounded by the enemy.

All of these factors combined to make Attila one of the most formidable military commanders of his time. His tactics and strategies were innovative and effective, and his ability to move and resupply his army over long distances gave him a crucial advantage over his enemies. While his reign was marked by violence and brutality, there is no denying his skill as a military leader and his enduring impact on the art of warfare.

The history of Attila the Hun is shrouded in myth and legend, but his military campaigns and tactics were remarkable for their effectiveness and brutality. Attila's success as a military leader was due in part to his ability to gather intelligence on his enemies and use this information to exploit their weaknesses. This allowed him to achieve victories against much larger and better-equipped armies, and to maintain a level of dominance over his conquered territories.

Attila's intelligence-gathering methods were varied and sophisticated. He employed spies, scouts, and informants to gather information about the movements and strengths of enemy armies, as well as their supply routes, defenses, and vulnerabilities. He also relied on interrogation of captured prisoners to gain valuable intelligence, and was known to be skilled at reading the signs of nature, such as the flight of birds or the behavior of animals, to predict the movements of his enemies.

One of Attila's most famous intelligence-gathering exploits was his capture of the Roman general Aetius' spy in his camp. Attila was able to extract valuable information from the spy about the Roman army's movements and strengths, which allowed him to plan and execute a surprise attack that resulted in a crushing defeat for the Romans.

Attila's use of intelligence was not limited to military operations. He also employed spies and informants to gather information on political and economic developments in the territories he conquered, which allowed him to better control and exploit these territories. He was known to use this information to identify and eliminate potential threats to his rule, and to extract tribute and resources from conquered peoples.

Attila's ability to use intelligence to his advantage was further enhanced by his mobility and speed. His army was comprised primarily of mounted archers and fast-moving horsemen, which allowed him to move quickly and resupply his army over long distances. This gave him a strategic advantage over his enemies, who were often weighed down by heavy armor and slow-moving infantry.

Attila's tactics also emphasized mobility and surprise. He was known for his ability to launch sudden and unexpected attacks on his enemies, often appearing where he was least expected and catching his enemies off guard. This tactic was particularly effective against larger and better-equipped armies, as it allowed Attila to strike quickly and avoid being pinned down or surrounded.

In addition to his intelligence-gathering and mobility tactics, Attila also relied heavily on psychological warfare. His reputation for brutality and violence was well-known, and he used this to his advantage to intimidate and demoralize his enemies. This often resulted in enemy armies surrendering or fleeing before battle was even joined, which allowed Attila to achieve victories without significant losses.

Attila's use of intelligence and psychological warfare set him apart from other military leaders of his time, and contributed to his remarkable success on the battlefield. However, his tactics were also brutal and often resulted in the slaughter of innocent civilians. While his military genius cannot be denied, his legacy is a mixed one, with some hailing him as a hero and others condemning him as a ruthless barbarian.

Chapter 3: The Invasion of the Roman Empire

In the 5th century AD, the Roman Empire was a shadow of its former self. Once a vast and mighty empire that spanned much of Europe, Asia, and Africa, it had been weakened by centuries of war, political instability, and economic decline. The empire had been split into two parts, with the Western Roman Empire centered in Rome and the Eastern Roman Empire centered in Constantinople.

The Western Roman Empire was in particular disarray, having suffered from numerous invasions, civil wars, and economic crises. Its once-mighty army had been weakened by years of warfare and was unable to defend the empire's borders from the numerous barbarian tribes that threatened to invade.

At the time of Attila's invasion, the Western Roman Empire was ruled by Emperor Valentinian III, a weak and ineffectual leader who was unable to provide strong leadership in the face of the empire's mounting challenges. The empire's military was led by a series of incompetent generals who were unable to effectively coordinate their forces to defend against barbarian attacks.

In addition to its military weaknesses, the Western Roman Empire was also plagued by economic problems. The empire had become heavily reliant on slave labor and had failed to develop new industries and technologies to keep up with the changing times. The empire's infrastructure was also deteriorating, with many of its roads and bridges in disrepair.

Despite these challenges, the Western Roman Empire still possessed significant resources and was able to mount a defense against Attila's invasion. The empire had a sizable army, with troops stationed along its borders and in strategic locations throughout the empire. The empire also possessed significant financial resources, with a large treasury and a network of taxation and tribute collection systems in place.

However, the empire's weaknesses would ultimately prove to be its undoing. Its lack of effective leadership, poor military coordination, and internal political divisions would make it easy for Attila to exploit the empire's vulnerabilities and mount a successful invasion. In the end, the Western Roman Empire would fall to Attila and his forces, marking the end of an era and the beginning of a new chapter in European history.

The early 5th century saw the Roman Empire weakened and vulnerable. Barbarian invasions and internal strife had left the empire divided and in a state of turmoil. It was during this time that a powerful Hunnic leader emerged in the steppes of Central Asia. His name was Attila, and he would become one of the most feared and respected conquerors in world history.

Attila's early military campaigns had brought him great success and his reputation as a fierce warrior had spread far and wide. He had established a powerful empire in the heart of Europe, stretching from the Danube River to the Baltic Sea. His next target was the Western Roman Empire, which he saw as weak and ripe for the taking.

Attila's invasion of the Western Roman Empire was swift and devastating. His armies moved quickly, capturing and pillaging towns and cities along the way. The Roman Empire was caught off guard, and its armies were unable to effectively counter Attila's tactics. As Attila's armies moved closer to Rome, panic began to spread throughout the empire.

The Roman general Aetius, a skilled military leader, knew that he had to act quickly to stop Attila's advance. Aetius was a veteran of many battles and had experience fighting against the Huns. He began to gather a coalition of forces from across the empire, including the Visigoths and other Germanic tribes.

The two armies met on the Catalaunian Plains, near the modern-day city of Châlons-en-Champagne in France. It was one of the most epic battles in ancient history, with over 300,000 men fighting on both sides.

Attila's army was made up primarily of mounted archers and light cavalry, while Aetius' forces were a mix of heavy and light infantry, cavalry, and archers. The battle was intense, with both sides taking heavy losses.

Attila himself fought bravely, leading his troops into battle and inspiring them with his bravery and skill. Aetius, on the other hand, was more cautious, relying on his superior tactics and strategy to outmaneuver Attila's army.

The battle lasted for several days, with neither side gaining a clear advantage. However, as the sun began to set on the second day of fighting, the Romans launched a surprise attack on Attila's camp, catching the Huns off guard and causing chaos in their ranks.

Attila was forced to retreat, and the battle ended in a stalemate. Both sides suffered heavy casualties, with estimates ranging from 20,000 to 100,000 dead. Despite the indecisive outcome, the battle had far-reaching consequences.

Attila's reputation as an unbeatable warrior was tarnished, and the Roman Empire had proven that it was still a force to be reckoned with. The battle also solidified the power of the Germanic tribes in Europe, who would eventually play a major role in the downfall of the Roman Empire.

Although Attila was not defeated at the Catalaunian Plains, his invasion of the Western Roman Empire was effectively halted. The empire was able to regroup and rebuild, thanks in part to the efforts of Aetius and his allies.

Attila would continue to wage war and expand his empire, but the Battle of the Catalaunian Plains marked a turning point in his reign. He would never again be able to mount a successful invasion of the Western Roman Empire, and his power would gradually decline in the years that followed.

The Battle of the Catalaunian Plains is a testament to the skill and bravery of both Attila and Aetius, and it remains one of the most significant battles in ancient history.

In the early 5th century, the Western Roman Empire was in a state of turmoil. Its territories were vulnerable to invasion, and its armies were in a state of disarray. In this time of crisis, a fearsome warrior emerged from the steppes of Central Asia. This was Attila, King of the Huns, and his conquests would leave an indelible mark on the history of Europe.

Attila's initial campaigns were directed towards the Eastern Roman Empire, where he encountered some success. However, it was his invasion of the Western Roman Empire that would make him a legend. In 452 AD, Attila set his sights on Italy, with the city of Aquileia as his primary target.

Aquileia was a major Roman city, situated in the northeast of Italy. It was a prosperous center of trade and culture, with a population of over 100,000 people. However, it was also a city with a long history of conflict. Over the centuries, Aquileia had been besieged and sacked by numerous invaders, including the Goths and the Huns.

Attila's army arrived outside Aquileia in the summer of 452 AD. The city was surrounded by a wall and a moat, but Attila was undeterred. He ordered his army to begin a siege, and the Huns immediately set to work building siege engines and preparing for an assault.

The siege of Aquileia lasted for several months. Attila's army launched numerous attacks on the city, but the defenders held firm. The Roman garrison was led by a general named Flavius Aetius, who was known for his military prowess and tactical brilliance. Aetius had previously fought alongside Attila, but had later become his enemy. He was determined to hold Aquileia at all costs.

Despite the efforts of Attila's army, the defenders of Aquileia refused to surrender. However, their situation was becoming increasingly dire. The

Huns had cut off their supply lines, and food and water were running low. Disease was also taking its toll on the defenders, and morale was beginning to wane.

Finally, after months of siege, the walls of Aquileia began to crumble. Attila's army had breached the defenses, and the defenders were overwhelmed. The Huns entered the city and began to loot and pillage. Many of the inhabitants were killed, and the survivors were taken captive.

The fall of Aquileia was a major victory for Attila. It was a blow to the prestige of the Roman Empire, and it showed that the Huns were a force to be reckoned with. Attila's reputation as a conqueror was further enhanced, and his name struck fear into the hearts of his enemies.

However, the victory at Aquileia would be the high point of Attila's campaign in Italy. His army was soon beset by disease and famine, and he was forced to withdraw back to his territories in Central Europe. Nonetheless, the legacy of Attila's siege of Aquileia would endure for centuries to come. The city was never fully restored to its former glory, and it remained a symbol of the vulnerability of the Roman Empire in the face of barbarian invasion.

In the year 435, a treaty was signed between Attila, the king of the Huns, and the Eastern Roman Empire, under Emperor Theodosius II. This treaty, known as the Treaty of Margus, was a significant moment in the history of the Roman Empire and the Huns. The negotiations and terms of the treaty reflect the balance of power and diplomacy that existed between the two sides at the time.

Attila's influence and military strength had grown considerably by the 430s. His conquests had reached as far as modern-day Bulgaria and Serbia, and his forces had defeated the Eastern Roman Empire in a series of battles. The Huns were a formidable force, and the Roman Empire had no choice but to negotiate with them.

The treaty was negotiated in the town of Margus, located in modern-day Serbia. The Roman Empire was represented by Flavius Aetius, a skilled general and diplomat, who was the most powerful man in the empire at the time. Attila was represented by his brother, Bleda.

The negotiations were tense and difficult. Attila demanded tribute payments from the Romans, which were to be paid annually. The Romans were also required to release all Huns who had been captured or enslaved, and to return all deserters who had fled to the Roman Empire. In return, Attila promised not to attack Roman territory and to maintain peaceful relations with the empire.

The terms of the treaty were harsh for the Romans, but they had little choice. Attila's forces were too strong, and the Roman Empire was too weakened by internal struggles and external threats. The tribute payments and other concessions made to the Huns were seen as necessary to maintain some level of stability and avoid further conflict.

The Treaty of Margus was a short-term solution, however. Attila's ambitions and the Huns' expansionist tendencies continued to be a threat to the Roman Empire. The tribute payments and other concessions did not stop Attila from invading Roman territory again in the future.

Nevertheless, the treaty did have some positive effects. It allowed for a period of relative peace between the two sides, which gave the Roman Empire some breathing room to recover and prepare for future threats. It also established a framework for diplomatic relations between the Huns and the Romans, which would continue to be important in the years to come.

The Treaty of Margus is significant for several reasons. Firstly, it reflects the balance of power and diplomacy between the Huns and the Roman Empire at the time. It shows the concessions and compromises that the Romans were willing to make in order to maintain some level of stability and avoid further conflict.

Secondly, it highlights the importance of diplomacy and negotiation in international relations. Attila was a formidable military leader, but he also recognized the importance of diplomacy and negotiation. His willingness to negotiate and sign a treaty shows that even the most ruthless and powerful leaders recognize the value of diplomacy and peaceful resolution of conflicts.

Finally, the Treaty of Margus is significant because it foreshadowed the decline of the Roman Empire and the rise of the Huns. Attila's ambitions and military strength continued to grow, while the Roman Empire struggled with internal problems and external threats. The treaty was a temporary solution to a larger problem, and it reflected the changing balance of power between the two sides.

In summary, the Treaty of Margus was a significant moment in the history of the Roman Empire and the Huns. It reflected the balance of power and diplomacy between the two sides, and highlighted the importance of negotiation and peaceful resolution of conflicts. It was a short-term solution to a larger problem, but it established a framework for diplomatic relations that would continue to be important in the years to come.

The name of Attila, king of the Huns, has become synonymous with barbarism and destruction. His invasion of the Roman Empire in the 5th century AD marked a turning point in the history of Europe, and his legacy still resonates today. Next, we will examine the impact of Attila's invasion and the lasting effects it had on the Roman Empire.

Attila was born into a royal family in the late 4th century on the Danube River. His uncle, Rugila, was the king of the Huns, and upon Rugila's death, Attila and his brother Bleda became joint rulers of the Hunnic Empire. From the beginning of his reign, Attila was known for his military prowess and his ability to unite the various Hunnic tribes under his rule.

Attila's early campaigns were aimed at expanding the Hunnic Empire and consolidating his power. He conquered numerous tribes and extended his rule over large parts of Eastern Europe. Attila's military strategy was based on the use of cavalry, and he was renowned for his ability to move his armies quickly over long distances.

However, Attila's reputation as a brutal and ruthless leader also played a significant role in his success. He was known for his use of scare tactics, such as burning entire villages and slaughtering their inhabitants, to intimidate his enemies. This tactic proved effective in sowing fear and panic among his opponents, making them more likely to surrender.

Attila's most famous campaign was his invasion of the Western Roman Empire in 451 AD. The Roman Empire was already in a state of decline, and the invasion of the Huns was one of the factors that hastened its downfall. Attila's army marched through the Balkans and Italy, pillaging and burning cities as they went. One of the most notable sieges was the siege of Aquileia, a major Roman city that was sacked and destroyed by Attila's forces.

The Roman Emperor at the time, Valentinian III, was unable to repel Attila's army and was forced to turn to the general Aetius for help. Aetius was able to gather a coalition of Roman, Visigothic, and Frankish forces to confront the Huns at the Battle of the Catalaunian Plains in modern-day France. The battle was fierce and bloody, with both sides suffering heavy losses. However, in the end, the Huns were defeated and forced to withdraw.

Despite this setback, Attila continued to pose a threat to the Roman Empire. In 452 AD, he launched a second invasion of Italy, but this time he was persuaded to withdraw by Pope Leo I, who is said to have met with Attila and convinced him to spare the city of Rome.

In 453 AD, Attila died unexpectedly, and his empire soon fell apart without his leadership. However, his legacy lived on, both in the tales of his exploits and in the impact his invasion had on the Roman Empire.

The invasion of the Huns marked a turning point in the history of the Roman Empire. It exposed the weaknesses of the empire and its inability to defend its borders against determined invaders. It also hastened the collapse of the Western Roman Empire, which would fall just a few decades later.

However, Attila's invasion also had a lasting impact on European culture and society. The Huns introduced new technologies and innovations, such as stirrups and composite bows, which would go on to shape the future of warfare in Europe. The invasion also led to the spread of new ideas and cultures, as the Huns brought with them their own customs and traditions.

Chapter 4: The Siege of Rome and Negotiations with the Empire

The ancient world was no stranger to military conquests and the rise of powerful empires. However, few conquerors have ever matched the ruthlessness and tenacity of the Hunnic king Attila. Born in the early 5th century in the region of modern-day Hungary, Attila was a fierce warrior who, from a young age, was destined to make his mark on history. As he grew older, Attila became more ambitious and began to envision a grand plan to conquer and dominate the Roman Empire, which he viewed as the most powerful force in the world.

Attila's motivation for attacking Rome was multifaceted. On the one hand, he was driven by a desire for wealth and glory, as well as a deep-seated belief in the superiority of his own people. The Huns had long been a nomadic tribe, roaming the plains of Central Asia and the steppes of Eastern Europe, and Attila felt that it was his destiny to lead them to greatness. He saw the Roman Empire as a prize ripe for the taking, with vast territories, rich cities, and an abundance of resources waiting to be plundered.

Moreover, Attila was also motivated by a deep-seated sense of resentment and hostility towards Rome. The Huns had long been a thorn in the side of the Roman Empire, launching raids and attacks on Roman territories throughout the 4th and 5th centuries. In response, the Romans had often resorted to diplomatic appeasement, paying tribute and offering concessions to the Huns in exchange for peace. However, Attila saw this as a sign of weakness and saw the Roman Empire as vulnerable and ripe for conquest.

Attila's decision to attack Rome was not made lightly. He spent years preparing and gathering his forces, building alliances with other tribes and armies and consolidating his power. He saw the invasion of Rome as a long-term project, one that required careful planning, strategic thinking, and a deep understanding of the enemy's strengths and weaknesses.

One factor that motivated Attila's attack on Rome was the perceived weakness of the Roman Empire at the time. The 5th century was a time of turmoil and instability for the empire, marked by political instability, economic decline, and military defeats. The empire had suffered a series of devastating defeats at the hands of various barbarian tribes, including the Goths and the Vandals, which had weakened its military and left it vulnerable to attack.

Another factor that motivated Attila's attack on Rome was his perception of the Roman Empire as a morally decadent and corrupt society. Attila saw the Romans as effeminate and soft, lacking the courage and strength of character that he felt was necessary to lead a successful empire. He saw their culture as decadent and depraved, full of moral decay and corruption, and saw his own people as a strong and noble contrast to this perceived decadence.

In addition to these factors, Attila was also driven by a deep-seated sense of pride and ambition. He saw the conquest of Rome as the ultimate achievement, one that would cement his place in history and elevate the status of his people to that of a world power. He saw himself as a conqueror on a par with Alexander the Great or Julius Caesar, and he was determined to make his mark on history.

Ultimately, Attila's decision to attack Rome was a complex and multifaceted one, driven by a combination of factors including ambition, pride, resentment, and a belief in the superiority of his own people.

It was the year 452 CE, and Attila, the fearsome Hun king, had set his sights on Rome. With a massive army at his command, Attila had already conquered much of the Western Roman Empire and seemed unstoppable in his quest for domination. Rome, the Eternal City, had long been a symbol of power and prestige, and Attila saw it as the ultimate prize.

Attila's decision to attack Rome was not made lightly. He knew that Rome was heavily fortified and defended, and that its armies were formidable. But he was determined to make his mark on history and cement his legacy as one of the greatest conquerors of all time.

The siege of Rome lasted for several months, and Attila's army launched a relentless assault on the city's defenses. But the Romans were not easily defeated, and they fought back fiercely. The two sides engaged in a brutal and bloody battle, with neither gaining a clear advantage.

Despite the ferocity of the fighting, Attila's forces were unable to breach the city's walls. The Romans had been preparing for this moment for years, and their fortifications proved to be too strong for Attila's army. Frustrated and unable to make progress, Attila eventually decided to abandon the siege and withdraw his forces.

Many historians believe that Attila's decision to withdraw from Rome was influenced by a number of factors. One of the most significant was the arrival of a delegation of Roman diplomats, led by Pope Leo I, who had traveled to Attila's camp to negotiate a peace treaty. The pope's presence was a powerful symbol of Roman authority and legitimacy, and it is said that Attila was so impressed by him that he agreed to withdraw his forces and leave Rome in peace.

Another factor that may have influenced Attila's decision was the increasingly dire state of his own empire. Attila had stretched his forces thin with his conquests, and his army was suffering from shortages of supplies and resources. With his armies weakened and his resources depleted, Attila may have realized that continuing to attack Rome was no longer a viable option.

Despite his failure to conquer Rome, Attila remained a formidable force in Europe for many years. He continued to wage war on the Roman Empire and other neighboring states, and his legacy as one of history's greatest conquerors remained intact. Today, he is remembered as a powerful and feared warrior, whose legacy lives on in the stories and legends of his exploits.

In the annals of Roman history, few stories are as enduring as the legend of Pope Leo the Great, who is said to have saved the city of Rome from the barbarian invader Attila the Hun. The tale of their encounter has been told and retold in countless works of literature, art, and popular culture, shaping the way that we think about the Roman Empire and its last great crisis in the 5th century CE.

The events leading up to their meeting began in the year 452 CE, when Attila, the powerful king of the Huns, embarked on a campaign to conquer Italy and plunder its wealth. Attila had already made a name for himself as one of the most fearsome warriors of his age, having conquered vast territories in eastern and central Europe and terrorized the Roman Empire for years. His invasion of Italy was seen as a direct challenge to the authority of the Roman Emperor Valentinian III, who struggled to muster the forces needed to stop him.

As Attila's army marched towards Rome, panic and fear spread throughout the city. The Romans had not faced such a threat since the sack of the city by the Visigoths in 410 CE, and they were ill-prepared to withstand the onslaught of the Huns. The citizens of Rome looked to their leaders for guidance and protection, but found little comfort in the cowardice and indecisiveness of the imperial court.

It was in this desperate moment that Pope Leo I, who had been elected to the papacy in 440 CE, emerged as a key figure in the defense of Rome. Leo was a learned and charismatic leader, who had earned a reputation for his piety, wisdom, and political skill. He had already played a crucial role in the church's efforts to combat heresy and maintain unity in the face of doctrinal disputes, and was highly respected by both Christians and pagans alike.

When Attila's army arrived at the gates of Rome, Leo made the bold decision to meet with the Hunnic king in person. He rode out of the city with a small retinue of priests and officials, dressed in his finest robes and carrying only his staff and the Book of the Gospels. As he approached the Huns' camp, he was met by Attila himself, who was struck by the pope's dignified bearing and impressive presence.

What transpired between the two men during their meeting is the subject of much speculation and legend. According to some accounts, Leo convinced Attila to spare Rome by invoking the wrath of Saint Peter and threatening the Hun with divine punishment if he dared to attack the holy city. Others suggest that Attila was simply impressed by Leo's bravery and eloquence, and decided to spare Rome out of respect for the pope's authority.

Whatever the truth of the matter, the fact remains that Attila did not attack Rome, and instead withdrew his army from Italy and returned to his kingdom in central Europe. The crisis was over, and Rome had been saved, thanks in large part to the courage and leadership of Pope Leo I.

The legacy of Leo's encounter with Attila has been profound and enduring. In the centuries that followed, the pope's heroism and diplomacy became the stuff of legend, inspiring countless works of art and literature, and earning him a place in the pantheon of great figures in the history of the Roman Catholic Church. The story of his meeting with Attila has also been seen as a testament to the power of faith and the triumph of good over evil, providing comfort and inspiration to Christians in times of crisis and uncertainty.

In the year 452 AD, the great Hunnic warlord Attila was poised to attack Rome, the seat of the mighty Roman Empire. The city had already been ravaged by the Visigoths just a few decades earlier, and the citizens were in a state of panic. But as fate would have it, Attila did not end up sacking the city, thanks to a remarkable meeting with the Roman delegation led by Pope Leo I.

The meeting between Attila and Pope Leo I took place on the banks of the River Mincio, near Mantua. The details of what was said at the meeting are not known for certain, but according to legend, the Pope convinced Attila not to attack Rome by invoking the power of Saint Peter, the patron saint of the city. The Hunnic king was said to have been so impressed by the Pope's piety and determination that he agreed to spare the city.

However, while the legend of Pope Leo I saving Rome is undoubtedly a compelling story, the reality of the situation was likely more complex. Attila was not the kind of man to be swayed by religious appeals alone, and there were likely other factors that played into his decision not to attack Rome.

One possible explanation for Attila's change of heart was that he had already achieved his main objective in Italy: to secure the release of the Roman princess Honoria, who had sent him a plea for help in escaping an unwanted marriage. Attila had used Honoria's plea as a pretext for his invasion of Italy, and once he had secured her release, he may have felt that he had accomplished what he had set out to do.

Another possibility is that Attila was simply running out of supplies and could not sustain a prolonged siege of Rome. The Hunnic army was accustomed to living off the land and plundering as they went, but Rome was a heavily fortified city with ample provisions and a well-trained army defending it. Attila may have realized that he did not have the resources to take the city by force.

Whatever the reasons behind Attila's decision, the result was a diplomatic agreement between the Huns and the Roman Empire, known as the Treaty of the River Mincio. The terms of the treaty were favorable to the Huns, who were granted a large sum of gold in exchange for their withdrawal from Italy. Attila also secured a promise from the Romans to pay an annual tribute to the Huns in exchange for peace.

The Treaty of the River Mincio marked a significant turning point in the relationship between the Huns and the Roman Empire. For the first time, the Romans had been forced to pay a tribute to a barbarian power, and the Huns had proven themselves to be a formidable foe capable of threatening the very heart of the Roman Empire. The treaty also allowed Attila to focus his attention on other regions, such as the Balkans and the Eastern Roman Empire, where he would continue his campaigns of conquest and terror.

In the end, while the legend of Pope Leo I saving Rome is a powerful symbol of Christian piety and devotion, the reality of the Treaty of the River Mincio is a more complex and nuanced story. Attila's decision not to attack Rome was likely influenced by a range of factors, including his own military objectives and the strategic considerations of his army. The treaty that emerged from the meeting between Attila and the Roman delegation marked a significant moment in the history of the Roman Empire and its relationship with the barbarian powers on its periphery.

At the dawn of the 5th century AD, the Roman Empire faced a new and formidable enemy: the Huns, a nomadic people from the steppes of Central Asia. Led by their fearsome warrior king Attila, the Huns launched a series of devastating attacks on the Roman Empire, leaving a trail of destruction and chaos in their wake.

Attila's motivations for invading the Roman Empire are a subject of much debate among historians. Some argue that he was driven by a desire for conquest and plunder, while others suggest that he was motivated by a more complex mix of political, economic, and cultural factors.

Whatever his reasons, there is no doubt that Attila was a formidable opponent. His army was highly mobile and skilled in the use of cavalry, allowing him to move quickly across vast distances and strike his enemies with lightning speed. He was also a master of psychological warfare, using his reputation for brutality and violence to intimidate and terrorize his opponents.

Despite his military prowess, however, Attila's invasion of Rome was not without its challenges. His failed attempt to conquer the city of Rome is perhaps the most famous example of this. According to legend, Attila was confronted by the Christian bishop Leo I, who convinced him to spare the city from destruction. While the truth of this story is difficult to confirm, there is no doubt that Attila's siege of Rome was ultimately unsuccessful.

The aftermath of Attila's invasion of Rome was profound. The Roman Empire was weakened by the constant attacks, and its people were left traumatized by the devastation wrought by the Huns. The once-great civilization was forced to confront the harsh reality that its power and influence were waning, and that it was vulnerable to attack from even the most primitive of foes.

Despite the long-term effects of Attila's invasion on the Roman Empire, however, there were also positive outcomes. The Huns' attacks on the Roman Empire helped to catalyze the decline of the Western Roman Empire, paving the way for the rise of new powers and civilizations in Europe.

In the end, Attila's legacy was mixed. He was a fearsome warrior and a master strategist, but he was also a ruthless and bloodthirsty conqueror. His invasion of the Roman Empire left an indelible mark on the course of Western history, and his story remains one of the most fascinating and enduring of all time.

Chapter 5: The Hunnic Empire and its Administration

In the annals of history, the Hunnic Empire stands out as a force that both intrigued and terrorized the ancient world. This nomadic confederation of tribes, led by charismatic figures such as Attila, swept across Eurasia in a seemingly unstoppable wave of conquest. But what was the structure of this enigmatic empire? How did it function, and how did it maintain its power over such a vast and diverse population?

To understand the Hunnic Empire, it is first necessary to examine the social and political structures that underpinned it. At the heart of Hunnic society was the clan system. Clans were led by chieftains, who were responsible for the governance of their members and the management of their resources. These chieftains formed the backbone of the Hunnic army, providing their own warriors as well as leading groups of allied tribesmen. At the top of this hierarchy was the khan, who was responsible for the overall leadership of the empire.

While the exact nature of the khanate's political structure is not entirely clear, it is generally agreed that the khan held absolute power over his people. He was advised by a council of elders, who were chosen from among the most respected chieftains and were responsible for assisting the khan in making decisions regarding matters of state. The khanate was divided into a number of provinces, each of which was governed by a local ruler, known as a shad or shah. These local rulers were responsible for the collection of taxes and the maintenance of order within their territories.

The Hunnic Empire was known for its skilled cavalry, which formed the backbone of its military might. Horses were bred for speed and endurance, and Hunnic warriors were trained from a young age in the arts of riding and archery. The cavalry was organized into units, each of which was led by a chieftain or high-ranking warrior. The Hunnic army was also composed of foot soldiers, although these were generally regarded as inferior to the cavalry and were often used in support roles, such as siege warfare or the provision of supplies.

The Hunnic Empire was not known for its great architectural achievements or its monumental buildings. Instead, it was a society that relied on mobility and the ability to move quickly across great distances. The Huns were known for their yurts, or felt tents, which they could quickly set up and take down as they moved from place to place. The yurt served as the center of Hunnic life, housing families and serving as a place for communal gatherings.

One of the unique features of the Hunnic Empire was its tolerance of other cultures and religions. The Huns themselves were animists, but they were willing to accept and even adopt aspects of other belief systems. For example, Attila was known to have had Christian advisors, and he even allowed Christian missionaries to enter his territory. Similarly, the Huns were known to have adopted aspects of Persian and Roman culture, particularly in the areas of dress and fashion. This tolerance of other cultures and beliefs is thought to have contributed to the Hunnic Empire's longevity and success.

In summary, the Hunnic Empire was a confederation of tribes that were united under the leadership of the khan. The empire was divided into provinces, each of which was governed by a local ruler. The Hunnic military was known for its skilled cavalry, which formed the backbone of its military might. The Hunnic Empire was a society that relied on mobility and the ability to move quickly across great distances. The Huns were known for their yurts, which served as the center of Hunnic life.

During the 5th century, the Hunnic Empire under Attila's leadership became a major power in Europe. The Huns were known for their fierce fighting spirit, but they also had a code of war that governed their society and behavior. Next, we will explore the laws and ethics that guided the Hunnic people in their military campaigns and daily life.

The Huns were a nomadic people who lived in the Eurasian steppes. They were known for their skill in horse riding and archery, and they were feared for their ability to strike quickly and unexpectedly. However, the Huns were not simply a band of marauders. They had a well-organized society and a code of conduct that governed their actions on and off the battlefield.

One of the key principles of the Hunnic code of war was the importance of honor. The Huns believed that it was important to uphold one's honor and reputation, even in the face of defeat. This meant that they were willing to fight to the death rather than surrender or retreat. In fact, the Huns considered surrender to be a shameful act, and they would often kill themselves or their families rather than be captured by their enemies.

Another important principle of the Hunnic code of war was the importance of loyalty. The Huns were fiercely loyal to their leaders, and they expected their leaders to be loyal to them in return. This meant that Attila had the unwavering support of his people, even during difficult times. The Huns were also loyal to their allies, and they would often come to the aid of their friends and neighbors in times of need.

The Huns also had a sense of fairness and justice. They believed that every member of their society had a right to justice and protection, regardless of their status or position. This meant that the Huns had a system of laws that governed their society and their interactions with others. They also had a system of punishment for those who broke the law, which ranged from fines to banishment to death.

Despite their reputation as fierce warriors, the Huns were not mindless killers. They had a sense of morality and ethics that governed their behavior on the battlefield. The Huns believed that certain actions were dishonorable, such as attacking unarmed civilians or prisoners of war. They also believed that certain tactics were unethical, such as using poison or attacking from ambush.

The Hunnic code of war was not just a set of abstract principles. It was a living tradition that was passed down from generation to generation. The Huns had a strong oral tradition, and their stories and legends helped to reinforce their values and beliefs. They also had a system of apprenticeship, where young men would learn from their elders how to be skilled warriors and honorable members of society.

In summary, the Hunnic code of war was a set of principles and values that governed the behavior of the Huns on and off the battlefield. It was based on the importance of honor, loyalty, fairness, and justice. Despite their reputation as savage barbarians, the Huns had a sense of morality and ethics that guided their actions. The Hunnic code of war was a living tradition that was passed down from generation to generation, and it played an important role in the success of the Hunnic Empire under Attila's leadership.

In the history of the Huns, one name stands out above all others: Attila. Often portrayed as a savage and barbaric warlord, Attila was in fact a complex and strategic leader whose legacy left a lasting impact on the history of Europe and Asia. Next, we will examine the role of Attila in the Hunnic Empire, exploring his leadership style and the ways in which he shaped the course of Hunnic history.

Attila was born in the early 5th century AD, the son of the Hunnic chieftain Mundzuk. As a child, he was raised in the nomadic lifestyle of the Huns, learning the art of horsemanship and the ways of warfare. As he grew older, he began to distinguish himself as a leader, commanding his own group of warriors and earning the respect of his fellow Huns.

When Mundzuk died, Attila and his elder brother Bleda inherited the leadership of the Hunnic Empire. Together, they set about consolidating their power, forging alliances with neighboring tribes and expanding their territory through a combination of diplomacy and force. Attila's particular talents lay in his ability to inspire loyalty among his followers, and his skill in forging alliances with other tribes.

Under the leadership of Attila and Bleda, the Hunnic Empire grew to encompass much of Eastern Europe and parts of Asia. Attila in particular was known for his strategic vision and his ability to coordinate complex military campaigns. He was a master of psychological warfare, using rumors and intimidation to sow fear among his enemies and destabilize their defenses.

One of Attila's most famous military campaigns was his invasion of the Roman Empire in 451 AD. Although he was ultimately defeated at the Battle of the Catalaunian Plains, his invasion had a profound impact on the Roman Empire, hastening its decline and contributing to its eventual collapse. Attila's tactics in this campaign were characteristic of his military strategy as a whole: he relied heavily on mounted archers and fast-moving horsemen, and he was skilled at laying siege to fortified cities and towns.

Attila's role in the Hunnic Empire was that of a charismatic leader and a skilled strategist. He was known for his ability to inspire loyalty among his followers, and he was revered for his military prowess and his skill in diplomacy. He was also a shrewd politician, negotiating treaties with neighboring tribes and maintaining a delicate balance of power within the empire.

Attila's legacy in the history of the Huns is complex and multifaceted. On the one hand, he is remembered as a powerful leader who expanded the Hunnic Empire and left his mark on the history of Europe and Asia. On the other hand, he is also remembered as a ruthless conqueror who was willing to use violence and intimidation to achieve his goals. The truth lies somewhere in between these two extremes.

In summary, the role of Attila in the Hunnic Empire was that of a skilled leader and strategist. He played a central role in the expansion of the empire, and his military campaigns had a lasting impact on the history of Europe and Asia. Although his legacy is sometimes clouded by myth and legend, it is clear that he was a complex and multifaceted leader who left an indelible mark on the history of the Huns.

The Huns, under the leadership of Attila, were a formidable force that threatened the stability of the Roman Empire. But how did they manage to sustain their military campaigns and maintain their dominance over their vast empire? The answer lies in the Hunnic economy, which was a complex system that relied on a variety of factors to support the empire's expansion.

At the core of the Hunnic economy was agriculture. The Huns were primarily nomadic pastoralists who relied on their herds of livestock for food and income. However, they also engaged in farming to supplement their food supply and provide raw materials for trade. The Hunnic Empire had a diverse range of crops and livestock that could be grown and raised in different regions, allowing for a degree of self-sufficiency in food production.

Trade was also a crucial aspect of the Hunnic economy. The Huns were situated at the crossroads of several major trade routes that connected Europe and Asia, allowing them to trade with a variety of peoples and regions. The Huns were known for their ability to control and tax trade routes, which provided them with a significant source of income. They also engaged in long-distance trade, exchanging luxury goods such as silk and spices from China for gold and other valuable commodities.

Taxes and tribute were another important aspect of the Hunnic economy. The Huns demanded tribute from the peoples they conquered, which consisted of goods, livestock, and people. The Huns also levied taxes on the people under their rule, which provided them with a steady source of income to support their military campaigns and administration. In addition to monetary and material tribute, the Huns also demanded military service from the peoples they conquered, which allowed them to supplement their own armies with local troops.

The Hunnic economy was also supported by a complex administrative system. The empire was divided into various administrative districts, each of which was headed by a chieftain or ruler appointed by Attila. These rulers were responsible for collecting taxes, enforcing the law, and maintaining order within their districts. The Hunnic administrative system allowed for a degree of decentralization and local autonomy, which helped to maintain stability within the empire.

The Hunnic economy was, however, heavily reliant on plunder and conquest. The Huns were known for their military prowess and ability to conquer and subjugate other peoples. They would raid and pillage towns and villages, taking whatever they could carry and leaving destruction in their wake. This provided them with a significant source of wealth and resources, but it also led to resentment and resistance from the peoples they conquered.

In summary, the Hunnic economy was a complex system that relied on agriculture, trade, taxes, tribute, and conquest to support the empire's expansion. The Huns were able to sustain their military campaigns and maintain their dominance over their vast empire through a diverse range of economic activities and a complex administrative system. However, their heavy reliance on plunder and conquest led to resentment and resistance from the peoples they conquered, ultimately contributing to their downfall.

The Huns, led by Attila, were a nomadic people that emerged in the 4th century and quickly became a powerful force in Europe and Asia. Their empire was vast and multicultural, stretching from the Black Sea to the Danube River and encompassing a diverse range of peoples and cultures. Despite their reputation as fierce warriors and conquerors, the Huns were surprisingly tolerant of the many peoples they conquered, creating a unique and diverse society that lasted for several centuries.

The Huns were a pastoral people, living in tents and herding livestock across the vast steppes of Eurasia. Their society was divided into tribes, each led by a chieftain who was responsible for the well-being of his people. These tribes were fiercely independent and often competed with one another, but they were also united by a common language and culture. Attila was one of the most successful of these chieftains, and he was able to unite many of the Hunnic tribes under his banner.

Attila was known for his military prowess and his ability to lead his people to victory in battle. He was a master of tactics and strategy, and his armies were feared and respected by all who faced them. However, Attila was not just a warrior; he was also a skilled diplomat and administrator, and he worked hard to maintain the stability and unity of his empire.

The Huns were a multicultural society, and Attila was keenly aware of the importance of maintaining good relationships with the many peoples he had conquered. He encouraged the adoption of local customs and languages, and he often appointed local leaders to positions of authority within his empire. This policy of tolerance and integration helped to foster a sense of unity and cooperation within the empire, and it allowed the Huns to maintain control over a vast and diverse territory.

The Huns were also known for their trading activities, and they played an important role in the commercial networks that crisscrossed Eurasia. They traded in luxury goods such as silk and spices, as well as more mundane items such as livestock and grains. They also collected tribute from the many peoples they conquered, which provided a steady stream of income for the empire.

Despite their reputation as ruthless conquerors, the Huns were surprisingly innovative when it came to governance and administration. They had a sophisticated system of government that was based on the rule of law, and they were skilled at maintaining order and stability within their empire. They also had a code of ethics that governed the behavior of their soldiers, which helped to prevent atrocities and maintain discipline within the ranks.

The relationship between the Huns and their conquered peoples was complex, and it evolved over time. In the early years of the empire, the Huns were often seen as brutal conquerors who had little regard for the lives and property of their subjects. However, as the empire grew and matured, the Huns became more tolerant and accommodating, and they worked hard to maintain good relationships with the many peoples they had conquered.

Overall, the Hunnic Empire was a unique and complex society that played an important role in shaping the history of Eurasia. Despite their reputation as fierce warriors and conquerors, the Huns were surprisingly tolerant and diverse, and they were able to maintain a stable and prosperous empire for several centuries. Attila was a key figure in the history of the Huns, and his leadership and guidance played a crucial role in the success of the empire.

Chapter 6: The Role of Women in Hunnic Society

The Hunnic Empire, under the rule of Attila, was characterized by its militarism and the significance it placed on warfare. Attila himself was a skilled military leader who commanded a fierce and powerful army, comprised of both men and women. Indeed, the role of women in the Hunnic military was a unique feature of their society, and one that set them apart from other contemporary cultures.

The Huns had a tradition of female warriors, which was rooted in their nomadic way of life. In Hunnic culture, women had a valued role as hunters and riders, and they were expected to be able to defend themselves and their families from attack. This tradition was carried over into their military campaigns, where women fought alongside men on the battlefield.

The participation of women in Hunnic warfare was not limited to one particular role or function. Some women served as archers or cavalry, while others fought as foot soldiers or even commanded armies themselves. One famous example is that of the legendary Hunnic warrior queen, Boudica, who led a rebellion against the Roman Empire in Britain in 60 AD.

The Huns did not discriminate against women in their military, and they were given the same training, equipment, and opportunities as their male counterparts. Women were respected and admired for their bravery and skill, and they were seen as essential to the success of the Hunnic military.

The role of women in the Hunnic military had a profound impact on their society as a whole. It challenged traditional gender roles and allowed women to assert their independence and strength. Women who fought in battles and achieved victory were celebrated and honored, and their actions served as a source of inspiration for future generations.

However, it is important to note that while the Huns valued the participation of women in their military, their society was still patriarchal and hierarchical. Women were not equal to men in all aspects of life, and their roles were still limited in many ways.

Despite these limitations, the Hunnic Empire remains a notable example of a society that recognized the strength and ability of women in warfare. The participation of women in their military campaigns challenged gender norms and contributed to the success and longevity of their empire.

The Huns, like many nomadic societies, held a deep respect for their religious and spiritual traditions. Among these traditions, the role of female shamans was particularly prominent. These women held significant power and influence within Hunnic society and played a crucial role in the spiritual and cultural practices of their people.

Hunnic shamans, both male and female, were known as "kam" or "qam" and were considered to be intermediaries between the human and spirit worlds. They were responsible for leading various rituals and ceremonies, such as sacrifices and divination, and were believed to have the ability to communicate with spirits and ancestors. It was through these practices that the Huns sought to gain favor and protection from their deities.

However, it was the female shamans who held a unique position within Hunnic society. Unlike in many other societies where women were relegated to secondary roles, the Huns believed that women were capable of possessing greater spiritual power than men. Female shamans were seen as particularly gifted in their ability to communicate with spirits and had a significant influence on the decisions made by Hunnic leaders.

One of the most famous female shamans in Hunnic history was the mother of Attila, whose name has been lost to history. According to ancient sources, she had a profound impact on her son's life and was responsible for instilling in him a deep respect for the spiritual traditions of their people. She was said to have prophesied that Attila would become a great leader and that he would be victorious in battle.

Female shamans were also known to participate in warfare alongside male warriors. They would chant and sing during battle, inspiring their fellow fighters and invoking the aid of the spirits. It was believed that they had the power to make their enemies afraid and to confuse and disorient them through magical means.

The role of women in Hunnic society was not limited to just shamanism and warfare. Women also played a significant role in other areas of Hunnic life, such as trade and agriculture. They were responsible for raising and herding livestock, tending to crops, and producing textiles and other goods for trade. They were also involved in the political and social life of their communities and had a say in the decisions made by their leaders.

The Huns were a society that valued strength and power, and it is no surprise that they held their female shamans in such high regard. The ability to communicate with the spirit world was seen as a source of strength and power, and women who possessed this ability were highly respected and valued. The legacy of these powerful women can still be seen in the spiritual and cultural practices of modern-day nomadic societies, where female shamans continue to play a significant role in their communities.

The role of women in leadership has been a topic of debate throughout history, and the Hunnic Empire is no exception. While it is true that the Huns were known for their military prowess and conquests, it is often overlooked that women played an important role in the leadership of the empire. Next, we will explore the examples of female rulers and advisors in Hunnic history, and examine the impact they had on the empire.

One of the most famous examples of a female ruler in the Hunnic Empire is that of Queen Amage. She was the wife of King Balamber, who ruled the Huns in the early 4th century. Amage was a strong and influential queen, who was known for her wisdom and political acumen. She played a key role in the governance of the empire, and was greatly respected by her subjects. According to some accounts, Amage was responsible for negotiating peace treaties with neighboring tribes, and was also involved in the education of her son, Attila.

Another example of a female ruler in the Hunnic Empire is that of Queen Krimhild. She was the wife of Attila, and is said to have been a formidable queen in her own right. Krimhild was known for her intelligence and her beauty, and was highly respected by her husband. According to some accounts, she played an important role in advising Attila on matters of state, and was also involved in military campaigns.

In addition to female rulers, there were also many examples of female advisors in the Hunnic Empire. One such example is that of Olga, who served as an advisor to Attila. She was known for her intelligence and her ability to read the stars, and was highly respected by Attila. According to some accounts, Olga played an important role in advising Attila on matters of war and diplomacy, and was instrumental in his success on the battlefield.

Another example of a female advisor in the Hunnic Empire is that of Aetia. She was a wise woman who was highly respected by the Huns. According to some accounts, she played an important role in advising Attila on matters of state, and was also involved in the education of his children.

It is clear from these examples that women played an important role in the leadership of the Hunnic Empire. While they may not have been rulers in their own right, they were still able to exercise significant power and influence in the governance of the empire. They were highly respected by their subjects, and were able to make important contributions to the success of the empire.

In summary, the role of women in leadership is an important and often overlooked aspect of Hunnic history. Female rulers and advisors played a crucial role in the governance of the empire, and their impact was felt throughout Hunnic society. It is important to remember the contributions of these women, and to recognize the importance of women in leadership in all societies throughout history.

In the annals of ancient history, few societies have left as profound a mark on the world as the Huns. Renowned for their military prowess, they conquered vast swaths of territory and established a powerful empire that stood the test of time. Yet, while much has been written about the Huns as warriors, little attention has been paid to the role of women in their society. This is a mistake, for the Huns were a society that placed great value on the contributions of women, both in the home and on the battlefield.

One of the most significant aspects of Hunnic society was the role of women in marriage and family life. Unlike other ancient societies, the Huns had a highly egalitarian approach to marriage. Women were not treated as property, but as equals to men, and had a great deal of agency in choosing their own partners. This is not to say that marriages were purely romantic affairs - alliances between clans and tribes were often cemented through marriage - but women had a say in the matter, and were not forced into unions against their will.

Once married, women played a vital role in child-rearing. Hunnic society placed a great deal of emphasis on the importance of family and the raising of children, and women were seen as central to this process. They were responsible for the day-to-day care of their children, and played a key role in teaching them the values and traditions of Hunnic culture. Moreover, women also had a role to play in the political life of the empire. The wives and mothers of Hunnic leaders were often highly respected figures, with significant influence over the decisions of their husbands and sons.

However, it was on the battlefield where Hunnic women truly came into their own. While other ancient societies relegated women to the sidelines of warfare, the Huns actively encouraged their participation in combat. Women were trained in the use of weapons and were expected to defend their homes and communities in times of war. In fact, there are many accounts of women who fought alongside their male counterparts in major battles. One such woman was Althaea, a Hunnic warrior who fought bravely at the Battle of Chalons, one of the most significant conflicts in Hunnic history.

Another notable aspect of Hunnic society was the power of female shamans. Shamanism was an integral part of Hunnic culture, and women played a significant role in the spiritual and cultural practices of the society. Female shamans were highly respected figures, revered for their ability to communicate with the spirit world and to provide guidance to their people. They were often consulted by Hunnic leaders before major battles or other significant events, and their counsel was highly valued.

Finally, it is worth noting that women also held positions of power in Hunnic society. While there were few female rulers, women did play an important role as advisors and confidantes to Hunnic leaders. One of the most famous examples of this is the story of Attila the Hun's wife, Ildico. According to legend, Ildico played a key role in advising her husband, and was one of the few people who could persuade him to change his mind.

In summary, the role of women in Hunnic society was multifaceted and significant. Women were not only responsible for the day-to-day running of households, but also played a key role in the military, spiritual, and political life of the empire. Their contributions helped to shape the culture and traditions of the Huns, and ensured that the empire remained strong and prosperous for centuries to come. As such, the importance of women in Hunnic society should not be overlooked or underestimated.

Throughout history, the role of women in society has varied greatly from culture to culture, and the Hunnic Empire was no exception. While the Hunnic people were known for their fierce and warlike nature, they also had a complex social structure that allowed for the participation of women in various aspects of their society. Next, we will explore the perception of women in Hunnic society, including the views of Hunnic men and women on the role and status of women in their culture.

In Hunnic society, women played a significant role in the family unit. They were responsible for domestic duties such as cooking, cleaning, and child-rearing, and were often tasked with the responsibility of managing the household. However, the role of women in Hunnic society was not limited to the domestic sphere. Women also played a role in politics and warfare, and there were several prominent female leaders and advisors throughout Hunnic history.

One such example is that of Queen Fredegund, the wife of the Hunnic king Chilperic I. Fredegund was known for her intelligence and political savvy, and was instrumental in helping her husband maintain his power and influence in the Hunnic Empire. Despite being a woman in a male-dominated society, Fredegund was respected and feared by her enemies and was known to be a skilled diplomat and strategist.

Another prominent female figure in Hunnic history was the shamaness Olga of Kiev. Olga was the wife of the Hunnic ruler Igor of Kiev and played a key role in the affairs of the empire. She was known for her cunning and ruthlessness, and was responsible for the subjugation of several neighboring tribes. Olga's power and influence were so great that she was able to rule the Hunnic Empire in her own right after the death of her husband.

Despite the prominent role of women in Hunnic society, there were still significant barriers to gender equality. Women were often seen as inferior to men, and were subjected to social and cultural norms that restricted their freedom and mobility. They were also frequently used as pawns in political marriages, and were expected to fulfill their duty to their husbands and families above all else.

One notable example of this is the story of Honoria, the sister of the Roman Emperor Valentinian III. Honoria was known for her rebellious nature and her desire for independence, and she attempted to gain her freedom by offering herself in marriage to Attila the Hun. However, her plan backfired, and she was punished for her defiance by being forced into a marriage with a man she did not love.

Despite these challenges, Hunnic women were able to exercise a significant degree of power and influence in their society. They were respected for their intelligence, cunning, and bravery, and were often able to use these qualities to gain the respect of their male counterparts. Additionally, the prevalence of shamanism in Hunnic culture allowed for the possibility of female religious leaders, which further expanded the role of women in society.

In summary, while the Hunnic Empire was a male-dominated society, women were still able to play a significant role in various aspects of their culture. Whether as domestic caretakers, political leaders, or religious figures, women were able to exercise a degree of power and influence that was not common in many other societies of the time. While there were still significant barriers to gender equality, the Hunnic Empire serves as a reminder that women have always played an important role in the shaping of human history, even in the face of adversity.

Chapter 7: Attila's Religion and Beliefs

The Huns, like many other nomadic peoples, held a complex set of religious beliefs that were intricately intertwined with their way of life. The exact nature of these beliefs is difficult to ascertain due to the lack of written sources from the Huns themselves. However, we can glean some information about their religion from contemporary accounts and later records.

The Huns are believed to have practiced a form of shamanism, which is the belief in communication with the spiritual world through a shaman or spiritual leader. These shamans were believed to have the power to communicate with spirits, both good and evil, and were consulted for guidance in matters such as hunting, warfare, and healing.

The Huns also believed in the existence of a supreme deity, whom they referred to as the Sky Father or Sky God. This deity was believed to be the creator of the world and all living beings, and was associated with the sky and the elements of nature. The Huns believed that the Sky Father was the most powerful deity and that he controlled the fate of all living things.

The Huns also worshiped various other deities and spirits, such as those associated with the sun, moon, and stars, as well as those associated with specific animals or natural phenomena. The worship of these deities was often accompanied by rituals and sacrifices, which were believed to appease or gain the favor of these powerful forces.

Attila himself is believed to have been a devotee of the god of war and hunting, which would make sense given his role as a warrior and leader of the Huns. It is also likely that he saw himself as a chosen representative of the Sky Father, and that he believed his conquests were ordained by divine will.

The Huns' religious beliefs were an important aspect of their culture and identity, and they played a significant role in shaping their worldview and guiding their actions. It is likely that these beliefs influenced the Huns' attitudes towards war and conquest, as well as their treatment of conquered peoples.

Despite the Huns' reputation as fierce and brutal conquerors, there is evidence to suggest that they were relatively tolerant of other religions and beliefs. They did not impose their own beliefs on conquered peoples, and in some cases even adopted the religious practices of their subjects. This may have been a pragmatic decision, designed to maintain the loyalty and cooperation of their conquered peoples, but it also reflects a certain degree of cultural flexibility and openness.

In summary, the religious beliefs of the Huns were a complex and multifaceted aspect of their culture, shaped by their nomadic way of life and their interactions with the natural world. These beliefs played an important role in guiding the Huns' actions and shaping their identity, and they continue to be an important part of the legacy of this enigmatic and fascinating people.

The beliefs and religious practices of Attila the Hun are shrouded in mystery and speculation. Little is known about Attila's personal religious beliefs, but what is clear is that religion played an important role in Hunnic society.

The Huns were a nomadic people, and their religious beliefs reflected their close connection to the natural world. They believed in a variety of deities, spirits, and supernatural forces that inhabited the world around them. The Huns believed that these forces could be harnessed or appeased through various rituals and offerings.

Attila himself was known to be superstitious and highly spiritual. He is said to have consulted with diviners and shamans before making important decisions, and he placed great stock in omens and signs. Attila was also known to be fiercely protective of his religious beliefs and traditions, and he was quick to punish anyone who violated them.

Despite his personal beliefs, Attila was also a pragmatist who recognized the importance of religion as a tool for political and social control. He understood that religion could be a powerful force in bringing people together and solidifying his rule, and he was not above using it to his advantage.

One example of this can be seen in Attila's treatment of the Roman Empire. While the Huns had their own religious traditions, Attila recognized the importance of Christianity to the Romans, and he allowed the Christian faith to flourish within the empire. This was a calculated move, as it helped to maintain stability within the Roman Empire and prevented the emergence of any anti-Hun factions.

At the same time, however, Attila also used religion as a means of intimidating his enemies. The Huns were known for their ferocity in battle, and they would often invoke their gods and spirits to strike fear into the hearts of their opponents. Attila himself was said to be a fearsome sight on the battlefield, adorned in his ritual armor and wielding his sacred sword.

Overall, while the specifics of Attila's personal beliefs remain a mystery, it is clear that religion played a significant role in Hunnic society and politics. Attila recognized the power of religion both as a personal belief system and as a tool for social and political control, and he used it to his advantage throughout his reign.

During the early centuries of the Common Era, the Huns, a nomadic people who originated from Central Asia, migrated westward and eventually established a powerful empire that spanned much of Europe and Asia. The Huns were a warrior people, renowned for their fierce fighting abilities and their mastery of horseback riding. However, their culture was not solely defined by their martial prowess; religion and spirituality also played a significant role in their society. In particular, shamanism held a central place in the spiritual life of the Huns.

Shamanism is a belief system that is often associated with indigenous peoples in various parts of the world, including the Siberian and Mongolian regions from which the Huns emerged. At its core, shamanism is characterized by the belief in spirits and the ability of certain individuals, known as shamans, to communicate with these spirits and use their powers for various purposes, including healing, divination, and protection. Shamanism also involves the use of rituals, chants, and other practices to access the spiritual realm.

For the Huns, shamanism was an integral part of their culture and way of life. According to historical accounts, Huns believed in a multitude of spirits, including ancestor spirits, nature spirits, and spirits of the underworld. These spirits were believed to have the power to influence events in the physical world and to provide protection and guidance to individuals and communities.

The role of the shaman was central to the Hunnic spiritual system. Shamans were seen as intermediaries between the spiritual and physical worlds and were believed to have the ability to communicate with the spirits and seek their favor. They also served as healers, using their knowledge of herbs and other natural remedies to cure illnesses and injuries. Additionally, shamans were responsible for conducting various rituals and ceremonies to ensure the well-being of the community, including animal sacrifices, feasts, and dances.

Attila the Hun, one of the most famous leaders of the Huns, was also known to be a practitioner of shamanism. According to some accounts, Attila was believed to have received supernatural powers from a shamanic source, which helped him become one of the most successful conquerors in history. Attila was also known to consult with shamans on matters of strategy and decision-making, indicating the significant role that shamanism played in his worldview.

While shamanism was a central aspect of Hunnic society, it was not the only religious system that the Huns practiced. As they expanded their empire, the Huns encountered various religious traditions, including Christianity and Zoroastrianism. However, rather than suppressing or replacing these traditions, the Huns often incorporated them into their own spiritual practices, resulting in a syncretic approach to religion that reflected the multicultural nature of their empire.

In summary, shamanism played a significant role in the spiritual life of the Huns. It was a system that provided guidance, healing, and protection to the Hunnic people and was a central aspect of their culture and way of life. Additionally, the syncretic approach to religion that the Huns employed, incorporating various traditions into their own practices, speaks to the multicultural nature of their empire and their willingness to incorporate and adapt to the beliefs and practices of the people they encountered.

The Huns were a nomadic people who roamed the vast plains of Central Asia. They were known for their ferocity in battle, their horse-riding skills, and their ability to adapt to different environments. As with other nomadic cultures, the religious practices of the Huns were shaped by their environment and their interactions with neighboring societies.

Shamanism was the predominant religion among the Huns. Shamans were individuals who had the ability to communicate with the spirit world, and they were respected and revered by the Hunnic people. Shamans played a vital role in Hunnic society, serving as healers, advisers, and mediators between the physical and spiritual worlds. They conducted ceremonies and rituals that were believed to bring good fortune and protection to the tribe.

Shamanism was a polytheistic religion, meaning that it involved the worship of multiple gods and spirits. The Huns believed in the existence of an afterlife and believed that the spirits of their ancestors played an important role in their lives. The spirits of ancestors were believed to protect and guide the living, and they were honored through rituals and offerings.

Although Shamanism was the dominant religion among the Huns, there is evidence to suggest that they were also exposed to other religions. The Huns came into contact with a variety of cultures during their migrations, including those of the Romans, the Goths, and the Chinese. As a result, they were exposed to different religions and belief systems.

One religion that is believed to have had an impact on Hunnic society was Zoroastrianism. Zoroastrianism was the religion of the Persians and was widespread throughout the Near East. The Huns may have encountered Zoroastrianism during their encounters with the Sassanid Empire, which was the main rival of the Roman Empire in the Near East.

Zoroastrianism was a monotheistic religion that worshiped the god Ahura Mazda. The religion placed an emphasis on morality and ethical behavior, and it was believed that individuals would be judged based on their actions in life. Zoroastrianism also included a belief in a final judgment and a resurrection of the dead.

There is evidence to suggest that the Huns may have adopted some elements of Zoroastrianism into their own belief system. For example, some Hunnic graves have been found that contain items associated with Zoroastrianism, such as silver and bronze bowls used for ritual offerings.

Another religion that may have influenced Hunnic society was Buddhism. Buddhism originated in India and spread throughout Central Asia during the early centuries of the Common Era. The Huns may have encountered Buddhism during their interactions with the Kushan Empire, which was a major Buddhist power in Central Asia.

Buddhism is a religion that places an emphasis on the attainment of enlightenment and the release from suffering. It includes a belief in karma, the idea that an individual's actions in this life will affect their future lives. There is evidence to suggest that some Huns may have embraced Buddhism and that it may have had an impact on their religious beliefs.

In summary, the Huns were a society with a predominantly shamanistic belief system. However, they were exposed to a variety of religions and belief systems during their migrations and interactions with neighboring societies. It is possible that they adopted elements of these religions into their own belief system, although the extent of this influence is not fully understood.

In the history of the Hunnic Empire, religion played a significant role in shaping its political landscape. The Huns were a polytheistic people who worshiped a variety of deities, spirits, and natural forces. At the same time, they were also heavily influenced by shamanistic beliefs and practices that emphasized the importance of divination, trance-induced visions, and ritual sacrifices. The role of religion in Hunnic politics was complex and multifaceted, reflecting the various religious beliefs and practices of the different tribes that made up the Hunnic confederation.

At the core of Hunnic religious beliefs was the worship of the sky god Tengri, who was believed to be the creator of the universe and the source of all life. Tengri was venerated as the supreme ruler of the heavens and was often invoked in prayers and offerings before battle.

Other important Hunnic deities included the sun god Utu, the moon goddess Ningal, and the god of war and hunting, Nergal.

The Huns also placed great importance on shamanism, which was practiced by both male and female shamans. These spiritual leaders acted as intermediaries between the human and spirit worlds, performing various rituals to seek guidance from the gods and ancestors. Shamanism was closely tied to the concept of fate, which the Huns believed to be determined by the spirits and influenced by the actions of individuals. Shamans played a significant role in Hunnic society, acting as advisers to rulers and offering their services as healers and diviners.

Religion played a significant role in Hunnic politics, as rulers often sought the support and guidance of the gods through various religious practices. Attila, for example, was known to consult with shamans and perform various rituals to ensure the success of his military campaigns. Similarly, the Hunnic nobility often relied on their personal connections to the gods to legitimize their rule and secure their positions of power.

Religion also played a role in diplomacy and alliances between the Huns and other groups. The Huns were known to adopt the religious practices of their conquered peoples, and they often formed alliances with groups that shared their religious beliefs. For example, the Huns formed an alliance with the Ostrogoths, who also worshiped Tengri, and this helped to solidify their power in Eastern Europe.

At the same time, religion also served as a source of conflict within Hunnic society. Different tribes within the confederation had their own religious beliefs and practices, and this sometimes led to tensions and even violence. For example, the Huns and the Alans had different religious beliefs, and this contributed to their conflict in the mid-4th century.

In summary, religion played a significant role in Hunnic politics and society, reflecting the complex and diverse religious beliefs and practices of the different tribes that made up the Hunnic confederation. The worship of Tengri, shamanism, and the concept of fate were all important elements of Hunnic religious beliefs, and rulers often relied on their personal connections to the gods to legitimize their rule and secure their positions of power. At the same time, religion also contributed to conflict and tension within Hunnic society, reflecting the complex and sometimes competing religious beliefs of the different tribes.

Chapter 8: Attila's Death and Succession

In the annals of history, few names have conjured up images of brutality and destruction like that of Attila the Hun. A fierce warrior and a skilled strategist, Attila was feared and reviled by his enemies, and his legacy has been the subject of countless tales and legends. But despite his fearsome reputation, the circumstances of Attila's death remain shrouded in mystery and conflicting accounts.

According to some historians, Attila died in 453 CE, while preparing for a new campaign against the Eastern Roman Empire. According to the Roman historian Priscus, Attila was in the midst of wedding his latest bride, a young girl named Ildico, when he suffered a violent nosebleed and died in his sleep. The Hunnic chieftain's sudden death threw his army and empire into chaos, and the Huns were never able to recover their former power and influence.

However, other accounts of Attila's death tell a different story. According to some sources, Attila was murdered by his own men, who had grown tired of his autocratic rule and bloodthirsty campaigns. This version of events suggests that Attila's death was the result of a power struggle within the Hunnic empire, rather than a natural or accidental occurrence.

Still other accounts of Attila's death suggest that he died in battle, fighting against his enemies on the field of combat. This version of events paints Attila as a valiant warrior, meeting his end in a final, epic struggle against his enemies. However, this version of events is perhaps the least likely, as there is little evidence to support the claim that Attila died in battle.

Regardless of the circumstances of his death, Attila's legacy continues to resonate today, as a symbol of ruthless conquest and savage warfare. Though his empire was short-lived, Attila's impact on world history cannot be denied, and his name remains synonymous with brutality and violence to this day.

The death of Attila the Hun, one of the most feared and respected leaders of his time, was a momentous event that left a lasting impression on the people of his era. The circumstances surrounding his death remain shrouded in mystery and legend, with conflicting accounts and various theories that have been proposed over the centuries.

According to some accounts, Attila died in his sleep, possibly as a result of a sudden illness or heart attack. Others suggest that he was assassinated by one of his own followers, possibly in a power struggle over the leadership of the Huns. Another theory proposes that he was killed by a combination of factors, including wounds sustained in battle and an alcohol-induced heart attack.

Despite the uncertain nature of his death, Attila's funeral was a grand and elaborate affair, befitting a leader of his stature and reputation. The funeral was held in the Hunnic capital, which at the time was located in modern-day Hungary, and was attended by thousands of mourners from all over the empire.

The funeral procession was led by Attila's favorite horse, which was said to have been specially trained to walk in the funeral procession without a rider. Behind the horse came a group of mourners, including Attila's wives, children, and closest advisors. The body of Attila was carried in a golden casket, adorned with precious gems and jewels, and was accompanied by a retinue of armed guards and honor guards.

As the procession made its way through the city, mourners wept and wailed, expressing their grief at the loss of their leader. The body of Attila was finally laid to rest in a grand tomb, which was said to have been filled with riches and treasures beyond measure.

The funeral of Attila was a fitting tribute to a leader who had brought the Huns to the height of their power and glory. Although his death marked the end of an era, the legacy of Attila and his empire lived on for centuries, inspiring countless legends, myths, and stories that continue to captivate the imagination of people around the world.

The death of Attila the Hun in AD 453 marked the end of an era and the beginning of a new phase in Hunnic history. With the loss of their charismatic leader, the Huns were faced with a succession crisis, which threatened to destabilize their already fragile empire. Attila's death left a power vacuum that needed to be filled, and the question of who would succeed him became a matter of great importance.

The Huns were a tribal confederation, and Attila's authority over them was not absolute. His power rested on a delicate balance of alliances, personal charisma, and military might. He had been able to maintain this balance during his lifetime, but with his death, the various factions within the Hunnic elite began to jockey for position and influence. The situation was made more complicated by the fact that Attila had left no clear heir to his throne.

According to some sources, Attila's sons had already died before him, leaving him with no direct heirs. This meant that the question of succession had to be decided by a council of Hunnic leaders, who would choose the next ruler based on their own interests and alliances. However, this process was fraught with danger, as it could lead to a power struggle between different factions within the Hunnic elite.

The council that was convened to choose Attila's successor was reportedly divided between two main factions: the Gepids and the Ostrogoths. The Gepids were a Germanic tribe that had been subjugated by the Huns, while the Ostrogoths were a powerful Gothic tribe that had allied with the Huns during Attila's reign. The Gepids supported Attila's brother Bleda, while the Ostrogoths backed a Hunnic noble named Ardaric.

The council eventually chose Ardaric as the new leader of the Huns, but the transition of power was not smooth. According to some accounts, Bleda refused to accept the council's decision and launched a rebellion against Ardaric. The rebellion was eventually suppressed, and Bleda was reportedly executed.

Ardaric's ascension to the throne marked a significant change in Hunnic history. Unlike Attila, who had been a charismatic and aggressive conqueror, Ardaric was a more cautious and conciliatory leader. He was able to maintain the fragile balance of power within the Hunnic confederation and avoid the kind of internal strife that had plagued the Huns in the past.

Under Ardaric's leadership, the Huns began to shift away from their traditional nomadic lifestyle and adopt a more settled existence. They began to establish permanent settlements and engage in agriculture and trade. This change in lifestyle marked the beginning of the decline of the Hunnic Empire, as it reduced the Huns' military mobility and weakened their ability to project power beyond their borders.

In summary, the death of Attila the Hun marked the end of an era and the beginning of a new phase in Hunnic history. The succession crisis that followed his death highlighted the delicate balance of power that had underpinned Attila's authority, and the challenges that the Huns faced in maintaining their empire without his leadership. The choice of Ardaric as Attila's successor marked a significant change in Hunnic leadership and marked the beginning of the decline of the Hunnic Empire.

The death of Attila the Hun in AD 453 marked the end of an era in European history. Attila was not only a skilled military commander but also a charismatic leader who had brought together disparate Hunnic tribes to form a formidable empire. After his death, his empire was divided among his sons, leading to a power struggle that ultimately weakened the Hunnic Empire and hastened its decline.

Attila had three sons - Ellac, Dengizich, and Ernak - all of whom were eager to take over their father's empire. However, the succession was not clear cut, and each son had his own supporters and ambitions. Ellac, the eldest son, was initially favored to succeed his father, but he died shortly after Attila's death in a battle against the Ostrogoths. Dengizich, the second son, then claimed the throne, but he faced opposition from his youngest brother, Ernak, and his own cousin, Bleda.

Bleda was the son of Attila's brother, Bleda, who had ruled alongside Attila until his death in AD 445. Bleda had been appointed by Attila to be the leader of the Eastern Huns, and he had significant support among the Huns in that region. Bleda and Dengizich clashed over the succession, and a civil war broke out between the two factions.

In the end, Dengizich emerged victorious and was proclaimed the new king of the Hunnic Empire. However, his reign was short-lived. He was killed just two years later in a battle against the Ostrogoths, and the empire was once again thrown into chaos.

Ernak, who had initially supported his brother Dengizich, then declared himself the new king. However, his claim was contested by Bleda, who had allied himself with another Hunnic leader, Ardaric of the Gepids. Ardaric and Bleda defeated Ernak in battle, and Bleda was crowned the new king of the Huns.

Bleda's reign was marked by instability and conflict. He faced opposition from several Hunnic leaders who resented his appointment, and he also faced external threats from neighboring tribes. In AD 469, Bleda was killed in a battle against the Ostrogoths, and the empire was once again thrown into disarray.

The Hunnic Empire continued to exist for several decades after Bleda's death, but it was never able to regain the power and influence it had enjoyed under Attila. The division of the empire among Attila's sons had weakened its unity and exposed its vulnerabilities to external threats. The Huns faced continued pressure from the Roman Empire, the Goths, and other barbarian tribes, and they were eventually absorbed into the surrounding cultures.

In summary, the succession crisis that followed Attila's death marked the beginning of the end for the Hunnic Empire. The power struggle between Attila's sons and the subsequent civil wars weakened the empire and made it vulnerable to external threats. The division of the empire among Attila's sons prevented the emergence of a strong, centralized leadership that could have maintained the unity of the Huns. Ultimately, the Hunnic Empire was unable to survive the challenges it faced and was absorbed into the surrounding cultures.

In the annals of history, few figures have cast as long a shadow as Attila the Hun. Born to a noble family in the early 5th century, Attila rose to power as the king of the Huns, a fierce warrior people who had long terrorized the Roman Empire and its neighbors. Attila's reign was marked by bloody warfare, military prowess, and a keen strategic mind. He led his people on campaigns of conquest that spanned much of Europe and Asia, leaving a legacy that would be felt for centuries to come.

However, Attila's death in 453 CE marked the end of an era, and with it, the end of the Hunnic Empire. The struggle for power and the division of the empire among Attila's sons would ultimately spell the downfall of the once-mighty Huns. Yet, despite the empire's eventual collapse, the legacy of Attila's reign endured, leaving an indelible mark on history.

Attila's death was shrouded in mystery and conflicting accounts. According to some sources, he died on his wedding night, having suffered a burst blood vessel while engaging in vigorous sexual activity. Other accounts suggest he was assassinated by his own men or fell from his horse and died of his injuries. Whatever the cause of his death, it marked the end of an era of Hunnic dominance, and his loss was deeply felt by his people.

In the aftermath of Attila's death, the Huns faced a succession crisis that would ultimately lead to the division of the empire among his sons. Attila had left no clear successor, and his empire was beset by internal rivalries and external pressures. The Romans, who had long been the Huns' primary enemy, saw Attila's death as an opportunity to strike back and launched a series of attacks on the weakened empire. At the same time, other tribes, such as the Ostrogoths and Gepids, began to assert their independence and challenge Hunnic dominance.

The struggle for power among Attila's sons ultimately led to the fragmentation of the Hunnic Empire. The eldest son, Ellac, was killed in battle soon after his father's death, leaving the two younger sons, Dengizich and Ernakh, to vie for control. Dengizich ultimately emerged victorious and became the new king of the Huns, but his reign was short-lived. He was killed in battle just a few years later, and the empire continued to splinter and decline.

Despite its eventual collapse, the legacy of the Hunnic Empire endured. Attila's conquests had left a profound mark on history, both in terms of the physical territory he had claimed and the cultural impact of his reign. The Huns' military tactics and weapons, such as their deadly use of mounted archers, would be emulated by other armies for centuries to come. Additionally, the Huns' influence on the culture and language of Europe and Asia is still felt today.

Attila's reign also had a profound impact on the Roman Empire. His campaigns of conquest had brought the Roman Empire to the brink of collapse, and the memory of his attacks would haunt the Romans for generations. The fall of the Western Roman Empire just a few decades after Attila's death has often been attributed, at least in part, to the damage wrought by the Huns.

In summary, the death of Attila the Hun marked the end of an era of Hunnic dominance and the beginning of a period of turmoil and decline. Despite the eventual collapse of the Hunnic Empire, Attila's legacy endured, leaving an indelible mark on history.

Chapter 9: The Legacy of Attila the Hun

It is difficult to overstate the impact that the Huns had on the history of Europe and Asia. At their peak, the Huns were the dominant power in Central Asia and Eastern Europe, and their influence extended far beyond their own borders. One of the key factors behind the Huns' success was their ability to spread their culture and values to the societies they conquered, leaving a lasting impact on the regions they controlled.

The Huns were a nomadic people who originated in the area that is now modern-day Mongolia. They were skilled horsemen and expert archers, and their mobility allowed them to conquer vast territories. As they expanded their territory, the Huns also spread their culture, language, and traditions.

One of the most notable aspects of Hunnic culture was their emphasis on horsemanship. Horses were central to the Hunnic way of life, and the Huns developed a unique style of mounted warfare that relied heavily on cavalry. This style of warfare was incredibly effective, allowing the Huns to quickly overrun their enemies and establish control over vast territories.

In addition to their military prowess, the Huns also had a distinct social and political structure. They were led by a single powerful leader, known as the khagan, who held absolute authority over the Hunnic tribes. This system of government was highly centralized and hierarchical, and it helped to keep the Huns united under a common banner.

The Huns were also known for their religious beliefs, which were heavily influenced by shamanism. Shamans played a central role in Hunnic society, serving as spiritual leaders and advisors to the khagan. Hunnic shamanism was a complex and intricate system that incorporated a variety of beliefs and practices, including divination, spirit possession, and ritual sacrifice.

As the Huns expanded their territory, they brought their culture and beliefs with them, leaving a lasting impact on the regions they conquered. In Europe, the Huns left a significant mark on the culture of the Germanic tribes they encountered. The Huns' emphasis on horsemanship and mounted warfare influenced the development of the medieval knightly class, while their hierarchical political structure helped to shape the feudal system that would dominate Europe for centuries to come.

In Asia, the Huns had a profound impact on the development of the Turkic peoples. The Huns' nomadic lifestyle and military tactics were adopted by many Turkic tribes, while their religious beliefs helped to shape the development of Turkic shamanism.

Despite their influence, the Huns' impact on history has been overshadowed by the exploits of their most famous leader, Attila the Hun. Attila is often remembered as a brutal and bloodthirsty conqueror, but his legacy extends far beyond his reputation as a fearsome warrior. Attila's leadership and military tactics helped to establish the Huns as a major power in Europe and Asia, while his impact on culture and society can still be felt today.

In summary, the Huns were a powerful and influential people whose impact on history cannot be underestimated. Through their conquests and cultural influence, the Huns left a lasting mark on the regions they controlled, shaping the development of Europe and Asia for centuries to come. While their reign was relatively short-lived, their legacy lives on in the traditions, languages, and beliefs of the peoples they conquered.

The fall of the Western Roman Empire is a story that has been told and retold countless times over the centuries. One of the most fascinating chapters in this story is the role played by Attila and the Huns in the decline of the once-great empire. Attila, known as the "Scourge of God," was a powerful warrior and leader of the Huns, a fierce and nomadic people from Central Asia. His invasions of the Roman Empire in the 5th century had a profound impact on the course of history.

Attila was born in what is now modern-day Hungary in the early 5th century. His early life is shrouded in mystery, but he rose to power as a leader of the Huns in the 430s or 440s. Attila was a brilliant military strategist and a charismatic leader, who united the various tribes of the Huns into a powerful confederation. Under his leadership, the Huns began a series of invasions of the Eastern Roman Empire, which would eventually culminate in the sack of Rome itself.

Attila's first major incursion into Roman territory occurred in 441, when he led a large force across the Danube River and into the Balkans. His target was the Eastern Roman city of Constantinople, which he hoped to sack and pillage. However, the Eastern Roman Emperor Theodosius II was able to negotiate a peace treaty with Attila, which included a substantial tribute payment to the Huns. This would become a pattern in Attila's dealings with the Romans – he would make demands, the Romans would pay him off, and he would return to the steppes of Central Asia.

Attila's next major campaign came in 447, when he led another invasion of the Eastern Roman Empire. This time, his target was the wealthy and strategically important city of Constantinople. However, he was once again forced to withdraw after a peace treaty was negotiated with the Eastern Roman Empire. Attila's attacks on the Eastern Roman Empire had weakened its defenses and left it vulnerable to other invaders, including the Goths and the Vandals.

In 450, Attila turned his attention to the Western Roman Empire, which was ruled by the weak and ineffective Emperor Valentinian III. Attila demanded a tribute payment from Valentinian, which the emperor was unable to pay. This led Attila to invade Gaul (modern-day France), where he sacked several cities and engaged in a series of battles with the Roman army. Attila was finally defeated in the Battle of the Catalaunian Plains in 451, in which the Roman general Aetius led a coalition of Roman and barbarian forces against the Huns.

Despite this setback, Attila was undeterred, and in 452 he launched a massive invasion of Italy. His target was Rome itself, which he hoped to sack and pillage. However, Attila was once again forced to withdraw after negotiations with Pope Leo I. According to legend, Leo convinced Attila to spare the city by promising him a vision of the saints Peter and Paul, who threatened to strike Attila down if he attacked the city.

Attila died shortly thereafter, in 453, under mysterious circumstances. Some sources claim that he was killed by his own men, while others suggest that he died of natural causes. Regardless of the cause of his death, Attila's legacy was profound. His invasions of the Roman Empire had weakened its defenses and left it vulnerable to other invaders, including the Goths and the Vandals.

In the 5th century AD, the world was witness to a great transformation in the political and military landscapes of Eurasia. At the heart of this transformation was the rise of the Huns and their great leader, Attila. The reign of Attila was marked by a series of conquests that led to the spread of Hunnic power throughout Europe and Asia. While Attila's death marked the end of his personal rule, it did not signal the end of Hunnic influence on the world stage. In the aftermath of Attila's reign, new political forces emerged, and the stage was set for a new era in world history.

Attila's reign was marked by a series of conquests that brought the Huns to the forefront of world affairs. His early campaigns were directed at the Eastern Roman Empire, where he sought to assert Hunnic dominance over the Balkans and the Black Sea region. These campaigns were marked by their brutality and ferocity, with Attila earning a reputation as a fearsome and ruthless conqueror. However, it was Attila's invasion of the Western Roman Empire that would ultimately bring the Huns to the height of their power.

Attila's invasion of the Western Roman Empire was marked by a series of victories over Roman forces. The Roman army was unable to match the mobility and speed of the Hunnic cavalry, and Roman cities and fortresses fell to Hunnic siege warfare. The Huns marched on Rome itself, and it seemed as though the ancient city would fall to the conqueror. However, Attila ultimately withdrew his forces from Italy, and the Roman Empire was spared complete destruction.

Attila's death marked the end of his personal rule, but it did not signal the end of Hunnic influence on the world stage. The succession crisis that followed Attila's death ultimately led to the splitting of the Hunnic Empire among his sons. The Eastern Huns, led by Attila's eldest son, Ellac, maintained their power in the Black Sea region, while the Western Huns, led by Attila's younger son, Dengizich, moved into Europe.

The division of the Hunnic Empire marked the beginning of a new era in world history. The Eastern Huns continued to exert their influence in the Black Sea region, while the Western Huns moved into Europe and came into contact with new political forces. The Visigoths, who had previously been a subject people of the Huns, were now free to pursue their own interests, and the Western Roman Empire was in a state of decline. New political forces, such as the Franks and the Saxons, were also emerging in Europe, and the stage was set for a new era of political and military conflict.

The fall of the Western Roman Empire and the rise of new political forces in Europe were directly related to the emergence of the Huns and their conquests under Attila. The Huns had brought a new style of warfare to Europe, one that emphasized mobility, speed, and surprise. The Romans were unable to adapt to this new style of warfare, and the fall of the Western Roman Empire was a direct result of their inability to match Hunnic military prowess. The emergence of new political forces in Europe was also a result of Hunnic conquests. The Huns had disrupted the existing political order in Europe, and the rise of new political forces was a direct result of this disruption.

In summary, the reign of Attila and the rise of the Huns marked a great transformation in the political and military landscapes of Eurasia. Attila's conquests brought the Huns to the forefront of world affairs, and the fall of the Western Roman Empire was a direct result of their military prowess.

The life of Attila the Hun is a captivating story of leadership, war, and conquest. His name has been remembered throughout history as a fierce warrior and a conqueror of great empires. However, the perception of Attila has varied over time and across cultures, and his reputation has often been shaped by myths and legends rather than historical facts.

One of the most significant ways that Attila has been remembered is through literature, art, and popular culture. From medieval epics to modern-day movies, Attila has been portrayed as a ruthless and barbaric warlord, leading his army on a relentless campaign of conquest and destruction. In many works of fiction, Attila is depicted as a savage, bloodthirsty warrior, leading hordes of barbarians to destroy civilized societies.

However, the romanticization of Attila as a heroic figure is a more recent development. In the 19th century, when nationalism was on the rise in Europe, Attila became a symbol of strength and independence. He was portrayed as a hero who fought against the oppression of the Roman Empire and who united the Huns into a powerful force that could rival the might of Rome. In this version of the story, Attila was seen as a symbol of resistance against foreign invaders and an inspiration to those who fought for their own freedom.

The romanticization of Attila continued into the 20th century, with the rise of fascist and nationalist ideologies. In Nazi Germany, Attila was celebrated as a symbol of Aryan power and a precursor to the Germanic tribes who had defeated the Roman Empire. He was depicted as a hero who had fought against the decadent and corrupt civilization of Rome, and who had sought to establish a pure and powerful empire.

However, the portrayal of Attila as a hero has been criticized by many historians and scholars. They argue that this image is based on myths and legends rather than historical facts, and that it ignores the brutal and violent nature of Attila's reign. They point out that Attila was responsible for the deaths of countless people, and that his conquests were often marked by cruelty and destruction.

Moreover, the romanticization of Attila has been used to justify political and military aggression. In the 20th century, his image was co-opted by fascist regimes to promote their own agendas, and his legacy has been invoked by modern-day nationalist and supremacist movements. This highlights the danger of romanticizing historical figures, as their image can be used to promote harmful and destructive ideologies.

In summary, the romanticization of Attila the Hun is a complex and controversial issue. While he is undoubtedly a fascinating figure who played a significant role in the history of Europe and Asia, his legacy has been shaped by myths and legends that have little basis in historical fact. While it is important to remember and learn from the past, it is equally important to approach historical figures with a critical eye, and to avoid the dangers of romanticization and myth-making.

Attila the Hun, the feared and powerful leader of the Hunnic Empire, has long been a subject of fascination and controversy in history. To some, he was a brutal barbarian, a scourge to civilization, while to others, he was a heroic leader, a symbol of strength and resilience in the face of adversity. The historical perception of Attila has shifted over time, reflecting changing attitudes towards him and his legacy.

During Attila's lifetime and in the immediate aftermath of his death, he was viewed with fear and loathing by many in the Roman Empire. To them, he was a ruthless conqueror who brought destruction and chaos wherever he went. Contemporary accounts describe him as a monster, a bloodthirsty savage who delighted in violence and cruelty. In the words of the Roman historian Priscus, "He was a man born into the world to shake the nations, the scourge of all lands, who in some way terrified all mankind by the dreadful rumors noised abroad concerning him."

However, even in his own time, Attila was not universally reviled. To the Huns and their allies, he was a great leader, a warrior king who led them to glory and power. The Huns had a different set of values and beliefs than the Romans, and Attila was revered in their society for his strength, courage, and strategic genius.

After Attila's death, his legacy was hotly debated. In the Roman Empire, he was still largely seen as a villain, a symbol of the barbarian threat to civilization. However, as time passed, attitudes towards him began to shift. In the Middle Ages, when Europe was experiencing a revival of interest in classical literature and art, Attila became a popular figure in literature and legend. He was portrayed as a fierce warrior, a conqueror who challenged the might of Rome and its successors. This romanticized view of Attila as a heroic figure would continue to influence popular culture for centuries to come.

In the 19th and 20th centuries, as nationalism and ethnic identity became more important, Attila was reevaluated once again. In Hungary, where he is still considered a national hero, he was celebrated as a leader who fought for the independence and autonomy of the Hunnic people. In Romania, where he is remembered as the "Scourge of God," he is seen as a symbol of resistance to foreign domination.

Today, the historical perception of Attila is more nuanced. While his brutal tactics and ruthless military campaigns are still condemned, he is also recognized as a skilled and innovative leader, a strategist who used his resources wisely and knew how to exploit his enemies' weaknesses. Attila's legacy is complex and multifaceted, reflecting the diversity of the societies and cultures that he affected.

In summary, the historical perception of Attila has evolved over time, reflecting changing attitudes towards him and his legacy. From a feared and reviled conqueror to a romanticized hero, and finally to a complex and multifaceted figure, Attila's place in history has been shaped by the values, beliefs, and biases of the societies that have remembered him. Despite the controversies and debates surrounding his legacy, Attila remains an important figure in the history of Europe and Asia, a symbol of the power and influence of the Huns and their impact on the world.

Chapter 10: Myths and Misconceptions about Attila the Hun

Attila the Hun, the great leader of the Hunnic Empire, is often remembered as a brutal and ruthless barbarian who brought terror and destruction to Europe. His name has become synonymous with barbarism, and his image has been romanticized as a savage and uncivilized warlord. However, this portrayal of Attila is an inaccurate and misleading one, created and perpetuated by biased and sometimes hostile historical accounts.

In reality, Attila was a complex and sophisticated leader, who led his people to great victories and established a powerful empire that spanned across Europe and Asia. He was a skilled military strategist and a shrewd politician, who was able to unite the various Hunnic tribes and build a formidable army that was feared by his enemies. Attila was also a patron of the arts and a lover of music and poetry, and he enjoyed the company of learned men and philosophers.

The image of Attila as a bloodthirsty barbarian can be traced back to the Roman historian Priscus, who wrote a biased account of Attila's meeting with the Roman ambassador Maximinus. Priscus depicted Attila as a savage and uncivilized warrior, who ate raw meat and drank blood from his enemies' skulls. However, this portrayal of Attila is now widely recognized as a fabrication, designed to demonize the Huns and justify the Roman Empire's hostility towards them.

Another factor that contributed to the negative portrayal of Attila was the Christian Church's perception of him as a heathen and a pagan. Attila's religious beliefs and practices were vastly different from those of the Christian Church, and he was often depicted as a demonic figure who was in league with the devil. The Christian Church's demonization of Attila contributed to his image as a barbarian and a savage.

Despite the negative portrayal of Attila, there is evidence that he was a skilled diplomat and a savvy negotiator. He was known to have formed alliances with other tribes and nations, and he was able to use diplomacy to achieve his goals as well as military force. Attila was also known to have shown mercy to his enemies on occasion, and he was willing to negotiate peace treaties and truces.

Attila's legacy is also evident in the modern world, particularly in the languages and cultures of the regions that were once part of the Hunnic Empire. The Hunnic language has had a lasting impact on the languages of Eastern Europe and Central Asia, and Attila's influence can be seen in the art, literature, and music of these regions.

In summary, the image of Attila as a barbarian and a savage is a gross oversimplification of the historical figure. Attila was a complex and multifaceted leader, who was skilled in military strategy, diplomacy, and cultural patronage. His legacy has had a lasting impact on the world, and his image as a brutal barbarian is a result of biased historical accounts and religious prejudices.

The story of Attila the Hun, known as the "Scourge of God," has become a legendary tale of a savage and bloodthirsty conqueror who laid waste to entire nations in his quest for power and glory. The very name Attila has come to be synonymous with cruelty and destruction. But how much of this is true, and how much is simply myth and legend?

One of the most enduring myths surrounding Attila is that he was somehow chosen by the gods to be their instrument of vengeance upon the Roman Empire. This idea is often attributed to a Latin phrase, "Flagellum Dei," or "Scourge of God," which was supposedly given to Attila by the Christian monk and historian, Jordanes.

However, this phrase is not actually found in any of Jordanes' writings. It first appears in a later Latin chronicle, the "Chronicon Gothanum," written in the 6th century, long after Attila's death. It is possible that this phrase was invented by later chroniclers as a way to explain Attila's success in conquering so much territory and defeating so many armies.

Another popular myth about Attila is that he was a merciless and bloodthirsty conqueror who took pleasure in slaughtering his enemies and leaving behind a trail of destruction. While it is true that Attila's campaigns were marked by violence and devastation, it is important to remember that this was not unusual for the time period. War was a brutal business, and Attila's contemporaries, such as the Roman generals Stilicho and Aetius, were also known for their ruthlessness and cruelty.

Moreover, there is evidence to suggest that Attila was not simply a mindless destroyer. He was a skilled military strategist who understood the importance of maintaining a supply chain and protecting his troops from disease and starvation. He also recognized the importance of diplomacy and negotiation, as demonstrated by his willingness to make peace with the Roman Empire on several occasions.

Perhaps the most enduring myth about Attila is that he was responsible for the downfall of the Roman Empire. While it is true that Attila's campaigns had a significant impact on the Roman Empire, it is important to remember that the decline of the Empire was a complex process that took place over centuries. Attila was simply one of many factors that contributed to this decline.

In fact, the Romans were able to resist Attila's invasion of Italy in 452 AD, and the subsequent death of Attila in 453 AD marked the beginning of a period of relative stability for the Western Roman Empire. It was not until several decades later, in 476 AD, that the Western Roman Empire finally fell to the Germanic tribes.

Despite the many myths and legends surrounding Attila, it is clear that he was a significant figure in world history. His campaigns and conquests had a profound impact on Europe and Asia, and his legacy continues to be felt to this day. However, it is important to separate fact from fiction and to recognize Attila as a complex and multifaceted figure, rather than simply a brutal barbarian.

In the annals of history, few figures have captured the imagination quite like Attila the Hun. Known as the "Scourge of God" and "Attila the Hun," his name has become synonymous with conquest, savagery, and destruction. Yet, as with many historical figures, the reality of Attila's life and reign is often far more complex than the myths and legends that have been passed down through the centuries.

Attila was born into a world that was already being transformed by the Huns, a nomadic people from Central Asia who were spreading across the Eurasian steppe. The Huns were known for their military prowess and their ability to ride and fight on horseback, and Attila quickly became known for his own skills as a warrior and leader. However, it was not until the death of his uncle Rugila that Attila emerged as the dominant figure among the Huns.

As Attila's power grew, so too did his ambitions. He sought to expand his territory and establish a Hunnic empire that would rival those of Rome and Persia. He launched a series of campaigns against the Eastern Roman Empire, including the famous Battle of Adrianople in 378 CE, which saw the defeat and death of the Roman Emperor Valens.

Attila's military campaigns were marked by his ruthlessness and brutality, and it is these qualities that have earned him his fearsome reputation. He was known to be merciless in his treatment of defeated enemies, and his armies were infamous for their pillaging and destruction. However, it is important to note that Attila was not simply a bloodthirsty conqueror; he was also a skilled strategist who understood the value of diplomacy and political maneuvering.

One example of Attila's political savvy was his approach to the Western Roman Empire. Unlike his campaigns against the Eastern Roman Empire, Attila did not seek to destroy the Western Empire outright. Instead, he used the threat of invasion as leverage to extract tribute and concessions from the Romans. In 452 CE, he launched a campaign into Italy and laid siege to the city of Rome, but ultimately withdrew his forces after negotiations with the Roman general Aetius.

Despite his successes, Attila's empire was short-lived. He died in 453 CE under mysterious circumstances, and his empire quickly fell apart in the years that followed. Nevertheless, his legacy would continue to be felt for centuries to come.

The image of Attila as a ruthless and bloodthirsty conqueror is not entirely unfounded, but it is an oversimplification of his character and achievements. Attila was a complex figure who was skilled in both warfare and diplomacy, and who was able to build a powerful empire that challenged the might of Rome and Persia. While his legacy may be mixed, there is no denying that Attila was a significant figure in world history, and his story continues to fascinate and inspire to this day.

Attila the Hun is a historical figure whose legacy has been both romanticized and demonized over the centuries. He is often depicted as a ruthless conqueror who committed atrocities on a massive scale, leaving death and destruction in his wake. However, the truth behind Attila's alleged war crimes and massacres is more complex than these simplified narratives suggest.

Attila was born into a prominent Hunnic family in the early 5th century, and rose to become king of the Huns in 434 AD, following the death of his uncle, King Rugila. As a ruler, Attila was known for his military prowess and his ability to unite the various Hunnic tribes under his leadership. He was a skilled strategist and tactician, and his campaigns brought him and his army across much of Europe and Asia.

One of the most famous and infamous events of Attila's reign was the sacking of the Roman city of Aquileia in 452 AD. The city was a major trading hub and a strategic point of defense for the Roman Empire, and its destruction was a significant blow. According to some historical accounts, Attila's forces killed or enslaved most of the city's population and left the city in ruins.

However, other historical sources suggest that the extent of the destruction at Aquileia has been exaggerated over time. While the city was certainly attacked and damaged, it is unclear whether the massacre was as large-scale as some accounts suggest. In fact, some historians argue that Attila's attack on Aquileia was a strategic move designed to weaken the Roman Empire's hold on the region, rather than a purely punitive act.

Another event that has been linked to Attila's reputation as a brutal conqueror is the Battle of the Catalaunian Plains in 451 AD. Attila and his forces clashed with a coalition of Roman and Germanic tribes, led by the

Roman general Aetius. The battle was a bloody and hard-fought one, with casualties on both sides. However, Attila's ultimate defeat has been attributed in part to the fact that his army was made up largely of horse archers, who were less effective in close combat.

Despite these mixed accounts of Attila's military campaigns, his reputation as a bloodthirsty conqueror persists in popular culture. He is often depicted as a savage and uncivilized warlord, driven by a desire for power and bloodshed. However, this portrayal ignores the complex social and political factors that shaped Attila's reign, as well as the various diplomatic and strategic moves he made throughout his career.

Furthermore, Attila was not simply a brute force, but a leader who understood the importance of alliances, negotiations, and cultural exchange. He was known to be a patron of the arts and a lover of music, and his court was a center of intellectual and artistic activity. Attila also maintained relationships with various non-Hunnic peoples, including the Romans, and worked to incorporate their cultures into his own.

While Attila's legacy as a conqueror is undeniably significant, it is important to recognize that his reign was not simply characterized by brutality and destruction. He was a leader who operated within a complex political and social framework, and whose decisions were shaped by a wide range of factors. By examining Attila's life and reign in a nuanced and comprehensive way, we can gain a deeper understanding of the historical and cultural forces that shaped the world in which he lived.

Attila, the King of the Huns, is a figure that has captured the imagination of people throughout history. His name is synonymous with barbarity, savagery, and ruthlessness. Yet, the true nature of Attila's character and achievements is shrouded in myth and legend. It is essential to understand Attila in the context of his times and the world he lived in to appreciate his legacy accurately.

Attila was born into a Hunnic tribe, the youngest son of Mundzuk, sometime in the late 4th century AD. His early years are shrouded in mystery, but it is known that he received an excellent education in military tactics and leadership from his uncle, King Rugila. After Rugila's death, Attila and his elder brother Bleda assumed the leadership of the Huns. The two brothers were known for their military prowess and diplomatic skills, and they quickly established themselves as the most dominant power in the region.

Attila's rule was characterized by his conquests of neighboring territories, including the Eastern Roman Empire, the Balkans, and Germany. He was a brilliant military strategist and tactician who used his army's mobility and speed to great advantage. Attila's use of psychological warfare was also a significant factor in his success. He cultivated an image of himself as a ruthless and bloodthirsty conqueror, capable of committing atrocities without mercy. This reputation made many of his enemies surrender without a fight, allowing him to expand his empire rapidly.

Attila's conquests came at a time when the Western Roman Empire was in decline. The empire was facing significant economic, military, and political challenges that made it vulnerable to external threats. Attila took advantage of this situation to launch a series of devastating attacks on the empire, culminating in his famous siege of Rome in 452 AD. Although Attila failed to capture the city, his campaign left the Roman Empire weakened and vulnerable.

Attila's death in 453 AD marked the end of his reign, and his empire quickly crumbled without his leadership. The Huns were unable to maintain their dominance, and their influence declined rapidly. Nevertheless, Attila's legacy lived on in the memory of people throughout history. He became a symbol of power, ruthlessness, and military might, inspiring countless legends, myths, and stories.

However, the true nature of Attila's character and achievements is more complex than the legends suggest. Attila was not a barbarian or a savage, as many have portrayed him. He was a skilled military strategist and leader who used his intelligence and charisma to build an empire that was the envy of his contemporaries. Attila's reputation as a bloodthirsty conqueror is also exaggerated. While he did commit atrocities during his conquests, it is important to remember that violence was a standard practice of war during his time.

Furthermore, Attila's legacy is more than just the memory of a conquering warlord. He was an influential figure who shaped the course of history. Attila's conquests had a significant impact on the fall of the Western Roman Empire, which marked the end of the ancient world and the beginning of the Middle Ages. Attila's legacy also extended to his people, the Huns, who were instrumental in the formation of the European identity.

In summary, Attila the Hun was a complex and multi-faceted figure whose legacy has been shrouded in myth and legend. While he was undoubtedly a skilled military leader and conqueror, he was not a barbarian or a savage. Attila's true character and achievements can only be understood in the context of his times and the world he lived in.

BOOK 3

ALEXANDER THE GREAT
FROM MACEDONIA TO THE INDUS

BY A.J. KINGSTON

Chapter 1: Early Life and Education

The Macedonian Kingdom in the 4th century BC was a land of contrasts. At its heart lay the city of Pella, where the royal court of the Argead dynasty held sway. Surrounded by rich agricultural lands and fertile forests, Pella was a center of trade and commerce, attracting merchants and artisans from all over Greece and beyond. Yet beyond its borders, the Macedonian Kingdom was a wild and rugged land, dominated by rugged mountains and dense forests, where bandits and brigands roamed free.

At the heart of the Macedonian Kingdom was the ruling Argead dynasty, which had come to power under the leadership of Alexander I in the early 5th century BC. The Argeads claimed descent from the mythical hero Heracles, and had consolidated their power through a combination of political maneuvering, military conquest, and strategic alliances. By the 4th century BC, the Argeads had established themselves as the preeminent power in Greece, with control over much of the Balkans and the northern Aegean.

Yet despite their power, the Argeads faced many challenges. One of the most pressing was the problem of succession. The Macedonian monarchy operated on a system of agnatic primogeniture, meaning that the eldest male heir would inherit the throne. This had led to a series of succession crises in the past, as rival claimants vied for power and support. To address this problem, the Argeads had developed a complex system of royal patronage and clientage, whereby the king would cultivate alliances with powerful nobles and military leaders, who would in turn pledge their loyalty to the monarch and his chosen heir.

This system of patronage and clientage was crucial to the stability of the Macedonian Kingdom, but it also created tensions and rivalries within the royal court. The most powerful nobles and generals, known as the "Companions," were often at odds with one another, competing for the favor of the king and the right to influence policy. These rivalries were exacerbated by the fact that the Macedonian court was often plagued by political intrigue and assassination, with ambitious courtiers and military leaders jockeying for position and power.

Despite these challenges, the Macedonian Kingdom remained a formidable power in the 4th century BC. Under the leadership of Philip II, who came to the throne in 359 BC, the kingdom underwent a period of rapid expansion and modernization. Philip II was a visionary ruler who recognized the need to strengthen the Macedonian army and economy, and he undertook a series of sweeping reforms to achieve these goals.

One of Philip's most important reforms was the creation of the Macedonian phalanx, a disciplined formation of heavy infantry armed with long spears and shields. The phalanx proved to be a formidable weapon on the battlefield, and it enabled the Macedonians to defeat much larger armies of the Greek city-states. Philip also introduced new methods of training and equipping his troops, and he invested heavily in the development of siege engines and other military technology.

Philip's reforms had a profound impact on the Macedonian economy as well. He encouraged the growth of industry and trade, and he established new mining and metallurgical centers to support the production of arms and armor. He also invested in the construction of new roads and infrastructure, which facilitated the movement of troops and goods throughout the kingdom. These reforms transformed the Macedonian Kingdom into a major power, and they laid the foundation for the conquests of Philip's son, Alexander the Great.

The childhood and education of Alexander the Great were crucial to his development as a military leader and statesman. Born in 356 BC in Pella, the capital of the Macedonian Kingdom, Alexander was the son of King Philip II and Queen Olympia. From an early age, he was surrounded by the trappings of power and privilege, and he was groomed for leadership from the moment he was born.

As a child, Alexander was precocious and intelligent, displaying a keen interest in literature, philosophy, and the arts. He was also a natural athlete and warrior, and he was trained in the art of horsemanship and archery from an early age. His father recognized his potential and appointed the great philosopher Aristotle as his tutor when he was just 13 years old.

Under the guidance of Aristotle, Alexander received a rigorous education in the classics and the natural sciences. Aristotle was a brilliant thinker and polymath who had studied under Plato and had a profound influence on Greek philosophy and thought. He taught Alexander a wide range of subjects, including mathematics, astronomy, biology, and ethics, and he instilled in him a deep appreciation for the values of reason, logic, and critical thinking.

Aristotle's influence on Alexander was profound, and it shaped his worldview and his approach to leadership for the rest of his life. Aristotle taught Alexander that the pursuit of knowledge and wisdom was the highest goal of human endeavor, and that leaders should be guided by reason and the common good rather than personal ambition and self-interest. He also instilled in him a love of Greek culture and a respect for the achievements of the past, which would later inform Alexander's policies as he sought to spread Hellenic culture and civilization throughout his empire.

In addition to his studies with Aristotle, Alexander also received a rigorous military education. His father had assembled one of the most formidable armies in the ancient world, and he recognized the importance of training his son to be a skilled and fearless warrior. Alexander was trained in the use of weapons and tactics, and he participated in mock battles and war games to hone his skills.

As he grew older, Alexander began to accompany his father on military campaigns, and he quickly distinguished himself as a brave and skilled leader. He participated in the famous Battle of Chaeronea in 338 BC, where he commanded the Macedonian left flank and helped to secure a decisive victory over the Greek city-states. This early experience in battle would prove invaluable to Alexander later in life, as he embarked on his legendary campaign of conquest across Asia.

Despite his privileged upbringing and education, Alexander was not without his faults and weaknesses. He had a volatile temper and a tendency towards excess, and he was prone to fits of rage and irrational behavior. He also had a complicated relationship with his mother, Queen Olympia, who was widely regarded as a scheming and ambitious figure. Some historians speculate that Alexander's desire to surpass his father's achievements and secure his own legacy was partly driven by a desire to outdo his mother's ambitions for him.

Nevertheless, Alexander's education and upbringing were crucial to his success as a military leader and statesman. His training in the classics and the natural sciences gave him a broad and deep understanding of the world and its workings, while his military education instilled in him the courage, discipline, and strategic thinking necessary to lead armies into battle. Under the guidance of Aristotle, he learned the importance of reason and the common good, and he came to see himself as a steward of Greek culture and civilization. These values would guide him as he embarked on his ambitious campaign of conquest, and they would shape the legacy he left behind as one of the greatest leaders in human history.

The assassination of King Philip II in 336 BC was a pivotal moment in the history of the Macedonian Kingdom, and it set the stage for Alexander the Great's ascension to the throne. Philip II had been one of the most successful and visionary leaders of his time, having transformed the Macedonian Kingdom into a major power through a series of military and political reforms. He had also paved the way for his son Alexander to succeed him as king, grooming him for leadership from an early age and appointing the great philosopher Aristotle as his tutor.

But on the day of Philip's assassination, all of his plans and ambitions were thrown into disarray. The king had been attending a wedding feast when he was stabbed to death by one of his own bodyguards, a man named Pausanias. The reasons for the assassination are still debated by historians, but it is clear that it was a deeply personal and political act, carried out by someone with a grievance against the king.

In the aftermath of Philip's assassination, the Macedonian Kingdom was thrown into chaos. There was no clear successor to the throne, and rival factions and claimants vied for power and support. Alexander, who was just

20 years old at the time, emerged as a leading contender for the crown. He was already a seasoned warrior and military leader, having accompanied his father on campaigns and battles since he was a teenager. He was also well-educated and charismatic, with a natural talent for leadership and diplomacy.

Despite his youth and inexperience, Alexander was able to win over key factions and supporters, and he quickly consolidated his position as the rightful heir to the Macedonian throne. He made strategic alliances with powerful nobles and generals, and he promised to continue his father's legacy of military expansion and modernization. He also made a show of force, leading a procession through the streets of the capital city of Pella, with the army marching in formation behind him.

In the end, Alexander's bid for power was successful, and he was crowned king of Macedon in the autumn of 336 BC. But his ascension to the throne was not without its challenges. He faced opposition from rival claimants and rebellious factions, and he was forced to suppress several uprisings in the early years of his reign. He also had to contend with the legacy of his father's assassination, which cast a shadow over his reign and made him keenly aware of the dangers of court intrigue and political assassination.

Nevertheless, Alexander was determined to continue his father's work and to fulfill his own ambitions for conquest and glory. He embarked on a series of military campaigns, beginning with a successful campaign against the rebellious city of Thebes in 335 BC. He then turned his attention to the Persian Empire, which had long been a thorn in the side of the Greek city-states and Macedonian Kingdom.

Over the next decade, Alexander would embark on one of the most ambitious military campaigns in history, conquering much of the Persian Empire and extending his empire all the way to India. He would earn a reputation as a brilliant military strategist and a fearless warrior, and he would inspire awe and admiration among his troops and his enemies alike.

But the legacy of his father's assassination would continue to haunt him, and it would ultimately contribute to his own downfall. In 323 BC, just a few years after completing his conquests in the east, Alexander died suddenly and mysteriously in Babylon, at the age of just 32. The circumstances of his death are still debated by historians, but it is clear that his reign and his legacy were cut short by the same forces of political intrigue and assassination that had plagued his father's reign.

Alexander the Great's military prowess and leadership skills were instrumental in his success as a conqueror and empire-builder. From an early age, he was trained in the art of war and taught the skills and strategies necessary to lead armies into battle. His military training was a key factor in his development as a leader and would shape his legacy as one of the greatest military commanders in history.

Alexander's military training began when he was a child. His father, King Philip II of Macedon, recognized the importance of training his son to be a skilled warrior and leader, and he made sure that Alexander received the best education and training available. He was taught the use of weapons and tactics, and he participated in mock battles and war games to hone his skills.

As he grew older, Alexander began to accompany his father on military campaigns, and he quickly distinguished himself as a brave and skilled leader. He participated in the famous Battle of Chaeronea in 338 BC, where he commanded the Macedonian left flank and helped to secure a decisive victory over the Greek city-states. This early experience in battle would prove invaluable to Alexander later in life, as he embarked on his legendary campaign of conquest across Asia.

When Alexander was 13 years old, his father appointed the great philosopher Aristotle as his tutor. Aristotle taught Alexander a wide range of subjects, including mathematics, astronomy, biology, and ethics. But he also recognized the importance of military training, and he instilled in Alexander a love of Greek culture and a respect for the achievements of the past. He also taught him the importance of reason and the common good, which would later inform Alexander's policies as he sought to spread Hellenic culture and civilization throughout his empire.

Under Aristotle's guidance, Alexander developed a deep appreciation for the values of reason, logic, and critical thinking, which would serve him well as a military leader. He learned to think strategically and to assess the strengths and weaknesses of his enemies. He also learned to inspire and motivate his troops, leading by example and earning their loyalty and respect through his bravery and skill.

As he grew older, Alexander's military training became more intense and focused. He continued to participate in military campaigns and battles, honing his skills as a warrior and leader. He also developed a deep understanding of the terrain and the logistics of warfare, which would prove crucial in his later campaigns.

When he became king, Alexander embarked on a series of ambitious military campaigns, beginning with a successful campaign against the rebellious city of Thebes in 335 BC. He then turned his attention to the Persian Empire, which had long been a thorn in the side of the Greek city-states and Macedonian Kingdom.

Over the next decade, Alexander would embark on one of the most ambitious military campaigns in history, conquering much of the Persian Empire and extending his empire all the way to India. He would earn a reputation as a brilliant military strategist and a fearless warrior, and he would inspire awe and admiration among his troops and his enemies alike.

Throughout his campaigns, Alexander remained intimately involved in the day-to-day operations of his armies, leading from the front and setting the example for his troops. He was a master of logistics and supply, and he understood the importance of morale and discipline in maintaining an effective fighting force.

But perhaps his greatest strength as a military leader was his ability to inspire and motivate his troops. He was a charismatic and eloquent speaker, able to rally his troops with speeches that were both passionate and persuasive. He also had a deep sense of empathy and compassion for his soldiers, often going out of his way to care for their needs and concerns.

The Battle of Chaeronea in 338 BC was a pivotal moment in the history of Greece and the Macedonian Kingdom. It was a decisive victory for the Macedonians over the Greek city-states, and it established Macedonian hegemony over Greece for the next several decades. For Alexander the Great, who participated in the battle as a young teenager, it was a formative experience that would shape his views on war and leadership for the rest of his life.

At the time of the battle, Greece was divided into a loose confederation of city-states, each with its own government and military. These city-states were often at odds with one another, and their constant conflicts made them vulnerable to external threats. King Philip II of Macedon recognized this vulnerability and saw an opportunity to expand his kingdom's power and influence.

Philip had spent years consolidating his power and modernizing his army, and he was now ready to take on the Greek city-states. He assembled a powerful army, consisting of heavy infantry and cavalry, and marched south towards Greece. His goal was to establish Macedonian hegemony over Greece and to secure his kingdom's borders from external threats.

The Greeks, meanwhile, were divided and disorganized. They lacked a unified leadership and a coordinated military strategy, and they were ill-prepared to face the Macedonian army. The Athenians, who were the most powerful city-state at the time, attempted to rally a coalition of states to resist the Macedonian advance, but their efforts were too little, too late.

The two armies met at the plain of Chaeronea in central Greece. The Macedonian army was led by King Philip II, while the Greek army was led by a coalition of city-states, with the Athenians playing a prominent role. The battle was fierce and bloody, with both sides fighting fiercely for victory.

In the end, the Macedonians emerged victorious, thanks in large part to their superior tactics and discipline. The Greek phalanxes were no match for the Macedonian heavy infantry, and the Macedonian cavalry was able to outflank and rout the Greek forces. The battle was a devastating defeat for the Greeks, and it marked the beginning of Macedonian hegemony over Greece.

For Alexander, who was just a teenager at the time, the battle was a formative experience that would shape his views on war and leadership for the rest of his life. He had accompanied his father on the campaign, and he had played a prominent role in the battle, commanding the Macedonian left flank. He had distinguished himself as a brave and skilled warrior, and he had earned the admiration of his troops and his father.

But the battle also taught Alexander the importance of strategy and discipline. He saw firsthand how the Macedonian army had used its superior tactics and discipline to defeat the Greeks, and he learned the importance of training and preparation in achieving victory. He also developed a deep respect for the Greeks and their culture, which would later inform his policies as he sought to spread Hellenic culture and civilization throughout his empire.

After the battle, Philip II went on to consolidate his power in Greece, establishing garrisons and allies in key cities and regions. He also imposed a series of reforms and institutions designed to integrate Greece into the Macedonian Kingdom, including the creation of a federal council and the establishment of Macedonian officials in key cities.

The conquest of Greece was a key step in Philip's grand strategy of expanding Macedonian power and influence. It gave him access to the resources and manpower of Greece, and it established the Macedonian Kingdom as the preeminent power in the region. It also set the stage for Alexander's later conquests, as he inherited his father's vision and ambition for conquest and empire-building.

Chapter 2: The Rise to Power and Unification of Greece

The inheritance of the Macedonian Kingdom was a complex and contested process, marked by intrigue, betrayal, and violence. When King Philip II of Macedon was assassinated in 336 BC, there was no clear successor to the throne, and the Macedonian Kingdom was plunged into uncertainty and chaos.

Philip II had been one of the most successful and visionary leaders of his time, having transformed the Macedonian Kingdom into a major power through a series of military and political reforms. He had also groomed his son, Alexander, for leadership from an early age, appointing the great philosopher Aristotle as his tutor and training him in the art of war and statecraft.

But on the day of Philip's assassination, all of his plans and ambitions were thrown into disarray. The king had been attending a wedding feast when he was stabbed to death by one of his own bodyguards, a man named Pausanias. The reasons for the assassination are still debated by historians, but it is clear that it was a deeply personal and political act, carried out by someone with a grievance against the king.

In the aftermath of Philip's assassination, the Macedonian Kingdom was thrown into chaos. There was no clear successor to the throne, and rival factions and claimants vied for power and support. Alexander, who was just 20 years old at the time, emerged as a leading contender for the crown.

Alexander was already a seasoned warrior and military leader, having accompanied his father on campaigns and battles since he was a teenager. He was also well-educated and charismatic, with a natural talent for leadership and diplomacy. He was able to win over key factions and supporters, and he quickly consolidated his position as the rightful heir to the Macedonian throne.

But his ascension to the throne was not without its challenges. He faced opposition from rival claimants and rebellious factions, and he was forced to suppress several uprisings in the early years of his reign. He also had to contend with the legacy of his father's assassination, which cast a shadow over his reign and made him keenly aware of the dangers of court intrigue and political assassination.

Despite these challenges, Alexander was able to establish himself as a strong and capable ruler, continuing his father's work and fulfilling his own ambitions for conquest and glory. He embarked on a series of military campaigns, beginning with a successful campaign against the rebellious city of Thebes in 335 BC.

Over the next decade, Alexander would embark on one of the most ambitious military campaigns in history, conquering much of the Persian Empire and extending his empire all the way to India. He would earn a reputation as a brilliant military strategist and a fearless warrior, and he would inspire awe and admiration among his troops and his enemies alike.

But his claim to the throne was not without controversy. Some factions within the Macedonian Kingdom continued to oppose him, and there were persistent rumors of plots and conspiracies against his rule. Alexander had to maintain a delicate balance of power, rewarding his supporters while suppressing his enemies and maintaining the loyalty of his troops.

In the end, Alexander's claim to the Macedonian throne was ultimately confirmed by his military conquests and his status as a great leader and warrior. He was able to establish his legitimacy through his accomplishments, winning the loyalty and support of his troops and his subjects.

The inheritance of the Macedonian Kingdom was a complex and contested process, marked by intrigue, betrayal, and violence. But in the end, Alexander's claim to the throne was established through his own abilities and accomplishments, as he became one of the greatest leaders in history and established an empire that would endure for centuries.

Alexander the Great's conquests and empire-building were marked by constant challenges and opposition from rival factions and rebellious subjects. One of the most significant challenges he faced was the need to suppress rebellion in Greece, where many city-states resisted Macedonian rule and sought to maintain their independence and autonomy.

After the Battle of Chaeronea in 338 BC, the Macedonians established hegemony over Greece, imposing a series of reforms and institutions designed to integrate Greece into the Macedonian Kingdom. But this integration was not always smooth, and many Greeks resented Macedonian rule and sought to challenge it through rebellion and uprisings.

Alexander recognized the importance of consolidating his rule in Greece, both for strategic and symbolic reasons. Greece was the birthplace of Hellenic culture and civilization, and its cities and states were seen as symbols of Greek identity and autonomy. By suppressing rebellion in Greece, Alexander hoped to demonstrate his strength and legitimacy as a ruler, and to show that he was capable of maintaining order and stability in a region that had long been divided and prone to conflict.

Alexander's efforts to suppress rebellion in Greece were marked by a combination of military force and political diplomacy. He used his armies to crush rebellious cities and states, but he also sought to win over key factions and leaders through diplomacy and negotiation.

One of the most significant rebellions that Alexander faced in Greece was the Theban uprising of 335 BC. The Thebans, who had played a leading role in the resistance against Macedonian rule, rose up in rebellion, hoping to overthrow the Macedonian garrison and reestablish their independence. Alexander responded with force, leading a siege of the city and ultimately conquering it through a combination of military skill and ruthless determination.

The Theban uprising was a major turning point in Alexander's efforts to consolidate his rule in Greece. It demonstrated his willingness to use force to suppress rebellion, and it sent a clear message to other cities and states that resistance would not be tolerated.

But Alexander's efforts to consolidate his rule in Greece were not limited to military force. He also used diplomacy and political maneuvering to win over key factions and leaders, and to establish himself as a legitimate ruler. He granted pardons and rewards to cities and states that pledged loyalty to him, and he established alliances and agreements with key leaders and factions.

One of the most significant examples of Alexander's use of diplomacy in Greece was his treatment of Athens. Athens had long been a center of resistance against Macedonian rule, and its leaders were deeply skeptical of Alexander's ambitions and policies. But rather than crush Athens through military force, Alexander sought to win over its leaders through diplomacy and political maneuvering.

He granted Athens a special status within the Macedonian Kingdom, allowing it to maintain a degree of autonomy and independence. He also granted citizenship and other rewards to key Athenian leaders and supporters, and he worked to establish a close relationship with the city.

These efforts paid off in the long run, as Athens became one of Alexander's key allies and supporters, providing him with troops and resources as he embarked on his campaigns of conquest and empire-building.

In the end, Alexander's efforts to suppress rebellion in Greece were largely successful, establishing Macedonian hegemony over the region and securing his rule as a legitimate and effective ruler. He used a combination of military force and political diplomacy to achieve his goals, demonstrating his strength and legitimacy as a ruler while also working to win over key factions and leaders. The suppression of rebellion in Greece was a crucial step in Alexander's grand strategy of conquest and empire-building. It allowed him to secure his borders and establish a firm foundation for his future campaigns, while also establishing himself as a legitimate and effective ruler in the eyes of his subjects and the wider world. The Battle of Issus in 333 BC was one of the most significant battles of Alexander the Great's conquests, and a turning point in the struggle between the Macedonian Kingdom and the Persian Empire. The battle was fought between the forces of Alexander and those of the Persian King Darius III, and it was a decisive victory for the Macedonians, securing their dominance over much of the Persian Empire.

At the time of the battle, Alexander had already established himself as a brilliant military strategist and a fearless warrior, having conquered much of Greece and Asia Minor in a series of lightning campaigns. But his conquests had brought him into conflict with the Persian Empire, which was then one of the most powerful and wealthy empires in the world.

Darius III, the Persian King, was determined to stop Alexander's advance and preserve his empire's power and influence. He assembled a massive army, consisting of tens of thousands of troops and hundreds of chariots and war elephants, and marched north to meet Alexander's forces.

The two armies met near the town of Issus in modern-day Turkey. Alexander's army was outnumbered and outgunned, but he had a secret weapon: his superior tactics and strategy. He had studied the Persian army's movements and weaknesses, and he had planned his attack carefully, seeking to exploit their vulnerabilities and outmaneuver their forces. The battle was fierce and chaotic, with both sides fighting fiercely for victory. The Persian chariots and elephants caused chaos and confusion in the Macedonian ranks, but Alexander was able to maintain his composure and rally his troops. In the end, it was Alexander's superior tactics and discipline that won the day. He used a combination of cavalry charges and infantry phalanxes to break the Persian lines, and he personally led his troops into the heart of the Persian army, engaging in hand-to-hand combat with Darius III himself. The battle was a devastating defeat for the Persians, and it marked a turning point in the struggle between the Macedonian Kingdom and the Persian Empire. Alexander's victory secured his dominance over much of the Persian Empire, and it allowed him to consolidate his power and expand his conquests even further. But the battle was also a significant moment in the history of warfare, demonstrating the importance of tactics and discipline in achieving victory. Alexander's ability to outmaneuver and outthink his opponents was a testament to his skill as a military strategist, and it inspired generations of generals and leaders to study his tactics and techniques.

The Battle of Issus also had significant political and cultural implications. It brought the Macedonian Kingdom into direct conflict with the Persian Empire, and it set the stage for Alexander's later campaigns of conquest and empire-building. It also marked the beginning of Alexander's efforts to spread Hellenic culture and civilization throughout the world, as he began to establish Greek-style cities and institutions in the conquered territories. In the end, the Battle of Issus was a pivotal moment in the history of Alexander the Great and the Macedonian Kingdom, demonstrating his skill as a military leader and his ambition as a conqueror. It secured his dominance over much of the Persian Empire, and it set the stage for his later conquests and empire-building. It was a testament to the power of tactics and strategy in warfare, and a reminder of the enduring legacy of Alexander's conquests and achievements. The Siege of Tyre in 332 BC was one of the most significant battles of Alexander the Great's conquests, and a testament to his military prowess and determination. Tyre was a major Mediterranean port city, strategically located on an island off the coast of modern-day Lebanon, and it was a key stronghold of the Persian Empire.

Alexander had already conquered much of the Persian Empire, including Egypt and Mesopotamia, and he was determined to secure his control over the Mediterranean by capturing Tyre. But the city was heavily fortified, with massive walls and a powerful navy, and it seemed impregnable to siege.

Undeterred, Alexander began a siege of the city, surrounding it with his armies and cutting off its supply lines. He also began building a causeway from the mainland to the island, in order to launch a direct assault on the city's walls.

The siege was long and grueling, lasting for seven months, and marked by fierce resistance from the defenders. The Tyrians launched a series of counterattacks, using their navy to harass Alexander's troops and block the causeway, and launching sorties against the Macedonian lines.

But Alexander was determined to succeed, and he used a combination of cunning and force to break through the city's defenses. He built siege engines and battering rams, using them to breach the city's walls and towers. He also launched a series of assaults on the city's gates and fortifications, using his troops to overwhelm the defenders.

In the end, it was Alexander's determination and skill that won the day. He was able to breach the city's walls and overwhelm the defenders, capturing the city and securing his control over the Mediterranean. The siege was a significant victory for the Macedonian Kingdom, and it marked a turning point in the struggle between Alexander and the Persian Empire.

The Siege of Tyre was also significant in the history of warfare, demonstrating the importance of siege engines and tactics in capturing fortified cities. Alexander's use of battering rams and siege towers was a testament to his military innovation and ingenuity, and it inspired generations of generals and leaders to study his techniques and strategies.

The conquest of Tyre also had significant political and cultural implications. It secured Alexander's control over the Mediterranean, and it allowed him to establish a network of Greek-style cities and institutions throughout the region. It also marked the beginning of his efforts to spread Hellenic culture and civilization throughout the world, as he began to incorporate Persian and other non-Greek cultures into his empire.

In the end, the Siege of Tyre was a significant moment in the history of Alexander the Great and the Macedonian Kingdom, demonstrating his skill as a military leader and his determination as a conqueror. It secured his control over the Mediterranean, and it set the stage for his later conquests and empire-building. It was a testament to the power of siege engines and tactics in warfare, and a reminder of the enduring legacy of Alexander's conquests and achievements.

The Battle of Gaugamela in 331 BC was one of the most significant battles of Alexander the Great's conquests, and a decisive victory in the struggle between the Macedonian Kingdom and the Persian Empire. The battle was fought between the forces of Alexander and those of the Persian King Darius III, and it was a stunning victory for the Macedonians, securing their control over much of the Persian Empire and cementing Alexander's reputation as one of the greatest military leaders in history.

At the time of the battle, Alexander had already established himself as a formidable conqueror, having defeated much of the Persian Empire and expanded his empire to include much of the Mediterranean and Middle East. But Darius III, the Persian King, was determined to resist Alexander's advances, assembling a massive army and challenging the Macedonians to battle.

The two armies met near the town of Gaugamela in modern-day Iraq. Darius III had a massive force, consisting of tens of thousands of troops and hundreds of chariots and war elephants, and he was confident in his ability to defeat the Macedonians.

But Alexander was not deterred. He had studied Darius III's tactics and movements, and he had a secret weapon: his superior military strategy and discipline. He had trained his troops to be agile and flexible, and he had developed innovative tactics and formations that would allow him to outmaneuver and outthink his opponents.

The battle was fierce and chaotic, with both sides fighting fiercely for victory. The Persian chariots and elephants caused chaos and confusion in the Macedonian ranks, but Alexander was able to maintain his composure and rally his troops.

In the end, it was Alexander's superior tactics and discipline that won the day. He used a combination of cavalry charges and infantry phalanxes to break the Persian lines, and he personally led his troops into the heart of the Persian army, engaging in hand-to-hand combat with Darius III himself.

The battle was a devastating defeat for the Persians, and it marked a turning point in the struggle between the Macedonian Kingdom and the Persian Empire. Alexander's victory secured his control over much of the Persian Empire, and it allowed him to consolidate his power and expand his conquests even further.

The Battle of Gaugamela was also significant in the history of warfare, demonstrating the importance of tactics and discipline in achieving victory. Alexander's ability to outmaneuver and outthink his opponents was a testament to his skill as a military strategist, and it inspired generations of generals and leaders to study his tactics and techniques.

But the battle also had significant political and cultural implications. It marked the beginning of Alexander's efforts to spread Hellenic culture and civilization throughout the world, as he began to incorporate Persian and other non-Greek cultures into his empire. It also had significant consequences for Greek hegemony, as it established the Macedonian Kingdom as the dominant power in the Eastern Mediterranean, displacing the Persians and other regional powers.

The Battle of Gaugamela was a pivotal moment in the history of Alexander the Great and the Macedonian Kingdom, demonstrating his skill as a military leader and his ambition as a conqueror. It secured his dominance over much of the Persian Empire, and it set the stage for his later conquests and empire-building. It was a testament to the power of tactics and strategy in warfare, and a reminder of the enduring legacy of Alexander's conquests and achievements.

Chapter 3: The Conquest of the Persian Empire

Alexander the Great's campaign in Asia Minor in the 4th century BC was a significant moment in the history of the Hellenic world, marking the beginning of his conquests and empire-building in the East. One of the key objectives of his campaign was the conquest of the Greek cities of Asia Minor, which were then under Persian control and resisted Macedonian rule.

At the time of Alexander's campaign, the Greek cities of Asia Minor were centers of Hellenic culture and civilization, and they had long been known for their wealth and influence. But they had also been subject to Persian rule for many years, and their leaders were deeply skeptical of Alexander's ambitions and policies.

Alexander recognized the importance of conquering these cities, both for strategic and symbolic reasons. They were important centers of trade and commerce, and they were also symbols of Greek identity and autonomy. By conquering these cities, Alexander hoped to demonstrate his strength and legitimacy as a ruler, and to show that he was capable of maintaining order and stability in a region that had long been divided and prone to conflict.

Alexander's campaign in Asia Minor was marked by a combination of military force and political diplomacy. He used his armies to crush resistant cities and states, but he also sought to win over key factions and leaders through diplomacy and negotiation.

One of the most significant cities that Alexander conquered in Asia Minor was Ephesus. Ephesus was a major commercial and cultural center, and it had long been a center of resistance against Macedonian rule. But rather than crush Ephesus through military force, Alexander sought to win over its leaders through diplomacy and political maneuvering.

He granted Ephesus a special status within the Macedonian Kingdom, allowing it to maintain a degree of autonomy and independence. He also granted citizenship and other rewards to key Ephesian leaders and supporters, and he worked to establish a close relationship with the city.

These efforts paid off in the long run, as Ephesus became one of Alexander's key allies and supporters, providing him with troops and resources as he embarked on his campaigns of conquest and empire-building.

But Alexander's campaign in Asia Minor was not without its challenges and setbacks. He faced fierce resistance from many of the Greek cities and states, who saw him as a foreign conqueror and resented his attempts to impose Macedonian rule.

One of the most significant challenges that Alexander faced was the siege of Halicarnassus. Halicarnassus was a key city in Asia Minor, strategically located on the coast and well-defended by Persian forces. Alexander led a prolonged siege of the city, lasting several months, and marked by fierce resistance from the defenders.

But in the end, it was Alexander's superior tactics and discipline that won the day. He used a combination of siege engines and tactics to breach the city's walls and overwhelm the defenders, securing his control over Halicarnassus and demonstrating his military skill and determination.

The conquest of the Greek cities of Asia Minor was a crucial step in Alexander's grand strategy of conquest and empire-building. It allowed him to secure his borders and establish a firm foundation for his future campaigns, while also establishing himself as a legitimate and effective ruler in the eyes of his subjects and the wider world.

The conquest of the Greek cities of Asia Minor also had significant political and cultural implications. It marked the beginning of Alexander's efforts to spread Hellenic culture and civilization throughout the world, as he began to establish Greek-style cities and institutions in the conquered territories. It also had significant consequences for Greek hegemony, as it established the Macedonian Kingdom as the dominant power in the Eastern Mediterranean, displacing the Persians and other regional powers.

The Battle of Granicus in 334 BC was one of the most significant battles of Alexander the Great's conquests, and marked his first decisive victory over the Persian Empire. The battle was fought between the forces of Alexander and those of the Persian satraps, or governors, who ruled the western provinces of the empire.

At the time of the battle, Alexander had already embarked on his ambitious campaign to conquer the Persian Empire, and had established a base of operations in Asia Minor. But the Persian satraps were determined to resist Alexander's advances, and they assembled a massive army to challenge him.

The two armies met near the town of Granicus in modern-day Turkey. The Persian army was massive, consisting of tens of thousands of troops and hundreds of chariots and cavalry, while Alexander's forces numbered only around 40,000.

But Alexander was not deterred. He had trained his troops to be agile and disciplined, and he had developed innovative tactics and formations that would allow him to outmaneuver and outthink his opponents.

The battle was fierce and chaotic, with both sides fighting fiercely for victory. The Persian chariots and cavalry caused chaos and confusion in the Macedonian ranks, but Alexander was able to maintain his composure and rally his troops.

In the end, it was Alexander's superior tactics and discipline that won the day. He used a combination of cavalry charges and infantry phalanxes to break the Persian lines, and he personally led his troops into the heart of the Persian army, engaging in hand-to-hand combat with the enemy leaders.

The battle was a stunning victory for the Macedonians, and it marked a turning point in the struggle between the Macedonian Kingdom and the Persian Empire. Alexander's victory secured his control over much of Asia Minor, and it allowed him to consolidate his power and expand his conquests even further.

The Battle of Granicus was also significant in the history of warfare, demonstrating the importance of tactics and discipline in achieving victory. Alexander's ability to outmaneuver and outthink his opponents was a testament to his skill as a military strategist, and it inspired generations of generals and leaders to study his tactics and techniques.

But the battle also had significant political and cultural implications. It marked the beginning of Alexander's efforts to spread Hellenic culture and civilization throughout the world, as he began to incorporate Persian and other non-Greek cultures into his empire. It also had significant consequences for Greek hegemony, as it established the Macedonian Kingdom as the dominant power in the Eastern Mediterranean, displacing the Persians and other regional powers.

In the end, the Battle of Granicus was a significant moment in the history of Alexander the Great and the Macedonian Kingdom, demonstrating his skill as a military leader and his ambition as a conqueror. It secured his dominance over much of Asia Minor, and it set the stage for his later conquests and empire-building. It was a testament to the power of tactics and strategy in warfare, and a reminder of the enduring legacy of Alexander's conquests and achievements.

The conquest of Egypt in 332 BC was a pivotal moment in the history of Alexander the Great and the Macedonian Kingdom. It marked the beginning of his conquests in the Middle East, and it allowed him to establish a firm foothold in the region, consolidating his power and extending his influence even further.

At the time of the conquest, Egypt was a key center of commerce and culture, and it was ruled by the Persian Empire. The Egyptians had long resented Persian rule, and they welcomed Alexander as a liberator and champion of their cause.

Alexander recognized the importance of Egypt, both for its strategic location and its cultural significance. He saw it as a key center of Hellenic culture and civilization, and he sought to incorporate it into his empire in order to spread Hellenic ideas and values throughout the region.

The conquest of Egypt was marked by a combination of military force and political diplomacy. Alexander used his armies to crush resistant cities and states, but he also sought to win over key factions and leaders through diplomacy and negotiation.

One of the most significant cities that Alexander conquered in Egypt was Memphis. Memphis was a key center of Egyptian culture and civilization, and it had long been a center of resistance against Persian rule. But rather than crush Memphis through military force, Alexander sought to win over its leaders through diplomacy and political maneuvering.

He granted Memphis a special status within the Macedonian Kingdom, allowing it to maintain a degree of autonomy and independence. He also granted citizenship and other rewards to key Memphis leaders and supporters, and he worked to establish a close relationship with the city.

These efforts paid off in the long run, as Memphis became one of Alexander's key allies and supporters, providing him with troops and resources as he embarked on his campaigns of conquest and empire-building.

But perhaps the most significant achievement of Alexander's conquest of Egypt was the foundation of Alexandria. Alexandria was a new city that Alexander founded on the Mediterranean coast, near the Nile Delta. It was strategically located at the crossroads of trade and commerce, and it quickly became a key center of Hellenic culture and civilization.

Alexander poured resources and manpower into the construction of Alexandria, building massive public works and institutions that would serve as a model for cities throughout the region. He also established a university and library in the city, known as the Library of Alexandria, which would become one of the most significant cultural institutions of the ancient world.

The foundation of Alexandria was a significant moment in the history of Hellenic culture and civilization, demonstrating Alexander's commitment to spreading Hellenic ideas and values throughout the world. It also had significant consequences for trade and commerce, as Alexandria quickly became a key center of economic activity and a hub of the Mediterranean trade network.

The conquest of Egypt and the foundation of Alexandria were crucial steps in Alexander's grand strategy of conquest and empire-building. They allowed him to secure his borders and establish a firm foundation for his future campaigns, while also establishing himself as a legitimate and effective ruler in the eyes of his subjects and the wider world.

In the end, Alexander's conquest of Egypt was a pivotal moment in the history of the Middle East and the Hellenic world, demonstrating his skill as a military leader and his ambition as a conqueror. It set the stage for his later conquests and empire-building, and it was a testament to the enduring legacy of Alexander's conquests and achievements.

The Battle of Issus in 333 BC was one of the most significant battles of Alexander the Great's conquests, and marked his decisive victory over the Persian Empire. The battle was fought between the forces of Alexander and those of Darius III, the king of Persia, who had assembled a massive army to challenge the Macedonian king.

At the time of the battle, Darius III had already amassed a large army, consisting of tens of thousands of troops and hundreds of chariots and cavalry. He was determined to defeat Alexander and drive him out of Asia Minor, and he was confident in his superior numbers and resources.

Alexander, however, was not deterred. He had already established a reputation as a master tactician and military strategist, and he had developed innovative tactics and formations that would allow him to outmaneuver and outthink his opponents.

The battle was fought near the town of Issus, near the northeastern coast of the Mediterranean. The Persian army had the advantage of the terrain, and they were able to position themselves on high ground overlooking the Macedonian forces.

But Alexander was not intimidated. He used his cavalry to launch a surprise attack on the Persian flank, catching them off guard and causing confusion and chaos in their ranks.

In the ensuing chaos, Alexander personally led his troops into the heart of the Persian army, engaging in hand-to-hand combat with the enemy leaders and fighting fiercely for victory.

The battle was fierce and intense, with both sides fighting fiercely for victory. The Persian chariots and cavalry caused chaos and confusion in the Macedonian ranks, but Alexander was able to maintain his composure and rally his troops.

In the end, it was Alexander's superior tactics and discipline that won the day. He used a combination of cavalry charges and infantry phalanxes to break the Persian lines, and he personally led his troops into the heart of the Persian army, engaging in hand-to-hand combat with the enemy leaders.

The battle was a stunning victory for the Macedonians, and it marked a turning point in the struggle between the Macedonian Kingdom and the Persian Empire. Alexander's victory secured his control over much of Asia Minor, and it allowed him to consolidate his power and expand his conquests even further.

The Battle of Issus was also significant in the history of warfare, demonstrating the importance of tactics and discipline in achieving victory. Alexander's ability to outmaneuver and outthink his opponents was a testament to his skill as a military strategist, and it inspired generations of generals and leaders to study his tactics and techniques.

But the battle also had significant political and cultural implications. It marked the beginning of Alexander's efforts to spread Hellenic culture and civilization throughout the world, as he began to incorporate Persian and other non-Greek cultures into his empire. It also had significant consequences for Greek hegemony, as it established the Macedonian Kingdom as the dominant power in the Eastern Mediterranean, displacing the Persians and other regional powers.

In the end, the Battle of Issus was a significant moment in the history of Alexander the Great and the Macedonian Kingdom, demonstrating his skill as a military leader and his ambition as a conqueror. It secured his dominance over much of Asia Minor, and it set the stage for his later conquests and empire-building. It was a testament to the power of tactics and strategy in warfare, and a reminder of the enduring legacy of Alexander's conquests and achievements.

The Siege of Babylon in 331 BC was a pivotal moment in the history of Alexander the Great and the Macedonian Kingdom. It marked the capture of the Persian capital, and the end of the Persian Empire, which had been a major power in the region for centuries.

At the time of the siege, Babylon was one of the most important cities in the Persian Empire, and it was a center of trade and commerce, as well as culture and learning. It was also the symbolic heart of the empire, and its capture was a major blow to the Persians and their supporters.

Alexander recognized the importance of Babylon, both for its strategic location and its cultural significance. He saw it as a key center of Hellenic culture and civilization, and he sought to incorporate it into his empire in order to spread Hellenic ideas and values throughout the region.

The siege of Babylon was marked by a combination of military force and political diplomacy. Alexander used his armies to lay siege to the city, but he also sought to win over key factions and leaders through diplomacy and negotiation.

One of the most significant figures in the siege was the Persian general Mazaeus, who had been appointed as the governor of Babylon by Darius III. Mazaeus was a skilled diplomat and military strategist, and he was able to hold off Alexander's forces for several months.

But Alexander was not deterred. He continued to press his attacks on the city, using a combination of military force and psychological warfare to wear down the defenders. He also worked to win over key factions and leaders within the city, offering them rewards and incentives to defect to his side.

In the end, it was Alexander's superior tactics and discipline that won the day. He used a combination of siege engines and psychological warfare to break the will of the defenders, and he personally led his troops into the heart of the city, engaging in hand-to-hand combat with the enemy leaders.

The fall of Babylon was a stunning victory for the Macedonians, and it marked the end of the Persian Empire. Alexander's victory secured his control over much of the Middle East, and it allowed him to consolidate his power and expand his conquests even further.

But the fall of Babylon was also significant in the history of Hellenic culture and civilization. It marked the beginning of Alexander's efforts to spread Hellenic ideas and values throughout the world, as he began to incorporate Persian and other non-Greek cultures into his empire.

It also had significant consequences for trade and commerce, as Babylon was a major center of economic activity and a hub of the regional trade network. The fall of the city disrupted the regional economy and trade, and it had significant implications for the wider world.

In the end, the Siege of Babylon was a significant moment in the history of Alexander the Great and the Macedonian Kingdom, demonstrating his skill as a military leader and his ambition as a conqueror. It marked the end of the Persian Empire, and it set the stage for Alexander's later conquests and empire-building. It was a testament to the power of tactics and strategy in warfare, and a reminder of the enduring legacy of Alexander's conquests and achievements.

Chapter 4: The Siege of Tyre and the Egyptian Campaign

The conquest of Tyre in 332 BC was a key moment in the history of Alexander the Great and the Macedonian Kingdom. Tyre was a major Mediterranean port, and it was a key center of commerce and trade, as well as culture and learning. Its capture was a significant achievement for Alexander, and it allowed him to establish a firm foothold in the region, consolidating his power and extending his influence even further.

At the time of the conquest, Tyre was a powerful city-state, and it was protected by a massive wall that surrounded the entire city. The wall was built on a rocky promontory that jutted out into the sea, and it was considered impregnable.

Alexander recognized the importance of Tyre, both for its strategic location and its cultural significance. He saw it as a key center of Hellenic culture and civilization, and he sought to incorporate it into his empire in order to spread Hellenic ideas and values throughout the region.

The siege of Tyre was marked by a combination of military force and political diplomacy. Alexander used his armies to lay siege to the city, but he also sought to win over key factions and leaders through diplomacy and negotiation.

One of the most significant figures in the siege was the Tyrian king, Azemilcus. Azemilcus was a skilled diplomat and military strategist, and he was able to hold off Alexander's forces for several months.

But Alexander was not deterred. He continued to press his attacks on the city, using a combination of siege engines and psychological warfare to wear down the defenders. He also worked to win over key factions and leaders within the city, offering them rewards and incentives to defect to his side.

In the end, it was Alexander's superior tactics and discipline that won the day. He used a combination of siege engines and psychological warfare to break the will of the defenders, and he personally led his troops into the heart of the city, engaging in hand-to-hand combat with the enemy leaders.

The fall of Tyre was a stunning victory for the Macedonians, and it marked the establishment of Alexander's control over much of the Eastern Mediterranean. It also had significant consequences for trade and commerce, as Tyre was a major center of economic activity and a hub of the regional trade network. The fall of the city disrupted the regional economy and trade, and it had significant implications for the wider world.

The conquest of Tyre was also significant in the history of Hellenic culture and civilization. It marked the beginning of Alexander's efforts to spread Hellenic ideas and values throughout the world, as he began to incorporate non-Greek cultures into his empire.

It also had significant political and cultural implications. It demonstrated Alexander's skill as a military leader and his ambition as a conqueror, and it established him as a legitimate and effective ruler in the eyes of his subjects and the wider world.

In the end, the conquest of Tyre was a significant moment in the history of Alexander the Great and the Macedonian Kingdom, demonstrating his skill as a military leader and his ambition as a conqueror. It secured his dominance over much of the Eastern Mediterranean, and it set the stage for his later conquests and empire-building. It was a testament to the power of tactics and strategy in warfare, and a reminder of the enduring legacy of Alexander's conquests and achievements.

Naval warfare played a crucial role in the conquests of Alexander the Great, and nowhere was this more evident than in the siege of Tyre in 332 BC. Tyre was a major Mediterranean port, and it was protected by a massive wall that surrounded the entire city. It was also surrounded by water on three sides, making it almost impregnable to land-based attacks.

Alexander recognized that the only way to capture Tyre was through a naval assault. He assembled a fleet of ships, consisting of both warships and transport vessels, and he launched a massive assault on the city from the sea.

The Tyrians were initially able to repel the Macedonian ships, using their own fleet and defensive measures to prevent the Macedonians from landing on the city's shores. But Alexander was not deterred. He used a combination of naval tactics and psychological warfare to wear down the defenders and gain the upper hand.

One of the key tactics he used was to construct a causeway, or mole, from the shore to the walls of the city. The causeway was constructed using debris from the ruined city of Old Tyre, which Alexander had destroyed in an earlier siege.

The construction of the causeway was a massive undertaking, and it took several months to complete. The Macedonians were constantly under attack from the Tyrian fleet, which tried to disrupt the construction and sink the ships carrying the materials.

But Alexander was determined to succeed. He used his superior naval tactics and discipline to protect the construction site and ensure the safety of his troops. He also used psychological warfare to break the will of the defenders, launching a series of surprise attacks and feints that kept the Tyrians off-balance and demoralized. In the end, the causeway proved to be the key to the Macedonian victory. It allowed Alexander to bring his siege engines and troops right up to the walls of the city, and it allowed him to launch a final assault that broke the will of the defenders and secured the city. The role of naval warfare in the siege of Tyre was a testament to Alexander's skill as a military leader and his willingness to innovate and adapt his tactics to suit the situation. It demonstrated the importance of naval power in the ancient world, and it showed the effectiveness of a well-trained and disciplined navy in achieving military objectives. The conquest of Tyre also had significant implications for trade and commerce, as it established Alexander's control over one of the major hubs of the Mediterranean trade network. The fall of Tyre disrupted the regional economy and trade, and it had significant implications for the wider world. In the end, the role of naval warfare in the conquests of Alexander the Great was a significant moment in the history of ancient warfare. It demonstrated the importance of innovation and adaptability in military tactics, and it showed the power of a well-trained and disciplined navy in achieving military objectives. It was a testament to the enduring legacy of Alexander's conquests and achievements, and a reminder of the ongoing importance of naval power in the modern world. The founding of Alexandria in 332 BC was one of the most significant achievements of Alexander the Great and the Macedonian Kingdom. The city was established as a center of commerce, culture, and learning, and it became one of the most important cities in the ancient world. At the time of its founding, Alexandria was located on the coast of Egypt, near the site of the ancient city of Rhakotis. The city was strategically located at the mouth of the Nile River, and it was ideally situated for trade and commerce with the Mediterranean world.

Alexander recognized the potential of the site, and he saw it as an opportunity to establish a new center of Hellenic culture and civilization in the region. He appointed his chief architect, Dinocrates, to design the city, and he provided him with generous resources to ensure the success of the project. The founding of Alexandria was marked by a combination of military force and political diplomacy. Alexander used his armies to secure the region and to protect the city from potential enemies, but he also worked to win over the local population and to build alliances with key factions and leaders. One of the key figures in the founding of Alexandria was the Macedonian general Ptolemy, who would later become the founder of the Ptolemaic dynasty in Egypt. Ptolemy played a key role in securing the region and in establishing the city as a center of

Hellenic culture and civilization. Under Alexander's leadership, Alexandria quickly became a major center of commerce and trade. Its location on the Mediterranean coast made it a key hub for the regional trade network, and its strategic position at the mouth of the Nile River made it a major center of agriculture and industry.

But Alexandria was more than just a center of commerce and trade. It was also a center of culture and learning, with some of the most important libraries and academic institutions in the ancient world. The famous Library of Alexandria, for example, was one of the largest and most comprehensive libraries in the ancient world, containing thousands of volumes of books and manuscripts.

The founding of Alexandria was a significant moment in the history of Hellenic culture and civilization. It marked the beginning of Alexander's efforts to spread Hellenic ideas and values throughout the world, as he sought to incorporate non-Greek cultures into his empire and to create a new world order based on Hellenic principles.

It also had significant implications for the wider world. The rise of Alexandria disrupted the existing balance of power in the region, and it set the stage for the later conflicts between the Hellenic world and the Roman Empire.

In the end, the founding of Alexandria was a significant moment in the history of Alexander the Great and the Macedonian Kingdom. It demonstrated his skill as a military leader and his vision as a statesman, and it marked the beginning of a new era in the history of Hellenic culture and civilization. It was a testament to the enduring legacy of Alexander's conquests and achievements, and a reminder of the ongoing importance of trade, commerce, and culture in shaping the world.

The Battle of the Nile in 332 BC was one of the most significant naval battles in the history of Alexander the Great and the Macedonian Kingdom. The battle was fought against the Persian navy, which had gathered at the Nile Delta in an attempt to stop Alexander's advance into Egypt.

The Persian navy was a formidable force, consisting of hundreds of ships and thousands of trained sailors and marines. It was led by the Persian admiral Memnon, who was known for his skill and expertise in naval warfare.

Alexander recognized the threat posed by the Persian navy, and he assembled a fleet of ships to meet them. He personally led the Macedonian navy, showing his determination and bravery in the face of overwhelming odds.

The battle was fierce and intense, with both sides using a variety of tactics and weapons to gain the upper hand. Alexander used a combination of boarding parties, naval artillery, and ramming attacks to inflict damage on the Persian fleet.

At the same time, he used his superior naval tactics and discipline to protect his own ships and troops, ensuring that they remained safe from harm. He also used psychological warfare to break the will of the enemy sailors and marines, launching surprise attacks and feints that kept the Persians off-balance and demoralized.

In the end, it was Alexander's superior tactics and discipline that won the day. He was able to break through the Persian lines and sink several key ships, effectively ending the Persian threat and securing control of the Nile Delta.

The Battle of the Nile was a significant moment in the history of naval warfare, demonstrating the power of a well-trained and disciplined navy in achieving military objectives. It was also a testament to Alexander's skill as a military leader and his willingness to innovate and adapt his tactics to suit the situation.

The battle had significant implications for the wider world, as it marked the establishment of Alexander's control over Egypt and the foundation of Alexandria as a major center of commerce, culture, and learning.

It also had significant implications for the Persian Empire, which was weakened by the loss of its navy and the disruption of its trade and commerce networks. The Persian defeat at the Battle of the Nile set the stage for Alexander's later conquests and the eventual collapse of the Persian Empire.

In the end, the Battle of the Nile was a significant moment in the history of Alexander the Great and the Macedonian Kingdom. It demonstrated the importance of naval power in the ancient world, and it showed the effectiveness of a well-trained and disciplined navy in achieving military objectives. It was a testament to the enduring legacy of Alexander's conquests and achievements, and a reminder of the ongoing importance of naval power in the modern world.

The Oracle of Siwa was one of the most important religious sites in ancient Egypt, and it played a significant role in the life of Alexander the Great and the Macedonian Kingdom. The oracle was located in the desert oasis of Siwa, and it was believed to be the home of the god Ammon.

In 332 BC, Alexander made a pilgrimage to the oracle in order to consult with the god and to seek his guidance on his campaign in Egypt. The journey was long and arduous, but Alexander was determined to receive the wisdom of the oracle and to establish his divine authority in the region. When he arrived at Siwa, Alexander was greeted by the priests of the temple and was given a royal reception. He was then led to the inner sanctum of the temple, where he underwent a series of rituals and ceremonies in order to prepare himself for the encounter with the god.

Finally, he was led into the presence of the oracle, and he was allowed to ask his questions and seek the wisdom of the god. The details of the conversation between Alexander and the god are not known, but it is believed that the oracle confirmed Alexander's divine status and blessed his campaign in Egypt.

The visit to the Oracle of Siwa was a significant moment in the life of Alexander and in the history of Egyptian religion. It demonstrated his commitment to the religious traditions of the region and his willingness to seek the guidance of the gods in his campaign.

It also had significant implications for the legacy of Alexander's conquests and the spread of Hellenic culture and religion. The encounter with the Egyptian religion and the acknowledgement of his divine status by the oracle served to legitimize Alexander's rule in the eyes of the Egyptian people and to establish his authority as a legitimate ruler in the region.

The visit to the oracle also had significant implications for the wider world, as it marked the beginning of a new era of religious and cultural syncretism. Alexander's encounter with the Egyptian religion and his subsequent incorporation of Egyptian elements into Hellenic culture paved the way for the later fusion of cultures and religions in the Hellenistic world.

The legacy of the visit to the Oracle of Siwa was a testament to Alexander's vision as a statesman and his willingness to embrace the cultural and religious traditions of the regions he conquered. It was a reminder of the power of religion and culture in shaping the world and of the enduring legacy of Alexander's conquests and achievements.

In the end, the visit to the Oracle of Siwa was a significant moment in the history of Alexander the Great and the Macedonian Kingdom. It demonstrated his commitment to the religious traditions of the region and his willingness to seek the guidance of the gods in his campaign. It also had significant implications for the legacy of his conquests and the spread of Hellenic culture and religion, paving the way for a new era of religious and cultural syncretism in the Hellenistic world.

Chapter 5: The Crossing of the Hindu Kush and Conquest of Bactria

The geopolitics of Central Asia in the 4th century BC were complex and ever-shifting, with various tribes, city-states, and empires vying for control of the region. It was into this environment that Alexander the Great launched his famous Eastern campaigns, seeking to expand the Macedonian Kingdom and to establish his dominance over the region.

At the time, the region was dominated by the Achaemenid Persian Empire, which had established its control over much of Central Asia and parts of India. The Persians were known for their military prowess and their ability to conquer and assimilate the various tribes and city-states in the region.

However, the Persian Empire was weakened by internal conflicts and political instability, and it was vulnerable to external threats. Alexander recognized this vulnerability and saw it as an opportunity to expand his empire and to challenge the Persian hegemony in the region.

To do this, Alexander relied on a combination of military force and political diplomacy. He used his army to conquer and subjugate the various tribes and city-states in the region, while also forging alliances with key leaders and factions.

One of the key challenges facing Alexander in his Eastern campaigns was the terrain and climate of the region. Central Asia is characterized by vast deserts, rugged mountain ranges, and harsh climates, which made it difficult for armies to traverse and maintain supply lines.

To overcome these challenges, Alexander relied on his military skill and leadership, as well as his ability to adapt to changing circumstances. He employed innovative tactics and strategies, such as the use of camels and other pack animals to transport supplies, and he relied on his cavalry and light infantry to outmaneuver and defeat the Persian forces.

The Eastern campaigns were marked by a series of battles and sieges, as Alexander sought to conquer and subjugate the various tribes and city-states in the region. The Battle of Gaugamela in 331 BC was one of the most significant battles of the campaign, as it marked the decisive defeat of the Persian Empire and the establishment of Macedonian control over the region.

The Eastern campaigns had significant implications for the wider world, as they marked the beginning of a new era of Hellenistic culture and civilization. Alexander's conquests and the establishment of the Hellenistic kingdoms paved the way for the later fusion of cultures and religions in the region, and they set the stage for the later conflicts between the Hellenistic world and the Roman Empire.

In the end, the Eastern campaigns were a significant moment in the history of Alexander the Great and the Macedonian Kingdom. They demonstrated his skill as a military leader and his ability to adapt to changing circumstances, and they marked the beginning of a new era of Hellenistic culture and civilization. They were a testament to the enduring legacy of Alexander's conquests and achievements, and a reminder of the ongoing importance of geopolitical strategy and military prowess in shaping the world.

The crossing of the Hindu Kush was one of the most significant moments in the Eastern campaigns of Alexander the Great and the Macedonian Kingdom. The Hindu Kush is a massive mountain range that stretches across Central Asia, forming a formidable barrier between the regions of modern-day Afghanistan and Pakistan.

In the spring of 329 BC, Alexander led his army across the Hindu Kush, seeking to extend his conquests into the eastern regions of the Persian Empire. The crossing was an arduous and dangerous journey, as the Macedonians had to traverse rugged mountain passes and endure harsh weather conditions.

Despite the challenges, Alexander pressed on, showing his determination and courage in the face of adversity. He led his troops through the treacherous mountain passes, using his military skill and leadership to navigate the difficult terrain and maintain the morale of his troops.

As they crossed the Hindu Kush, the Macedonians encountered fierce resistance from the local tribes and city-states, who sought to protect their independence and resist the advance of the Macedonian army. The battles were fierce and intense, with both sides using a variety of tactics and weapons to gain the upper hand.

In the end, it was Alexander's superior military tactics and discipline that won the day. He was able to outmaneuver and defeat the local forces, securing his control over the region and extending the reach of the Macedonian Kingdom into the east.

The crossing of the Hindu Kush had significant implications for the wider world, as it marked the extension of Hellenistic culture and civilization into the eastern regions of the Persian Empire. It also set the stage for the later conflicts between the Hellenistic world and the Roman Empire, and it demonstrated the importance of geopolitical strategy and military prowess in shaping the world.

In the end, the crossing of the Hindu Kush was a significant moment in the history of Alexander the Great and the Macedonian Kingdom. It demonstrated his determination and courage in the face of adversity, and it showed his ability to adapt to changing circumstances and to overcome the challenges of difficult terrain and fierce resistance.

It was a testament to the enduring legacy of Alexander's conquests and achievements, and a reminder of the ongoing importance of military prowess and strategic thinking in shaping the world. The crossing of the Hindu Kush was a defining moment in the history of Central Asia and the wider world, and it remains a symbol of Alexander's enduring legacy and impact on the course of human history.

The Battle of the Hydaspes was one of the most significant battles in the Eastern campaigns of Alexander the Great and the Macedonian Kingdom. The battle was fought against the Indian king Porus, who ruled over the region of modern-day Punjab.

Porus was known for his military prowess and his ability to resist foreign invasions, and he posed a formidable challenge to Alexander and his army. The battle took place in 326 BC, and it was marked by a series of intense clashes between the Macedonian and Indian forces.

The Macedonian army was outnumbered and outgunned, facing an Indian army that was larger and better equipped. However, Alexander used his military skill and leadership to outmaneuver and outflank the Indian forces, using a combination of cavalry charges, infantry assaults, and artillery bombardments to wear down the enemy.

The battle was a grueling and intense affair, with both sides suffering heavy casualties and enduring the brutal conditions of the battlefield. However, it was Alexander's superior tactics and discipline that ultimately won the day, as he was able to break through the Indian lines and defeat Porus and his forces.

The Battle of the Hydaspes had significant implications for the wider world, as it marked the extension of Macedonian control over the region of Punjab and the establishment of Alexander's dominance in the eastern regions of the Persian Empire. It also set the stage for the later fusion of Hellenistic and Indian cultures and religions, paving the way for the later syncretism of the Hellenistic world.

The battle was also significant for the legacy of Alexander and the Macedonian Kingdom, demonstrating his skill as a military leader and his ability to adapt to changing circumstances. It was a testament to the enduring legacy of his conquests and achievements, and a reminder of the ongoing importance of military prowess and strategic thinking in shaping the world.

In the end, the Battle of the Hydaspes was a defining moment in the history of Alexander the Great and the Macedonian Kingdom. It marked the extension of Macedonian control over the eastern regions of the Persian Empire and the establishment of Hellenistic culture and civilization in the region.

It was a testament to Alexander's military skill and leadership, and it demonstrated the importance of geopolitical strategy and military prowess in shaping the world. The Battle of the Hydaspes remains one of the most significant battles in the history of the ancient world, and it serves as a reminder of the enduring legacy of Alexander the Great and his conquests.

The conquest of Bactria was a significant moment in the Eastern campaigns of Alexander the Great and the Macedonian Kingdom. Bactria was a region located in modern-day Afghanistan and Uzbekistan, and it was known for its rich history and culture.

At the time, Bactria was ruled by the Bactrian Empire, a powerful state that had established its control over much of Central Asia and parts of India. The Bactrians were known for their military prowess and their ability to resist foreign invasions.

However, Alexander saw the conquest of Bactria as a key objective in his campaign, as it would allow him to extend his control over the eastern regions of the Persian Empire and to establish his dominance in the region.

To do this, Alexander relied on a combination of military force and political diplomacy. He used his army to conquer and subjugate the various tribes and city-states in the region, while also forging alliances with key leaders and factions.

The conquest of Bactria was marked by a series of battles and sieges, as Alexander sought to defeat the Bactrian forces and establish Macedonian control over the region. The battles were intense and grueling, with both sides using a variety of tactics and weapons to gain the upper hand.

However, it was Alexander's superior military tactics and discipline that ultimately won the day. He was able to outmaneuver and defeat the Bactrian forces, securing his control over the region and extending the reach of the Macedonian Kingdom into the east.

The conquest of Bactria had significant implications for the wider world, as it marked the extension of Hellenistic culture and civilization into the eastern regions of the Persian Empire. It also set the stage for the later fusion of cultures and religions in the Hellenistic world, paving the way for a new era of religious and cultural syncretism in the region.

The conquest of Bactria was also significant for the legacy of Alexander and the Macedonian Kingdom, demonstrating his skill as a military leader and his ability to adapt to changing circumstances. It was a testament to the enduring legacy of his conquests and achievements, and a reminder of the ongoing importance of military prowess and strategic thinking in shaping the world.

In the end, the conquest of Bactria was a defining moment in the history of Alexander the Great and the Macedonian Kingdom. It marked the extension of Macedonian control over the eastern regions of the Persian Empire and the establishment of Hellenistic culture and civilization in the region.

It was a testament to Alexander's military skill and leadership, and it demonstrated the importance of geopolitical strategy and military prowess in shaping the world. The conquest of Bactria remains one of the most significant moments in the history of the ancient world, and it serves as a reminder of the enduring legacy of Alexander the Great and his conquests.

The legacy of Alexander's eastern campaigns was far-reaching and profound, shaping the course of history and leaving an indelible mark on the peoples and cultures of Central Asia. Alexander's conquests had significant implications for the wider world, as they marked the expansion of Hellenistic culture and civilization into the eastern regions of the Persian Empire and beyond.

One of the most significant effects of Alexander's conquests was the establishment of a new era of cultural and religious syncretism in Central Asia. As the Macedonian Kingdom extended its reach into the east, it encountered a diverse range of cultures and peoples, each with their own unique traditions and beliefs.

Alexander's conquests sparked a process of cultural exchange and cross-fertilization, as the Hellenistic world encountered and absorbed the various traditions and practices of the peoples it conquered. This process of syncretism led to the emergence of new forms of art, architecture, literature, and philosophy, as well as the fusion of religious and spiritual beliefs.

The legacy of Alexander's conquests was also felt in the political and military sphere. The Macedonian Kingdom's expansion into Central Asia had significant geopolitical implications, as it disrupted the established balance of power in the region and challenged the dominance of the Persian Empire.

The legacy of Alexander's conquests was felt most acutely in the emergence of new political and military structures in Central Asia. The Hellenistic world's influence led to the emergence of new states and empires, each with its own unique blend of Hellenistic and local traditions.

The legacy of Alexander's conquests was also felt in the economic sphere. The expansion of the Macedonian Kingdom into Central Asia led to the integration of local economies into the wider world, creating new opportunities for trade and commerce and leading to the emergence of new forms of economic organization and exchange.

Overall, the legacy of Alexander's eastern campaigns was far-reaching and profound, shaping the course of history and leaving an indelible mark on the peoples and cultures of Central Asia. The emergence of new forms of cultural and religious syncretism, the establishment of new political and military structures, and the integration of local economies into the wider world were all significant legacies of Alexander's conquests.

The enduring legacy of Alexander's eastern campaigns serves as a reminder of the ongoing importance of geopolitical strategy and military prowess in shaping the world. It is a testament to the enduring legacy of his conquests and achievements, and a reminder of the ongoing importance of cultural and political exchange in shaping the course of human history.

Chapter 6: Alexander's Military Tactics and Strategies

The Macedonian phalanx was one of the most iconic and formidable military formations in the ancient world. Originating in Greece, the phalanx was adapted and refined by the Macedonian Kingdom, becoming the backbone of the Macedonian army and a key factor in its military successes.

The phalanx was a formation of heavily armed infantry soldiers, arranged in ranks and files, and armed with a long spear known as a sarissa. The soldiers were protected by a large, circular shield known as a hoplon, and were trained to fight in close formation, using their spears to create a wall of overlapping points that could effectively ward off enemy attacks.

The Macedonian phalanx was distinctive in several respects. First, it was organized into smaller units known as syntagmata, which were highly mobile and adaptable, allowing for rapid changes in formation and tactics. Second, it made use of longer spears than those used by the Greek phalanxes, with the sarissa being up to 18 feet in length.

The use of the longer spear was a key factor in the success of the Macedonian phalanx. The longer spear allowed Macedonian soldiers to reach over the heads of the front rank of enemy soldiers and strike at the enemy from a distance, effectively neutralizing their attacks.

Another key factor in the success of the Macedonian phalanx was the discipline and training of its soldiers. Macedonian soldiers were trained to fight in close formation, to maintain their ranks and files, and to respond to the commands of their officers quickly and effectively.

The Macedonian phalanx was put to the test in a series of battles against the armies of the Persian Empire, including the Battle of Issus and the Battle of Gaugamela. In these battles, the Macedonian phalanx proved its worth, using its superior discipline, tactics, and equipment to overcome larger and better-equipped Persian armies.

The Macedonian phalanx was not without its limitations, however. Its heavy reliance on close formation and the sarissa made it vulnerable to flanking attacks and ambushes. Additionally, its effectiveness was largely dependent on the quality and training of its soldiers, making it difficult to replicate in other contexts.

Despite its limitations, the Macedonian phalanx was a key factor in the success of the Macedonian Kingdom and the legacy of Alexander the Great. Its use and adaptation of the traditional Greek military formation represented a significant evolution in the history of warfare, and its legacy can still be seen in modern military tactics and formations.

In the end, the Macedonian phalanx was a testament to the enduring legacy of military innovation and adaptation. Its use and refinement by the Macedonian Kingdom represented a key turning point in the history of warfare, paving the way for new forms of military organization and tactics that would continue to shape the course of human history.

The Companion Cavalry was one of the most important and elite units in the army of Alexander the Great. Composed of some of the most skilled and experienced horsemen in the Macedonian Kingdom, the Companion Cavalry played a key role in many of Alexander's most important military campaigns and battles.

The Companion Cavalry was a highly mobile and adaptable unit, capable of moving rapidly across the battlefield and outmaneuvering enemy forces. They were armed with long spears and swords, and were trained to fight both in close combat and at a distance.

The Companion Cavalry was also highly disciplined and well-trained, with a strict hierarchy of officers and a deep sense of camaraderie and loyalty. This loyalty was strengthened by the fact that many of the soldiers in the Companion Cavalry were members of the Macedonian aristocracy, with close personal ties to Alexander himself.

The role of the Companion Cavalry in Alexander's campaigns was multifaceted. On the one hand, they were used as shock troops, charging into enemy lines and breaking their formations. On the other hand, they were used for reconnaissance, scouting out enemy positions and providing crucial intelligence to Alexander and his generals.

Perhaps their most important role, however, was as a reserve force. The Companion Cavalry was often held in reserve, waiting for the right moment to launch a devastating charge against the enemy. This tactic proved highly effective, as the sight of the Companion Cavalry charging across the battlefield was often enough to break the morale of even the most seasoned enemy soldiers.

The Companion Cavalry played a key role in many of Alexander's most famous battles, including the Battle of Issus, the Battle of Gaugamela, and the Battle of the Hydaspes. In each of these battles, the Companion Cavalry proved itself to be a highly effective and formidable force, capable of turning the tide of battle in Alexander's favor.

The importance of the Companion Cavalry in Alexander's campaigns cannot be overstated. Their mobility, discipline, and skill as horsemen made them a highly versatile and adaptable unit, capable of fulfilling a wide range of roles on the battlefield. Their loyalty and devotion to Alexander also made them a key factor in the cohesion and morale of the Macedonian army as a whole.

The legacy of the Companion Cavalry can still be seen in modern military tactics and formations, with many modern armies utilizing highly trained and specialized units for specific roles on the battlefield.

In the end, the Companion Cavalry was a testament to the enduring legacy of military innovation and adaptation. Its role and importance in the campaigns of Alexander the Great represented a key turning point in the history of warfare, paving the way for new forms of military organization and tactics that would continue to shape the course of human history.

Siege warfare was a crucial aspect of ancient military strategy, and Alexander the Great was no stranger to this form of combat. The techniques and strategies used by Alexander's army in laying siege to fortified cities were highly developed and sophisticated, allowing them to overcome some of the most formidable defenses in the ancient world.

One of the key elements of Alexander's approach to siege warfare was the use of extensive preparatory work. Before launching a siege, Alexander's army would typically establish a camp outside the city walls, and then proceed to build a series of siege engines and other structures necessary for the assault.

These structures included battering rams, siege towers, and mobile artillery, as well as tunnels and other underground passages designed to undermine the city walls. Alexander's engineers were highly skilled, and their designs were often highly innovative, incorporating new technologies and techniques to overcome even the most formidable defenses.

Once the preparatory work was complete, Alexander's army would typically launch a coordinated assault on the city walls. This assault would involve a combination of siege engines and infantry units, with the aim of creating breaches in the walls and allowing the Macedonian soldiers to enter the city.

Alexander's army was highly adaptable, and they were able to adjust their tactics to suit the specific challenges presented by each individual siege. For example, when besieging the city of Tyre, which was located on an island off the coast of modern-day Lebanon, Alexander's army built a causeway connecting the island to the mainland, allowing them to launch a full-scale assault on the city's defenses.

Another key element of Alexander's approach to siege warfare was the use of psychological tactics. Alexander understood that a well-timed threat or show of force could often be enough to break the morale of the city's defenders, and he was not afraid to use these tactics to his advantage.

One of the most famous examples of Alexander's use of psychological tactics occurred during the siege of the city of Gaza. As his army was preparing to assault the walls, Alexander himself rode up to the city on horseback, armed only with a spear. This bold display of courage and determination was enough to inspire his soldiers to redouble their efforts, and the city was quickly taken.

Overall, the techniques and strategies used by Alexander's army in laying siege to fortified cities were highly effective, allowing them to overcome some of the most formidable defenses in the ancient world. The combination of extensive preparatory work, sophisticated siege engines and tactics, and psychological warfare made Alexander's army a formidable force, capable of conquering even the most heavily fortified cities.

The legacy of Alexander's approach to siege warfare can still be seen in modern military tactics and strategies. The use of preparatory work, siege engines, and psychological tactics remains a key component of modern siege warfare, demonstrating the enduring legacy of Alexander's military innovations and the ongoing importance of military strategy in shaping the course of human history.

In the ancient world, intelligence gathering was a crucial component of military strategy, and Alexander the Great was no exception. The Macedonian king relied heavily on scouts and spies to gather information about enemy movements, fortifications, and weaknesses, allowing him to make strategic decisions that would ultimately lead to his victories on the battlefield.

One of the key elements of Alexander's intelligence gathering strategy was the use of scouts. These were highly skilled soldiers who were tasked with scouting out enemy positions, monitoring troop movements, and gathering information about the terrain and climate.

Scouts were often sent out in small groups, armed with nothing more than their wits and their knowledge of the terrain. They were trained to move quickly and quietly, avoiding detection by enemy forces, and to gather as much information as possible before returning to the Macedonian camp.

In addition to scouts, Alexander also made extensive use of spies. These were individuals who were sent into enemy territory, often disguised as civilians or traders, with the aim of gathering information about enemy movements and intentions.

Spies were often highly skilled in the art of deception, using their charm and charisma to gather information from enemy officials and soldiers. They were also skilled in the use of code and cipher, allowing them to communicate their findings back to the Macedonian camp without fear of detection.

The information gathered by scouts and spies was used by Alexander to make strategic decisions about his military campaigns. For example, in the lead-up to the Battle of Issus, Alexander received intelligence that the Persian army was planning to attack him from behind. This information allowed Alexander to adjust his strategy and to position his troops in a way that would ultimately lead to his victory.

Similarly, in the lead-up to the siege of Tyre, Alexander received intelligence that the city's walls were heavily fortified and that the only way to breach them would be to build a causeway across the water. This information allowed Alexander to plan and execute a successful assault on the city's defenses, leading to its eventual capture.

Overall, the use of intelligence gathering was a crucial component of Alexander's military strategy, allowing him to make strategic decisions that would ultimately lead to his victories on the battlefield. The combination of scouts and spies, along with their specialized training and skills, allowed Alexander to gather the information he needed to make informed decisions about his military campaigns.

The legacy of Alexander's use of intelligence gathering can still be seen in modern military tactics and strategies. The use of scouts and spies, as well as the importance of gathering and analyzing intelligence, remains a key component of modern military strategy, demonstrating the enduring legacy of Alexander's military innovations and the ongoing importance of military intelligence in shaping the course of human history.

Logistics played a crucial role in the success of Alexander the Great's military campaigns. The Macedonian king was a master of supply lines and transportation, and his ability to keep his army well-fed, well-equipped, and well-supplied was a key factor in his ability to conquer much of the known world.

One of the key elements of Alexander's logistics strategy was his use of a highly organized and efficient supply chain. This involved a vast network of pack animals, carts, and boats, as well as a dedicated corps of supply officers and quartermasters who were responsible for overseeing the movement of supplies and equipment.

The supply chain was designed to be as efficient and streamlined as possible, with supplies and equipment moving quickly and easily from one location to another. This required careful planning and coordination, as well as a deep understanding of the terrain and climate.

Alexander's army was also highly mobile, able to move quickly and easily across long distances. This mobility was crucial in allowing Alexander to launch surprise attacks on enemy forces, and to quickly respond to changes in the battlefield.

To maintain this mobility, Alexander's army was equipped with a wide range of transportation options, including horses, mules, carts, and boats. These were carefully managed and maintained, with a dedicated corps of transport officers responsible for their care and upkeep.

In addition to transportation, Alexander also paid close attention to the supply of food and water for his troops. He understood that a well-fed and hydrated army was a more effective and resilient fighting force, and he made sure that his troops were always supplied with plenty of fresh food and water.

This required careful planning and coordination, as well as a deep understanding of the local terrain and climate. Alexander's army was able to make use of local resources wherever possible, and his soldiers were trained in a variety of survival skills that allowed them to thrive even in the harshest of conditions.

Overall, the role of logistics in Alexander's military campaigns cannot be overstated. The efficient and effective movement of supplies and equipment, as well as the careful management of transportation and supply lines, allowed Alexander to maintain a highly mobile and effective fighting force, capable of conquering much of the known world.

The legacy of Alexander's logistics strategy can still be seen in modern military tactics and strategies. The importance of supply chains and transportation, as well as the need for careful planning and coordination, remains a key component of modern military logistics, demonstrating the enduring legacy of Alexander's military innovations and the ongoing importance of logistics in shaping the course of human history.

Chapter 7: The Administration and Governance of the Empire

One of the most significant decisions that Alexander the Great made in the latter stages of his military campaigns was the division of his empire among his generals. This decision was made shortly before Alexander's death in 323 BC and would have a lasting impact on the political landscape of the ancient world.

The division of the empire was a complex process, involving a careful balance of power and influence among Alexander's closest advisers and generals. Alexander had no clear heir, and his decision to divide the empire was driven by a number of factors, including his desire to maintain the loyalty of his most trusted advisers and to ensure the continued stability of the empire after his death.

The division of the empire was carried out in a series of agreements, known as the Diadochi, among Alexander's generals. These agreements established the territorial boundaries of each general's domain and set out the terms of their relationship with one another.

One of the key considerations in the division of the empire was the strategic value of each territory. Some territories were more valuable than others, either because of their strategic location, their resources, or their economic importance. Alexander's generals understood this, and they were careful to negotiate for territories that would provide them with the greatest strategic advantage.

Another key consideration was the loyalty and influence of each general. Alexander's generals were a diverse group, each with their own strengths and weaknesses. Some were more loyal to Alexander than others, and some had greater influence and power within the empire. These factors played a significant role in determining the division of the empire, as each general sought to establish a territory that would maximize their power and influence.

Despite the complexities involved in the division of the empire, Alexander's generals were largely successful in maintaining the stability of the empire in the years following his death. The territories established in the Diadochi remained largely intact, and the empire continued to prosper under the leadership of Alexander's most trusted advisers.

The legacy of Alexander's division of the empire can still be seen in the political landscape of the modern world. The idea of dividing a large empire among multiple leaders has been used throughout history, from the Roman Empire to the British Empire. The division of the empire also had significant implications for the development of Hellenistic culture and the spread of Greek language and philosophy throughout the ancient world.

Overall, the division of the empire was a complex and carefully negotiated process that had significant implications for the political and cultural landscape of the ancient world. Alexander's decision to divide the empire among his generals was driven by a desire to maintain the stability and prosperity of the empire, and it remains a testament to his strategic thinking and leadership abilities.

It is a truth universally acknowledged that an empire in possession of vast territories must be in want of a system of governance. Such was the case with the empire of Alexander the Great, who, in his bid for world conquest, found himself in control of lands stretching from Greece to India. To rule such a vast domain, Alexander relied on a system of satraps, or provincial governors, who served as his representatives in the various regions of his empire.

The satraps were appointed by Alexander himself, and their primary function was to collect taxes, maintain order, and ensure loyalty to the central government. Each satrap was responsible for a particular province, which could vary greatly in size and population. Some of the more important provinces, such as Egypt or Babylon, were ruled by multiple satraps, while smaller provinces might be governed by a single individual.

The satraps held a position of considerable power within the empire, and they were often drawn from the local aristocracy or other influential families. However, their authority was always subject to the will of the king, and they could be removed from office at any time if they failed to meet the demands of the central government. To ensure their loyalty, Alexander required them to send regular reports on their activities and to provide him with troops and resources when needed.

Despite the centralization of power under Alexander, the satraps were granted a significant degree of autonomy in their local affairs. They were allowed to enforce their own laws and customs, provided they did not conflict with those of the central government. This policy of cultural accommodation was a shrewd move on Alexander's part, as it allowed him to maintain the loyalty of the local population while also asserting his authority as the ultimate ruler of the empire.

The satraps were not just administrators; they were also military commanders, responsible for raising and maintaining troops within their provinces. In times of war, they would be called upon to contribute soldiers and supplies to the king's army. They also had the power to make alliances with neighboring states or engage in diplomacy on behalf of the empire.

The system of satraps was not without its challenges. As with any system of local government, there was always the risk of corruption, abuse of power, or rebellion. Some satraps were more loyal to their own interests than to the empire as a whole, and there were cases where they defied or even fought against the central government. Nevertheless, the satrapal system proved remarkably durable and adaptable, surviving even after Alexander's death and the subsequent fragmentation of his empire.

In the years after Alexander's death, the satraps continued to play a prominent role in the affairs of the successor kingdoms. Some of the more ambitious satraps even carved out their own empires, such as Seleucus I Nicator, who founded the Seleucid Empire in the eastern provinces. The satrapal system also provided a model for later empires, such as the Parthians and the Sassanids, who adopted similar systems of local governance.

In summary, the satraps were a crucial component of Alexander's empire, providing a means of governing the vast territories he conquered. They were responsible for maintaining order, collecting taxes, and providing troops and resources to the central government. Their position of power and autonomy allowed for cultural accommodation and ensured the loyalty of the local population. Despite the challenges they faced, the satraps proved remarkably adaptable and durable, and their legacy can be seen in the systems of local governance that followed in the centuries after Alexander's death.

The empire of Alexander the Great was a vast and diverse entity that spanned across multiple regions and cultures. One of the key factors that allowed the empire to thrive and expand was its ability to incorporate and integrate the customs and practices of the conquered peoples into its own administration and governance.

At the heart of this system was the role of satraps, who were appointed by Alexander to govern the various provinces and regions that he had conquered. These satraps were typically drawn from the local nobility or ruling class, and were given a certain degree of autonomy and authority to govern their provinces according to their own customs and traditions.

This system of local governance was essential to the success of Alexander's empire, as it allowed for the continuation of existing power structures and the preservation of local identities and cultures. By appointing local rulers as satraps, Alexander was able to gain the support and loyalty of the conquered peoples, while also ensuring that the empire remained stable and cohesive.

However, while the satraps were given a degree of autonomy, they were still ultimately answerable to Alexander and his central administration. The satraps were required to pay tribute and provide troops to support Alexander's military campaigns, and were subject to regular inspections and audits to ensure that they were governing their provinces effectively and efficiently.

In addition to the satraps, Alexander also appointed a number of Greek officials to key positions within the empire, particularly in the areas of finance and administration. These officials brought with them the administrative systems and practices of the Greek city-states, which were renowned for their efficiency and effectiveness.

This integration of local customs and Greek administrative practices was a key factor in the success of Alexander's empire, as it allowed for the efficient management of a vast and diverse territory. The administrative systems put in place by Alexander and his officials were able to maintain order and stability, while also allowing for the continued development and growth of local cultures and identities.

Despite this system of integration, however, there were still tensions and conflicts between the conquered peoples and the Greeks who had come to govern them. Many of the local rulers and nobility resented the intrusion of the Greeks into their traditional power structures, and there were frequent rebellions and uprisings throughout the empire.

Nonetheless, the system of satraps and Greek officials remained in place throughout Alexander's lifetime, and was even continued by his successors after his death. This system allowed the empire to survive for several centuries, and had a lasting impact on the cultures and societies of the regions that Alexander had conquered.

In summary, the role of satraps and the integration of local customs and practices was a key factor in the success of Alexander's empire. This system allowed for the continuation of existing power structures and the preservation of local identities, while also ensuring the stability and cohesion of the empire. While there were tensions and conflicts between the conquered peoples and their Greek rulers, the system of satraps and Greek officials remained in place throughout Alexander's lifetime and had a lasting impact on the cultures and societies of the regions he conquered.

In the annals of history, few figures have left as profound an impact as Alexander the Great. In just a few short years, Alexander transformed the Greek city-state of Macedon into an empire that spanned three continents, from the Ionian Sea to the Himalayas. His military conquests and administrative reforms set the stage for the Hellenistic Age, a period of cultural and scientific progress that lasted for centuries after his death. Next, we will examine the legacy of Alexander's empire and explore the ways in which his conquests shaped the course of history.

One of the most significant contributions of Alexander's empire was the system of local government and administration that he established. Under his rule, conquered territories were governed by satraps, or regional governors, who were responsible for maintaining order and collecting taxes. These satraps were chosen for their loyalty and ability, rather than their social status or family connections, and were required to report directly to Alexander himself. This system allowed for greater efficiency and control, as well as greater cultural and political integration between different regions and peoples.

Another key aspect of Alexander's empire was its policy of incorporating local customs and practices into its administration. Rather than imposing a rigid system of government or culture, Alexander and his generals sought to respect the traditions and beliefs of conquered peoples. This policy allowed for a degree of religious and cultural diversity within the empire, which in turn helped to promote trade and cultural exchange. For example, Alexander allowed conquered peoples to continue worshipping their own gods and practicing their own religious rituals, as long as they did not interfere with the peace and stability of the empire.

The legacy of Alexander's empire was profound and far-reaching. Perhaps its most lasting impact was the spread of Greek culture and language throughout the Mediterranean and beyond. As the empire expanded, Greek became the language of trade and diplomacy, and the culture of the Greeks began to influence the cultures of other regions. This led to a period of cultural and intellectual flourishing known as the Hellenistic Age, in which Greek ideas and concepts were combined with local traditions to create a new synthesis of culture.

Another important legacy of Alexander's empire was its impact on the political and military structures of the ancient world. Prior to Alexander's conquests, the Mediterranean world was dominated by city-states and small kingdoms, with little centralization or coordination. Alexander's empire introduced a new model of government and administration, one that was based on a strong central authority and a professional army. This model would be imitated by later empires, such as the Roman Empire and the Byzantine Empire, and would serve as a template for many modern states.

Finally, Alexander's empire had a profound impact on the course of world history. His conquests and subsequent rule helped to spread Greek culture and language throughout the world, paving the way for the development of Western civilization. His administration and military strategies set the stage for the rise of the Roman Empire, which would go on to dominate Europe for centuries. And his legacy inspired countless leaders and conquerors throughout history, from Julius Caesar to Napoleon Bonaparte.

In summary, the legacy of Alexander's empire was vast and multifaceted. His system of local government and administration, as well as his policy of incorporating local customs and practices, helped to create a more integrated and diverse empire. His conquests and administration transformed the political and military structures of the ancient world, paving the way for the rise of great empires and states. And his influence on culture and language helped to shape the course of world history, creating a legacy that would endure for centuries to come.

Chapter 8: The Hellenistic Age and the Spread of Greek Culture

The death of Alexander the Great in 323 BC marked the end of an era, but also the beginning of a new one. With no clear heir, his vast empire was divided among his generals, who became known as the Diadochi, or successors. The Diadochi fought amongst themselves for control of the empire, eventually establishing their own kingdoms and empires. The legacy of Alexander's empire can be seen in the various kingdoms that emerged, such as the Seleucid Empire, the Ptolemaic Kingdom, and the Antigonid Empire.

The division of Alexander's empire among his generals was not without conflict. The Diadochi fought against each other, often in brutal and bloody battles, to establish their own power and influence. The struggles between these generals continued for decades after Alexander's death, with shifting alliances and betrayals as each sought to gain the upper hand. The wars between the Diadochi ultimately weakened the empire, making it vulnerable to invasion and conquest.

Despite the conflicts and turmoil that followed Alexander's death, his legacy had a profound impact on the world. His conquests and administration brought together various cultures and civilizations, creating a cosmopolitan society that spanned from Greece to India. The spread of Greek culture and language, known as Hellenism, had a lasting influence on the regions that Alexander conquered. Greek became the common language of trade, diplomacy, and culture, and the ideas and philosophy of the ancient Greeks spread throughout the world.

The successors of Alexander continued his legacy, spreading Hellenism and the Greek way of life throughout their empires. The Seleucid Empire, founded by Seleucus I Nicator, was the largest of the successor kingdoms, encompassing much of Alexander's former empire in the east. The Ptolemaic Kingdom, founded by Ptolemy I Soter, ruled over Egypt and parts of the eastern Mediterranean. The Antigonid Empire, founded by Antigonus I Monophthalmus, controlled much of Greece and Macedonia.

Under the rule of the Diadochi, the various kingdoms and empires that emerged continued the trend of cultural and economic exchange that had begun under Alexander. Trade routes were established between the various regions, and a thriving trade in goods and ideas emerged. Hellenistic art and architecture flourished, as did philosophy, literature, and science.

The legacy of Alexander's empire can also be seen in the continued expansion of the Roman Empire. Rome, which had been a minor power during Alexander's time, gradually rose to dominance in the Mediterranean world. The influence of Hellenism can be seen in the art, architecture, and philosophy of the Roman Empire, and the Greek language became the language of scholarship and education.

Alexander's empire was short-lived, but its legacy had a lasting impact on the world. The spread of Hellenism and Greek culture transformed the regions that Alexander conquered, creating a cosmopolitan society that brought together various cultures and civilizations. The Diadochi, in their struggles for power, continued this legacy, spreading Hellenism and Greek culture throughout their own empires. The legacy of Alexander's empire can be seen in the continued influence of Greek culture and language, and in the lasting impact of his conquests and administration on the subsequent history of the world.

The spread of Greek language and education played a crucial role in the Hellenization of the East. Alexander's conquests established Greek culture as a dominant force in the regions he had conquered. The success of his military campaigns allowed him to expand the reach of Greek language and education, which facilitated the spread of Hellenistic culture throughout the eastern Mediterranean.

The Greek language was the primary medium through which Greek culture and values were disseminated across the Eastern world. Greek became the language of trade, diplomacy, and education, and was widely spoken in major cities and centers of learning throughout Alexander's Empire. Greek language and culture were particularly influential in the urban centers of Alexandria, Antioch, and Seleucia, where a vibrant intellectual and cultural life flourished.

Greek language was introduced into the Eastern regions that Alexander conquered as part of a broader policy of cultural assimilation. Alexander recognized the importance of promoting Greek culture and language as a means of integrating conquered territories into his empire. He encouraged Greek settlers to establish colonies in conquered territories and granted them special privileges to help promote the use of Greek language and customs.

Alexander's successors continued his policy of promoting Greek language and culture. The Seleucid Empire, which was founded by Seleucus I after Alexander's death, was particularly successful in spreading Greek culture throughout the eastern Mediterranean. Seleucus encouraged the establishment of Greek-style cities, such as Antioch and Seleucia, and promoted the use of Greek language and education in the administration of his empire.

The Hellenization of the East was not just limited to language, however. Greek education and philosophy also had a significant impact on the intellectual and cultural life of the Eastern Mediterranean. The teachings of Greek philosophers such as Aristotle and Plato were studied and debated in centers of learning throughout the Hellenistic world. Greek educational institutions, such as the famous Library of Alexandria, attracted scholars and students from all over the Mediterranean, and contributed to the development of a vibrant intellectual culture in the region.

The spread of Greek language and education had a profound impact on the Eastern Mediterranean. Greek became the lingua franca of the region, and played a key role in the development of a cosmopolitan culture that drew on the rich diversity of Eastern and Greek traditions. The integration of Greek culture into the Eastern world facilitated the spread of new ideas, technologies, and social practices, and contributed to the formation of a dynamic and diverse civilization that had a lasting impact on the history of the world.

In summary, the spread of Greek language and education played a critical role in the Hellenization of the East. Greek culture became a dominant force in the Eastern Mediterranean, and helped to integrate conquered territories into Alexander's empire. The legacy of Greek language and education continued to shape the intellectual and cultural life of the Eastern Mediterranean long after Alexander's death, and contributed to the development of a vibrant and cosmopolitan civilization that had a lasting impact on the world.

In the aftermath of Alexander the Great's conquests, a new era of cultural and artistic innovation was unleashed, known as the Hellenistic period. This period was marked by a fusion of Greek and non-Greek cultures and the development of new artistic styles and techniques. The Hellenistic world produced some of the most magnificent works of art and architecture in history, and their influence can still be seen today.

The Hellenistic period saw the emergence of new artistic forms and styles, such as the realistic and emotive portrayal of human figures, which was a departure from the idealized forms of earlier Greek art. Sculptors and painters began to depict their subjects in more lifelike poses and with more attention to detail, creating works that were both beautiful and realistic. This trend was reflected in the famous statue of the Winged Victory of Samothrace, which portrayed the Greek goddess

Nike in a dynamic and fluid pose that captured the movement of her flowing robes.

Another important development in Hellenistic art was the use of new materials and techniques. Sculptors began to experiment with new materials such as bronze and marble, which allowed them to create more intricate and detailed works. They also developed new techniques, such as the use of molds to create multiple copies of a single work, which allowed for wider dissemination of artistic styles and ideas.

The Hellenistic period also saw the rise of great architects, who produced some of the most impressive buildings and structures in history. Perhaps the most famous example is the Great Library of Alexandria, which was one of the largest and most comprehensive libraries in the ancient world. It was home to hundreds of thousands of books, scrolls, and other documents, and was a center of learning and scholarship for centuries.

Another important architectural achievement of the Hellenistic period was the construction of the Pharos Lighthouse, which was one of the tallest and most impressive structures of its time. The lighthouse was built in the city of Alexandria and stood over 400 feet tall, making it one of the tallest man-made structures in the world at the time.

The Hellenistic period also saw the development of new forms of architecture, such as the use of columns and arches in public buildings and monuments. These structures were designed to convey a sense of grandeur and power, and were often decorated with intricate carvings and sculptures that depicted scenes from Greek mythology and history.

The legacy of Hellenistic art and architecture can still be seen today in many of the world's greatest cultural treasures. The influence of Greek art can be seen in the works of Renaissance artists such as Michelangelo and Leonardo da Vinci, while the use of columns and arches in public buildings is still a hallmark of many modern cities. The Hellenistic period was a time of great artistic and cultural achievement, and its legacy has had a lasting impact on the world.

The Hellenistic Age, which spanned from the death of Alexander the Great in 323 BC to the conquest of Egypt by Rome in 30 BC, was a period of great cultural and intellectual achievement. It was during this time that Greek civilization spread across the Eastern Mediterranean and beyond, leaving a lasting impact on the world. In particular, the Hellenistic period was marked by significant developments in philosophy and science, as scholars from Greece and the Eastern Mediterranean exchanged ideas and developed new ways of thinking about the world.

One of the most significant developments in philosophy during the Hellenistic Age was the emergence of Stoicism, which was founded by the Greek philosopher Zeno of Citium in the 4th century BC. Stoicism was characterized by its emphasis on living in accordance with reason, and on the belief that people could achieve inner peace and tranquility through the cultivation of virtue. Stoic philosophy had a profound impact on the Hellenistic world, and its ideas continued to influence Western philosophy for centuries to come.

Another important philosophical movement that emerged during the Hellenistic period was Epicureanism. Founded by the Greek philosopher Epicurus in the 3rd century BC, Epicureanism was characterized by its emphasis on pleasure as the ultimate good, and on the belief that people should strive to live a simple and peaceful life. Epicureanism also had a significant influence on Hellenistic culture, and its ideas were particularly popular among the educated classes.

In addition to philosophy, the Hellenistic period was marked by significant advances in science, particularly in the fields of mathematics and astronomy. Greek scholars such as Euclid and Archimedes made important contributions to the study of geometry and mechanics, while astronomers such as Hipparchus and Ptolemy made groundbreaking discoveries about the movements of the planets and stars. These discoveries would have a lasting impact on scientific thought, and would pave the way for the development of modern science.

The Hellenistic period was also marked by significant developments in medicine. Greek physicians such as Hippocrates and Galen made important contributions to the field of medicine, and their works continued to be studied and translated long after the end of the Hellenistic period. The development of anatomy and the study of disease were important areas of focus during this time, and the Hellenistic period saw the emergence of new medical practices and techniques that would continue to be used for centuries to come.

The Hellenistic period was also marked by significant cultural achievements, particularly in the fields of art and architecture. Greek artists and architects produced some of the most beautiful and enduring works of art in history, and their influence can be seen in the art and architecture of the Hellenistic world and beyond. The Hellenistic period saw the emergence of new artistic styles, such as the Hellenistic baroque, which was characterized by its dramatic and emotional expression.

In summary, the Hellenistic Age was a period of great intellectual and cultural achievement, marked by significant advances in philosophy, science, medicine, art, and architecture. The exchange of ideas and the blending of cultures that occurred during this time had a profound impact on the development of Western civilization, and the legacy of the Hellenistic world continues to be felt today.

The Hellenistic Age, which spanned from the death of Alexander the Great in 323 BCE to the Roman conquest of Egypt in 30 BCE, left an indelible mark on the history of the world. Under the leadership of Alexander, the Greek Empire had expanded to encompass much of the known world, spreading Greek culture, language, and customs far and wide. Following Alexander's death, his generals fought bitterly for control of his empire, with the result being a series of successor states that spanned from Greece and Egypt to Central Asia and India. Despite the political instability of the era, the Hellenistic Age was a time of great cultural and intellectual ferment, with Greek thought and traditions blending with those of the many different peoples and cultures that came under Greek rule.

One of the most significant legacies of the Hellenistic Age was the spread of Greek language and culture throughout the Mediterranean world and beyond. Alexander's conquests had brought Greek culture into contact with the diverse cultures of the Persian Empire, India, and beyond, creating a rich blend of influences and ideas. In the centuries that followed, Greek language became the lingua franca of the eastern Mediterranean and beyond, with people from all walks of life learning to speak and write in Greek. This had a profound impact on the way people communicated and thought about the world, with Greek ideas and concepts becoming central to the intellectual and cultural life of the Hellenistic world.

The spread of Greek culture was accompanied by a flourishing of art and architecture, which drew on the rich traditions of Greece and the cultures it had come into contact with. Hellenistic art was marked by a heightened sense of realism and drama, with artists striving to capture the complex emotions and experiences of their subjects. This was reflected in the creation of monumental sculptures, such as the famous Colossus of Rhodes, as well as in the development of new forms of architecture, such as the Corinthian order of columns. The impact of Hellenistic art and architecture can still be seen today in the many surviving examples of Greek temples, public buildings, and statues that dot the landscape of the Mediterranean world.

In addition to art and architecture, the Hellenistic Age was a time of great scientific and philosophical inquiry. Greek philosophers such as Aristotle and Plato had laid the groundwork for a tradition of rigorous philosophical inquiry, and in the Hellenistic Age this tradition was continued and expanded upon by a host of new thinkers. One of the most influential of these was the philosopher Epicurus, who developed a system of thought that emphasized the pursuit of pleasure and the avoidance of pain as the keys to a good life. Other important thinkers of the era included Zeno of Citium, the founder of the Stoic school of philosophy, and the mathematician Euclid, who wrote one of the most important texts on geometry ever written.

The legacy of the Hellenistic Age can still be seen in the world today. The spread of Greek language and culture laid the foundation for the development of a shared European identity, while the art and architecture of the era continue to inspire and captivate people around the world. The scientific and philosophical innovations of the Hellenistic Age, meanwhile, continue to shape the way we think about the world and our place in it. From literature to politics, from art to science, the legacy of the Hellenistic Age remains an integral part of the cultural and intellectual history of the world.

Chapter 9: Alexander's Legacy and Influence on World History

The conquest of the Persian Empire by Alexander the Great is one of the most significant events in world history. The victory not only marked the end of the Persian Empire but also signaled the emergence of a new world power. The impact of Alexander's conquests is still felt today, more than two thousand years later. Next, we will examine the importance of Alexander's victory over the Persians for world history.

The Persian Empire was one of the largest and most powerful empires in the ancient world. It had a long and rich history, stretching back to the Achaemenid dynasty in the 6th century BCE. By the time of Alexander's invasion, the Persian Empire had become the dominant power in the Near East, controlling territories that spanned from modern-day Greece to India.

Alexander's conquest of the Persian Empire was a remarkable achievement. He led his army across the Hellespont and into Asia Minor, defeating the Persian forces at the Battle of Granicus in 334 BCE. He then proceeded to conquer the rest of Asia Minor, Syria, and Egypt, before finally defeating the Persians at the decisive Battle of Gaugamela in 331 BCE. With this victory, Alexander effectively ended the Persian Empire and established himself as the new ruler of the region.

The importance of Alexander's victory over the Persians lies in its far-reaching consequences. Firstly, it established the Greek world as the dominant cultural and intellectual force in the Near East. Alexander's conquests led to the spread of Greek culture and ideas throughout the region, creating a new era of cultural exchange and synthesis. Greek language, literature, philosophy, and art became the basis for the emerging Hellenistic culture of the Near East.

Secondly, Alexander's victory over the Persians marked the emergence of a new world power. The Macedonian Empire that Alexander established was the first truly global empire in history, stretching from Greece to India. It was a vast and diverse empire, incorporating people of different cultures, religions, and languages. The Macedonian Empire was a model for later empires, such as the Roman and Byzantine Empires, which also sought to establish control over vast territories and diverse populations.

Thirdly, Alexander's conquests had a significant impact on the course of world history. The Macedonian Empire created a new political and economic order in the Near East, which would shape the region for centuries to come. The spread of Hellenistic culture and ideas led to a period of great intellectual and cultural flourishing, with major advances in science, mathematics, and philosophy.

Finally, Alexander's conquest of the Persian Empire had a profound impact on the development of Christianity. The Hellenistic culture that emerged in the Near East following Alexander's conquests provided the intellectual and cultural context in which Christianity emerged. The early Christian Church adopted many of the ideas and concepts of Hellenistic philosophy, such as the idea of a transcendent God and the concept of an afterlife. The spread of Christianity in the Roman Empire was facilitated by the common language and cultural context created by the spread of Hellenistic culture.

In summary, Alexander's conquest of the Persian Empire was a defining moment in world history. It marked the emergence of a new world power and established the Greek world as the dominant cultural and intellectual force in the Near East. The spread of Hellenistic culture and ideas created a new era of cultural exchange and synthesis, leading to major advances in science, mathematics, and philosophy. The Macedonian Empire created a new political and economic order in the Near East, which would shape the region for centuries to come. The legacy of Alexander's conquests is still felt today, more than two thousand years later, and it remains one of the most significant events in world history.

In the wake of Alexander the Great's unprecedented conquests, a new era in world history dawned. The spread of Greek culture, language, and thought would come to define the period known as the Hellenistic age, lasting from the death of Alexander in 323 BC to the rise of the Roman Empire in the 1st century BC. The legacy of this period is still felt today in the fields of art, literature, philosophy, and politics.

At the heart of the Hellenistic age was the spread of Greek culture. Alexander the Great, in his conquest of the Persian Empire, brought with him Greek language and customs. The cities he founded, such as Alexandria in Egypt, became centers of Greek culture, populated by Greek-speaking citizens who brought with them the arts, sciences, and literature of their homeland. The result was a new cultural fusion, where Greek and local traditions mixed to create a unique synthesis of styles and ideas.

In the field of art and architecture, the influence of Greek culture was profound. The period saw the creation of new styles, such as the Hellenistic baroque, which emphasized realism and drama. Greek sculpture, with its focus on the human form and its naturalism, came to dominate the art of the period. The Hellenistic age also saw the rise of great architectural achievements, such as the Library of Alexandria and the Mausoleum at Halicarnassus.

In literature, the Hellenistic age saw the continuation and expansion of Greek epic poetry, as well as the development of new forms such as the novel. The works of writers such as Homer, Hesiod, and Euripides continued to be studied and revered, while new writers such as Apollonius of Rhodes and Callimachus emerged, introducing new themes and styles.

Philosophy and science also flourished in the Hellenistic age. The period saw the development of new schools of thought, such as Stoicism and Epicureanism, as well as the continuation of Platonic and Aristotelian philosophy. The works of mathematicians such as Euclid and Archimedes, as well as the groundbreaking scientific works of Ptolemy and Galen, influenced scientific thinking for centuries to come.

The spread of Hellenistic culture was not limited to the Mediterranean world. As Alexander's empire expanded eastward, it came into contact with the great civilizations of India and China. The influence of Greek thought and culture can be seen in the art, literature, and philosophy of these regions. The Mauryan Emperor Ashoka, for example, was influenced by the teachings of the Stoic philosopher Epictetus, while the Chinese philosopher Wang Chong wrote extensively on the works of the Greek philosopher Democritus.

The legacy of the Hellenistic age can also be seen in the development of political institutions. The period saw the rise of powerful city-states, as well as the establishment of large empires, such as the Seleucid Empire and the Ptolemaic Kingdom. These states were characterized by a complex system of government, which often blended Greek and local traditions.

The Hellenistic age also saw the rise of cosmopolitanism, a belief in the essential unity of humanity and the interdependence of cultures. This idea was reflected in the widespread use of the Greek language as a common tongue, as well as the promotion of trade and commerce between different regions. The result was a new sense of cultural unity, which paved the way for the later Roman Empire and the spread of Christianity.

In summary, the Hellenistic age was a time of great cultural and intellectual achievement, characterized by the spread of Greek culture and thought throughout the ancient world.

The campaigns of Alexander the Great, beyond their military and political impact, also played a significant role in the expansion of knowledge and the spread of ideas. The Greeks had a long-standing tradition of intellectual inquiry, and Alexander's conquests opened up new horizons for scientific exploration and geographical discovery. As a result, the Hellenistic age witnessed a remarkable growth in knowledge, as scholars from all over the Mediterranean world sought to understand the new lands and peoples that Alexander's empire had brought into contact with Greek culture.

One of the most notable contributions of Alexander's campaigns was the expansion of geographical knowledge. Prior to Alexander's conquests, the Greeks had a limited understanding of the world beyond the Mediterranean. However, through his military campaigns, Alexander and his army traveled through vast regions of Asia, including modern-day Turkey, Iraq, Iran, and Afghanistan. As a result, Greek scholars gained new insights into the geography of these regions, including the locations of cities, rivers, and mountains.

In addition to the expansion of geographical knowledge, Alexander's conquests also had a significant impact on the development of science. The Greeks had a strong tradition of scientific inquiry, and the Hellenistic age saw a flourishing of scientific thought, as Greek scholars built on the discoveries of earlier thinkers and combined them with new knowledge gained through their encounters with other cultures.

One area of scientific exploration that was greatly influenced by Alexander's conquests was medicine. Greek physicians had long been interested in the study of anatomy and the treatment of disease, and Alexander's campaigns brought them into contact with new medical traditions, including those of the Persians and Egyptians. As a result, Greek medicine became more sophisticated and began to incorporate new ideas and techniques.

Another area of scientific inquiry that was influenced by Alexander's conquests was astronomy. Greek astronomers had long been interested in the study of the stars and planets, and Alexander's campaigns brought them into contact with new astronomical traditions, including those of the Babylonians and Egyptians. As a result, Greek astronomy became more sophisticated, and new discoveries were made about the movements of celestial bodies.

Beyond the expansion of knowledge in specific fields, Alexander's conquests also had a profound impact on the spread of ideas and culture. Greek culture had already spread throughout the Mediterranean world prior to Alexander's conquests, but his empire brought Greek ideas and practices into contact with a much wider range of peoples and cultures. As a result, the Hellenistic age saw a flourishing of cultural exchange, as Greek ideas were adopted and adapted by other peoples.

One example of the impact of Greek culture on other peoples can be seen in the spread of the Greek language. The conquests of Alexander and his successors brought Greek language and culture into contact with a wide range of peoples, including Persians, Egyptians, and Indians. As a result, Greek became a common language of administration and trade throughout much of the Mediterranean world, and Greek culture became a model for other cultures to emulate.

In summary, the campaigns of Alexander the Great had a profound impact on the expansion of knowledge and the spread of ideas. Through his conquests, Greek scholars gained new insights into geography and science, and Greek culture and language spread throughout the Mediterranean world and beyond. The legacy of Alexander's conquests can still be seen today, in the enduring influence of Greek culture and thought on Western civilization.

In the annals of history, few military leaders have been as influential as Alexander the Great. From his remarkable conquests to his innovative military tactics, Alexander left an indelible mark on the ancient world. However, perhaps one of his greatest legacies was his impact on political and military strategy. Alexander's strategies and tactics have influenced military leaders and empires throughout the ages, shaping the course of history.

Alexander's military genius was rooted in his ability to adapt to changing circumstances and to think creatively about his tactics. He recognized that a one-size-fits-all approach to warfare was not effective, and instead he tailored his tactics to suit the terrain and the strengths and weaknesses of his opponents. For example, in his conquest of the Persian Empire, Alexander recognized the importance of defeating the Persian cavalry, which was a key component of the Persian army. To do so, he utilized his own cavalry to lure the Persians into battle on open ground, where his superior mobility and tactics would give him the advantage.

Alexander was also known for his boldness and willingness to take risks. He was not afraid to make unconventional choices, such as his decision to cross the Gedrosian Desert, which had never been traversed by a large army before. This willingness to take risks and push the boundaries of what was considered possible inspired future military leaders to think outside the box and take bold actions.

Alexander's influence on military strategy extended beyond his own campaigns. His tactics and strategies were studied and emulated by military leaders in subsequent centuries, including Julius Caesar, Napoleon Bonaparte, and even modern military commanders. For example, Napoleon is said to have been a great admirer of Alexander, and he often incorporated Alexander's tactics into his own military campaigns. In addition to his impact on military strategy, Alexander also influenced political strategy. He recognized the importance of establishing good relationships with conquered peoples and of using diplomacy and alliances to maintain control over large territories. He also recognized the importance of cultural assimilation, encouraging his soldiers to marry local women and promoting the spread of Greek culture and language throughout his empire. These tactics would later be emulated by other conquerors, including the Roman Empire.

Furthermore, Alexander's conquests and the subsequent spread of Greek culture had a profound impact on the political and social structures of the ancient world. The Hellenistic era, which followed Alexander's death, saw the emergence of new political entities and the spread of Greek culture throughout the eastern Mediterranean and beyond. This cultural exchange and blending of ideas would shape the course of world history, influencing everything from literature and philosophy to art and architecture. In summary, Alexander the Great's impact on political and military strategy is immeasurable. His innovative tactics and bold decision-making have inspired military leaders throughout the ages and shaped the course of history. His legacy continues to be felt in the modern world, where his ideas and tactics are still studied and emulated by military strategists and historians alike. Alexander's genius lies not only in his remarkable conquests, but in his ability to think creatively and adapt to changing circumstances, making him one of the most influential military leaders in history.

In the annals of history, few figures have captured the imagination of scholars, artists, and the general public alike as much as Alexander the Great. His legendary military conquests, his dazzling charisma, and his enduring impact on the world continue to fascinate and inspire us to this day. But what was it about Alexander that made him so extraordinary, and how did his legacy shape the course of world history?

To fully appreciate Alexander's significance, we must first understand the historical context in which he lived. Born in 356 BC in the ancient kingdom of Macedon, Alexander was the son of King Philip II, who had recently succeeded in uniting the fractious Macedonian tribes into a powerful kingdom. From a young age, Alexander was groomed for leadership and received a rigorous education under the tutelage of Aristotle, one of the greatest philosophers of his time.

When Alexander ascended to the throne in 336 BC at the age of 20 following his father's assassination, he inherited a kingdom with ambitions of expanding its borders and spreading its influence. However,

Alexander had greater ambitions than his father and was determined to conquer the entire known world. Thus, he embarked on a campaign of conquest that would take him and his army across the breadth of Asia, from Greece to Egypt to Persia and beyond.

What made Alexander's conquests so remarkable was not just their sheer scope but also his unconventional military tactics and strategies. Unlike many ancient generals who relied on brute force and attrition, Alexander favored speed, maneuverability, and surprise. He pioneered the use of the phalanx, a tightly-packed formation of infantry soldiers armed with long spears, which he would deploy alongside swift-moving cavalry and archers. He also recognized the importance of psychological warfare, often employing elaborate deceptions and feints to unsettle his enemies and demoralize their troops.

But Alexander's legacy goes beyond just his military prowess. His conquests paved the way for the spread of Hellenistic culture, language, and philosophy throughout the ancient world. Under Alexander's rule, Greek became the lingua franca of the eastern Mediterranean and beyond, and many non-Greek cultures came to adopt Greek customs and traditions. This cultural fusion gave rise to a new era of intellectual and artistic flourishing, as artists, philosophers, and scientists from all over the Mediterranean world converged in the cosmopolitan centers of Alexandria and Athens.

Moreover, Alexander's campaigns also had far-reaching geopolitical consequences. By toppling the Persian Empire and carving out a vast empire of his own, Alexander created a power vacuum in the eastern Mediterranean that would be filled by a succession of empires and kingdoms over the centuries, including the Seleucid Empire, the Ptolemaic Kingdom of Egypt, and the Parthian Empire. This political fragmentation contributed to the decline of Greek civilization as a dominant force in the Mediterranean world, paving the way for the rise of Rome and the eventual spread of Christianity.

Despite his early death at the age of 32 in 323 BC, Alexander's impact on the world was profound and enduring. His conquests and the Hellenistic culture he fostered left an indelible mark on the ancient world and continued to shape the course of history for centuries to come. Even today, Alexander's legacy remains an object of fascination and study, inspiring countless books, films, and works of art, and serving as a touchstone for those seeking to understand the power and complexity of ancient civilizations.

Chapter 10: Myths and Misconceptions about Alexander the Great

The story of Alexander the Great is one of the most fascinating in all of human history. His conquests and accomplishments have earned him a place among the most legendary figures of all time. But among the many tales and legends that surround him, one in particular stands out - the story of his supposed belief in his own divinity.

According to some ancient sources, Alexander came to believe that he was the son of the god Zeus, and that he was therefore himself divine. This belief is said to have developed over time, as Alexander's military successes and personal charisma led his followers to view him as something more than a mere mortal.

The most famous incident associated with Alexander's alleged belief in his own divinity is the story of his visit to the Oracle of Amun at Siwa in Egypt. According to the story, Alexander sought out the oracle in order to confirm his belief in his own divine parentage. The oracle reportedly greeted him as the son of Zeus, and Alexander left convinced that he was indeed a god.

It is not clear whether Alexander truly believed himself to be divine, or whether these stories were simply part of a propaganda campaign designed to boost his own reputation and authority. Some historians have suggested that Alexander's supposed divinity may have been little more than a convenient myth, used to justify his conquests and impress his followers.

Regardless of whether or not Alexander truly believed himself to be divine, his alleged belief had significant consequences. For one thing, it helped to solidify his hold over his followers, who saw him not just as a military leader, but as a god among men. This in turn allowed him to maintain control over his vast empire, even in the face of significant challenges and rebellions.

In addition, Alexander's alleged divinity helped to establish him as a cultural and religious icon. In the centuries following his death, he became a subject of fascination and veneration among the people of Greece and Rome, who saw him as a symbol of their own cultural and military superiority. His conquests and accomplishments were celebrated in art, literature, and poetry, and his story became a key part of the cultural heritage of the Western world.

Despite the enduring legacy of Alexander's supposed belief in his own divinity, it is worth noting that many modern scholars are skeptical of the idea. Some have suggested that the stories of Alexander's divinity were exaggerated or invented by his followers after his death, in order to enhance his reputation and ensure his place in history.

Ultimately, whether or not Alexander truly believed himself to be divine is something that may never be fully known. But regardless of the truth behind the legends, there can be no doubt that his legacy as a military leader, cultural icon, and symbol of human achievement will continue to endure for centuries to come.

The figure of Aristotle looms large in the popular imagination when it comes to the life and career of Alexander the Great. Many people believe that Aristotle was Alexander's personal tutor, and that the philosopher played a key role in shaping the young prince's worldview and military strategy. However, while there is no doubt that Aristotle and Alexander had a relationship, the extent of the philosopher's influence on the king has been greatly exaggerated over the years.

To begin with, it is important to understand the context in which Aristotle and Alexander met. Aristotle was born in Stagira, a city in northern Greece, in 384 BC. He studied under Plato at the Academy in Athens before founding his own school, the Lyceum, in 335 BC. Alexander, meanwhile, was born in 356 BC and became king of Macedon in 336 BC following the assassination of his father, King Philip II. At the time of Alexander's ascension to the throne, Aristotle was already an accomplished philosopher, and his reputation as a teacher had begun to spread throughout the Greek world.

According to some accounts, Aristotle was invited to become Alexander's personal tutor shortly after the young prince became king. However, there is little evidence to support this claim, and it is more likely that Aristotle and Alexander's relationship was more informal. It is known that Aristotle sent a copy of his book "Politics" to Alexander when the king was campaigning in Asia, and it is also possible that the two corresponded on other matters of philosophy and governance. However, it is unlikely that Aristotle had much direct influence on Alexander's military strategy, which was based on the Macedonian model of phalanx warfare rather than any specific philosophical or tactical approach.

In fact, there is evidence to suggest that Alexander was already a seasoned military commander by the time he met Aristotle. As a young man, Alexander had been trained in the art of war by his father, King Philip II, who was one of the most accomplished military strategists of the time. Under Philip's tutelage, Alexander had learned the basics of phalanx warfare and cavalry tactics, as well as the importance of logistics and supply lines. By the time he became king, Alexander was already well-versed in the art of war, and he had a keen understanding of the political and military realities of the time.

That being said, it is possible that Aristotle had some influence on Alexander's broader worldview. Aristotle was one of the most influential philosophers of the ancient world, and his ideas on politics, ethics, and metaphysics had a profound impact on Western thought. It is possible that Alexander was exposed to some of these ideas through his correspondence with Aristotle, and that this exposure helped shape his thinking on matters of governance and morality. However, there is little evidence to suggest that Aristotle had any direct influence on Alexander's military strategy or his conduct on the battlefield.

In summary, while it is true that Aristotle and Alexander had a relationship, the extent of the philosopher's influence on the king has been greatly exaggerated over the years. While it is possible that Aristotle had some impact on Alexander's broader worldview, there is little evidence to suggest that he played a key role in shaping the young king's military strategy or tactics. Rather, it was Alexander's own experience and training, as well as the political and military realities of the time, that shaped his approach to warfare and conquest.

The conquest of India by Alexander the Great remains a fascinating and controversial topic in the study of ancient history. Many accounts of this campaign have been written, but few are entirely accurate, and many are entirely fictional. Nevertheless, it is clear that Alexander's campaign in India was one of the most challenging and significant of his career, and it had a profound impact on the history of the Indian subcontinent.

Alexander's campaign in India began in 327 BC, after he had conquered much of the Persian Empire and established himself as the ruler of a vast empire stretching from Greece to Egypt and beyond. At this point, he was determined to expand his conquests even further, and he set his sights on the rich and fertile lands of India.

Alexander's Indian campaign was not an easy one. The Indian subcontinent was home to a number of powerful kingdoms, each with its own formidable army and well-trained warriors. Alexander's forces were greatly outnumbered, and they faced many challenges, including the harsh terrain and unfamiliar flora and fauna of India.

Despite these difficulties, Alexander was determined to succeed, and he led his army deep into India, conquering kingdom after kingdom and defeating countless armies along the way. He established a number of new cities and fortifications, including Alexandria on the Indus, which served as a key center of Greek culture and learning in India for many years.

However, Alexander's Indian campaign was not without its controversies. Many historians have argued that his conquest of India was a futile and costly endeavor, and that it had little lasting impact on the history of the region. Others have suggested that Alexander's campaign was a failure, and that it ultimately contributed to the downfall of his empire.

Despite these criticisms, it is clear that Alexander's campaign in India had a profound impact on the region's history. It introduced Greek culture and learning to India, and it established a lasting legacy of cross-cultural exchange and dialogue between the Greeks and Indians. It also paved the way for later invasions of India by foreign powers, including the Mongols and the British.

Ultimately, the conquest of India by Alexander the Great remains one of the most fascinating and controversial episodes in ancient history. While the historical facts surrounding this campaign are often shrouded in myth and legend, there is no denying the profound impact that Alexander's conquests had on the history of the Indian subcontinent, and on the world as a whole.

In the ancient world, the Library of Alexandria was a renowned center of learning and scholarship, attracting scholars and intellectuals from all over the Mediterranean world. Today, it is remembered as one of the greatest achievements of the Hellenistic age, a symbol of the power and sophistication of the Greek world. However, there are many misconceptions about the library, including the role of Alexander the Great in its foundation and destruction.

It is commonly believed that Alexander the Great was the founder of the Library of Alexandria, and that he was responsible for its destruction. However, these beliefs are largely based on myth and exaggeration. In reality, the library was not founded by Alexander, but rather by his successor, Ptolemy I Soter, who established it as a research institution and repository for all the books of the known world.

Furthermore, the destruction of the Library of Alexandria was not a singular event, nor was it caused by a single individual. Rather, it was a gradual process that occurred over many years, as a result of a variety of factors, including political instability, civil unrest, and neglect. The library was damaged and rebuilt several times throughout its history, and it ultimately fell into disrepair and obscurity after the Arab conquest of Egypt in the 7th century.

Despite the myths and misconceptions that surround the Library of Alexandria, its legacy is undeniable. It was the most important center of learning and scholarship in the ancient world, and it was responsible for preserving many of the greatest works of Greek literature, philosophy, and science. It was a symbol of the power and sophistication of the Hellenistic world, and it continues to inspire scholars and intellectuals to this day.

The library housed a vast collection of books and manuscripts, including works by some of the greatest thinkers and writers of the ancient world, such as Homer, Plato, Aristotle, and Euclid. It was a hub of intellectual activity, attracting scholars and intellectuals from all over the Mediterranean world, who came to study, learn, and share their knowledge.

In addition to its collection of books and manuscripts, the Library of Alexandria was also home to a number of other important institutions, including a museum, a botanical garden, and an astronomical observatory. These institutions helped to foster the growth of new ideas and disciplines, and they contributed to the advancement of knowledge in a wide range of fields.

The legacy of the Library of Alexandria continues to be felt today, not only in the preservation and dissemination of ancient texts and knowledge, but also in the development of new ideas and disciplines. The library served as a model for future institutions of learning and scholarship, and it inspired generations of scholars and intellectuals to push the boundaries of human knowledge and understanding.

In summary, the Library of Alexandria is one of the most enduring symbols of the Hellenistic age, a testament to the power and sophistication of the Greek world. While the myths and misconceptions that surround its foundation and destruction are many, its legacy as a center of learning and scholarship continues to inspire scholars and intellectuals around the world.

The death of Alexander the Great, one of history's greatest conquerors, has been the subject of much debate and speculation over the centuries. The circumstances surrounding his sudden and unexpected death have given rise to a number of theories and legends, some more plausible than others.

According to the most widely accepted account, Alexander died on June 10, 323 BC, in the palace of Nebuchadnezzar II in Babylon, at the age of 32. He had spent much of the previous year consolidating his empire, and had planned to continue his campaigns eastward into Arabia and Africa. But his health had been failing for some time, and in the spring of 323 he fell seriously ill.

The exact cause of Alexander's death is not known for certain, but it is widely believed to have been due to natural causes, possibly exacerbated by his heavy drinking and hard living. According to the historian Plutarch, Alexander had been suffering from a fever for several days before his death, and had become delirious and unresponsive. His condition rapidly deteriorated, and he died on the eleventh day of his illness.

Despite the apparent natural causes of Alexander's death, a number of legends and theories have arisen over the years to explain his sudden demise. One of the most famous is the theory that he was poisoned, possibly by one of his own generals or advisors. This theory gained credence in the 20th century, when a number of studies suggested that Alexander may have been suffering from arsenic poisoning, possibly from contaminated drinking water.

Another theory is that Alexander died from a rare autoimmune disease known as Guillain-Barre syndrome, which can cause sudden paralysis and respiratory failure. This theory is based on the accounts of several ancient historians, who describe Alexander's symptoms as including a loss of sensation and control in his limbs.

Yet another theory is that Alexander died from a combination of illnesses and injuries, including malaria, typhoid fever, and a series of wounds sustained in battle. This theory is based on the fact that Alexander was known to have suffered from a number of illnesses and injuries throughout his life, including malaria, dysentery, and several serious battle wounds.

Whatever the true cause of Alexander's death, there is no denying the enduring fascination that his life and achievements continue to hold for people today. His legacy as one of history's greatest conquerors and cultural icons remains as strong today as it did over two thousand years ago, and his influence can be seen in countless aspects of modern life, from politics and art to literature and popular culture.

BOOK 4

NAPOLEON BONAPARTE
FROM REVOLUTION TO EMPIRE

BY A.J. KINGSTON

Chapter 1: Early Life and Rise to Power

Napoleon Bonaparte, one of the most renowned military commanders and statesmen in history, had a humble beginning in the island of Corsica. Born on August 15, 1769, he was the second surviving child of Carlo Buonaparte and Letizia Ramolino. Despite the modest background of his family, young Napoleon received an exceptional education that would shape his future as a leader.

As a child, Napoleon showed a prodigious mind and a strong will. He was interested in history, mathematics, and geography, and would spend hours studying books and maps. His father recognized his intellectual potential and enrolled him at the Ecole Militaire in Brienne, France, at the age of nine. The school was a prestigious institution that provided education to the sons of noble and wealthy families. Despite being an outsider from Corsica, Napoleon excelled in his studies and showed a remarkable talent for mathematics and military strategy.

Napoleon's years at the Ecole Militaire were challenging, both intellectually and socially. He faced discrimination from his peers, who mocked him for his accent and Corsican origins. However, he was determined to prove himself and to rise above his humble background. He immersed himself in his studies, and his academic achievements earned him the respect and admiration of his teachers.

After completing his studies at Brienne, Napoleon continued his education at the Ecole Militaire in Paris, where he studied artillery and engineering. He graduated at the age of 16 with a commission as a second lieutenant in the French army. Despite his youth, he was already showing signs of his future military genius, and he quickly rose through the ranks.

Napoleon's education was not limited to academic studies. He was also exposed to the ideas and values of the Enlightenment, which had a profound influence on his worldview. He read extensively on the subject of government and society, and developed a deep appreciation for the concepts of liberty, equality, and democracy. These ideas would later inform his political and social reforms in France and the territories under his rule.

Napoleon's early education also instilled in him a sense of discipline and perseverance. He was taught to be resilient in the face of setbacks and to never give up on his goals. These qualities would serve him well throughout his military campaigns and his political career.

In summary, Napoleon's early education was a crucial factor in his rise to power and his lasting legacy as a military and political leader. Despite his humble origins, he received an exceptional education that provided him with the intellectual and moral foundation to become one of the most brilliant minds of his time. His education instilled in him the values of the Enlightenment, the discipline to overcome obstacles, and the determination to pursue his ambitions. These qualities would be instrumental in his future achievements, and in shaping the course of history.

The late 18th century was a time of great upheaval in France, as the French Revolution shook the country to its core and changed the course of European history. The Revolution was a complex and multifaceted event, driven by a variety of political, social, and economic factors. At its heart was a desire for greater democracy, equality, and justice, as well as a rejection of the ancien régime, the corrupt and repressive feudal system that had ruled France for centuries.

In the years leading up to the Revolution, France was facing a number of challenges. The country was heavily in debt, due in part to its involvement in the American War of Independence, which had drained its resources. At the same time, the French economy was struggling, with widespread poverty, unemployment, and social unrest. The monarchy was also facing a crisis of legitimacy, as many French citizens grew increasingly disillusioned with the excesses and abuses of the Bourbon kings.

The Revolution began in 1789, when the French people rose up against the monarchy and established a new democratic government. Over the course of the next few years, the Revolutionaries implemented a series of sweeping reforms, including the abolition of feudalism and the establishment of equal rights for all citizens. They also introduced a new system of government, with a constitution that enshrined the principles of liberty, equality, and fraternity.

However, the Revolution was also marked by violence and turmoil. The Reign of Terror, which began in 1793, saw the execution of thousands of people, including many who were perceived to be enemies of the Revolution. The Revolution also led to the rise of Napoleon Bonaparte, a military leader who would go on to become one of the most famous and controversial figures in European history.

Napoleon rose to prominence during the Revolutionary Wars, a series of conflicts that pitted France against a coalition of European powers. He proved to be a brilliant military strategist, and by 1799 he had risen to the rank of First Consul, effectively making him the leader of France. In

1804, he crowned himself Emperor of France, and went on to conquer much of Europe before finally being defeated at the Battle of Waterloo in 1815.

The French Revolution and its aftermath had a profound impact on European history. It marked the end of the old order and the beginning of a new era of democracy and nationalism. It also helped to spread revolutionary ideas and principles across Europe, inspiring a wave of political and social change that would continue for decades to come. And while the Revolution was a time of great turmoil and suffering, it also produced some of the most important and influential figures in modern European history, including Napoleon Bonaparte.

The year was 1793 and the French Revolution was in full swing. The country was in chaos and turmoil, with different factions fighting for power and control. It was in this environment that a young Corsican artillery officer named Napoleon Bonaparte first gained prominence.

Napoleon's early years were spent in Corsica, a rugged and mountainous island in the Mediterranean Sea. He was born into a noble family that was supportive of Corsican independence from France. However, when Corsica was sold to France in 1768, Napoleon's family became loyal French subjects.

Napoleon received his education in France, first at a military school in Brienne and later at the Ecole Militaire in Paris. He was an exceptional student, excelling in mathematics and history, and showing a talent for leadership and strategy.

It was during the French Revolution that Napoleon first made his mark on the world stage. In 1793, he was sent to Toulon, a strategic port city on the Mediterranean coast that had been seized by royalist forces. Napoleon was put in charge of the artillery that was to be used in the siege of the city.

Napoleon quickly distinguished himself in Toulon, showing both his military genius and his ability to inspire and lead his troops. He devised a plan to bombard the city's defenses from the surrounding hills, and his accurate and relentless artillery fire ultimately forced the royalist forces to surrender.

This victory in Toulon propelled Napoleon to national fame and established him as a rising star in the French military. His success in Toulon earned him a promotion to brigadier general, and he was given command of the army in Italy just two years later.

The French Revolution continued to rage on, and Napoleon's military career flourished. He led successful campaigns in Italy, Egypt, and Syria, cementing his reputation as one of the greatest military leaders of all time.

However, Napoleon's ambition and desire for power ultimately led to his downfall. He became the Emperor of France in 1804, and his aggressive military expansion throughout Europe ultimately resulted in his defeat at the Battle of Waterloo in 1815.

Despite his ultimate defeat, Napoleon's military successes and his impact on French and European history cannot be overstated. His rise to prominence at the Siege of Toulon was just the beginning of a legendary career that forever changed the course of history.

In the history of warfare, few campaigns have had the impact of the Italian Campaign of Napoleon Bonaparte. The young Corsican general, only in his late twenties, took command of the French army in Italy and transformed it into an unstoppable force that shattered the power of Austria and brought Italy under French control. His success in Italy established him as a military genius and set the stage for his rise to power in France and the creation of the Napoleonic Empire.

Napoleon's Italian Campaign began in 1796, shortly after he had been appointed commander of the French Army of Italy. His mission was to drive the Austrians out of northern Italy and secure the French position in the region. Napoleon quickly proved himself to be a brilliant military strategist, and his innovative tactics and aggressive approach caught the Austrians off guard. He scored a series of stunning victories, first at Lodi and then at Castiglione and Arcola, and quickly gained control of much of northern Italy.

Napoleon's success in Italy was due in large part to his ability to innovate and adapt his tactics to the situation at hand. He was not bound by traditional military thinking or conventional strategies, and he was willing to take risks and try new approaches. He used his knowledge of geography to outmaneuver his opponents, and he employed surprise attacks and swift movements to keep his enemies off balance. He also understood the importance of propaganda and the power of public opinion, and he used his victories to build his own reputation and undermine the morale of his enemies.

One of Napoleon's most significant innovations was his use of artillery. He recognized the importance of artillery in modern warfare and developed new tactics for its use on the battlefield. He concentrated his artillery in a single position and used it to create a devastating barrage that could break through enemy lines and allow his infantry to advance. This strategy proved highly effective, and it helped him win several key battles, including the Battle of Rivoli, which secured his position in northern Italy.

Napoleon's success in Italy was also due in part to his ability to forge alliances with local leaders and gain their support. He understood the importance of winning the hearts and minds of the people he was trying to conquer, and he worked hard to build relationships with Italian politicians and intellectuals. He also recognized the value of cultural exchange, and he encouraged French artists and intellectuals to come to Italy and experience the culture and history of the region. This cultural exchange helped to create a new sense of identity and community in Italy, and it played a significant role in the development of Italian nationalism.

Napoleon's Italian Campaign was not without its challenges and setbacks. He faced a number of tough opponents, including the skilled Austrian general Dagobert von Wurmser, and he struggled with issues of supply and logistics. He also faced resistance from local populations, who were often reluctant to support the French invaders. Despite these challenges, however, Napoleon persevered, and he ultimately succeeded in establishing French control over northern Italy.

The impact of Napoleon's Italian Campaign was significant and far-reaching. It established Napoleon as a military genius and a rising star in French politics, and it helped to pave the way for his eventual rise to power as Emperor of France. It also marked a significant turning point in European history, as it signaled the decline of the old order and the rise of a new era of nationalism and revolutionary thinking. The Italian Campaign inspired similar movements in other countries, including Spain and Portugal, and it set the stage for the wave of nationalist revolutions that would sweep across Europe in the 19th century.

It was the year 1799 when France, embroiled in the chaos of the French Revolution, found itself in dire need of a strong and stable leader. The Directory, a group of five men who had been elected to govern France, were plagued by corruption and inefficiency, leaving the nation vulnerable to invasion and internal dissent. It was in this climate of political and social unrest that a young and ambitious military commander named Napoleon Bonaparte seized the opportunity to establish himself as the supreme ruler of France.

The events leading up to Napoleon's rise to power began with his victory at the Siege of Toulon in 1793, where he displayed his military prowess by successfully capturing the heavily fortified city from the British. This triumph brought him to the attention of the revolutionary government in Paris, and he was quickly promoted through the ranks of the army.

By 1796, Napoleon had been appointed commander of the French Army in Italy, where he would go on to achieve a series of stunning victories against the Austrians and their allies. It was during this time that he established himself as a brilliant military strategist and charismatic leader, admired by his soldiers and feared by his enemies.

With his military successes and growing popularity, Napoleon began to turn his attention towards politics. In 1799, he joined forces with two other influential politicians, Sieyès and Ducos, to stage a coup against the Directory. On November 9, 1799, the coup was carried out, and the Directory was overthrown.

In the aftermath of the coup, a new government was established, known as the Consulate. Napoleon was appointed First Consul, effectively making him the most powerful man in France. He wasted no time in consolidating his power, implementing a series of reforms and initiatives aimed at restoring order and stability to the country.

Under his leadership, the French economy was restructured, education was reformed, and the legal system was overhauled. He also established a new constitution, which granted him sweeping powers as First Consul, effectively making him a dictator.

Despite his growing authoritarianism, Napoleon remained popular with the French people, who saw him as a strong and capable leader. He continued to lead the French Army in a series of successful military campaigns, expanding the reach of the French Empire and establishing his dominance over much of Europe.

However, his unchecked ambition and relentless pursuit of power would ultimately lead to his downfall. In 1804, he crowned himself Emperor of the French, a move that alienated many of his former supporters and solidified his reputation as a power-hungry dictator.

Despite his many successes, Napoleon's legacy remains a controversial and divisive subject. While some view him as a brilliant military strategist and visionary leader, others see him as a ruthless tyrant who caused untold suffering and destruction.

Regardless of one's opinion of him, however, there is no denying the enduring impact that Napoleon had on the world. His military campaigns and political reforms shaped the course of European history and established France as a major player on the world stage. And while his reign may have been marked by controversy and conflict, his legacy continues to be felt to this day.

Chapter 2: The French Revolution and the Rise of Napoleon

In the late 18th century, the social and political climate of France was one of turmoil and unrest. The people were growing increasingly discontent with the absolute monarchy that had been in place for centuries, and calls for reform were growing louder by the day. This discontent was exacerbated by a number of factors, including economic hardships, high taxes, and a corrupt and ineffective government.

The French Revolution was the result of this discontent, and it had far-reaching implications for the rest of Europe and the world. The revolution was marked by violence, as the people rose up against the ruling class and demanded greater rights and freedoms. The Reign of Terror, a period of extreme violence and bloodshed, saw thousands of people executed by the guillotine, including King Louis XVI and his queen, Marie Antoinette.

The French Revolution also had a profound impact on the economy of France. The old feudal system, in which the peasants were tied to the land and subject to the whims of the nobility, was abolished, and a new system of land ownership was introduced. The French government also introduced a number of economic reforms, including the introduction of a national bank and a system of paper currency.

In the midst of this chaos, a young artillery officer named Napoleon Bonaparte was rising to prominence. Born on the island of Corsica, which had only recently been acquired by France, Napoleon was a product of the revolutionary era. He was a brilliant military strategist and leader, and he quickly rose through the ranks of the French army.

Napoleon's military victories, including his successful campaign in Italy and his defeat of the British at the Battle of the Nile, made him a national hero in France. His popularity grew even further after he led the French army to victory in the coup of 18 Brumaire, which saw the establishment of the Consulate and the consolidation of his power.

Despite his military success, however, Napoleon faced a number of challenges during his rule. The constant wars and military campaigns he waged drained the resources of France and left the country deeply in debt. His attempts to establish a European-wide empire also brought him into conflict with other nations, leading to a series of costly and devastating wars.

In the end, Napoleon's legacy was a mixed one. He was a brilliant military leader and strategist, and his achievements in battle cannot be denied. However, his attempts to establish a French-dominated empire in

Europe ultimately failed, and his legacy is tainted by the immense human cost of his wars and his authoritarian rule. Nonetheless, his influence on French and European history cannot be denied, and his name remains one of the most recognizable in history.

The French Revolution was a period of political and social upheaval that had profound implications not just for France, but for the rest of Europe and the world. It was a time of radical change and transformation, characterized by the overthrow of the Bourbon monarchy and the rise of the Jacobin government, which was dedicated to the creation of a new, democratic France.

One of the most significant aspects of the French Revolution was the series of wars that it sparked, both within France itself and throughout Europe. These wars were fought for a variety of reasons, including territorial expansion, ideological conflict, and the desire for power and influence.

The Revolutionary Wars began in 1792, shortly after the execution of King Louis XVI, when France declared war on Austria. The war quickly spread, with other European powers, including Prussia, Great Britain, and Spain, joining the conflict. The wars continued for more than two decades, and by the time they ended in 1815, they had reshaped the political and social landscape of Europe.

One of the most important figures to emerge during the Revolutionary Wars was Napoleon Bonaparte. Born on the island of Corsica in 1769, Napoleon was educated in France and joined the French army in 1785. He quickly rose through the ranks, and by 1796, he was commanding the French army in Italy.

Napoleon's military prowess was on full display during the Italian Campaign, which began in 1796. Over the course of several months, Napoleon and his troops defeated a series of Austrian armies, culminating in the Battle of Marengo in 1800. The Italian Campaign was a resounding success for the French, and it established Napoleon as one of the most brilliant military commanders of his time.

The Revolutionary Wars, also known as the French Revolutionary Wars, were a series of conflicts fought between France and various European powers from 1792 to 1802. These wars were a direct result of the French Revolution, which had begun in 1789 and had seen the overthrow of the French monarchy and the establishment of a republic.

At the start of the Revolutionary Wars, France was in a state of political turmoil. The country was divided into two factions, the Girondins and the Jacobins, who held opposing views on how the country should be governed. The Girondins favored a moderate approach, while the

Jacobins were more radical and sought to establish a democratic government.

In 1792, the Girondin-led government declared war on Austria, which was then allied with Prussia. The French army, led by General Charles Dumouriez, achieved a series of victories in Belgium and the Rhineland. However, the French were defeated by the Austrians at the Battle of Neerwinden in March 1793, and Dumouriez defected to the Austrians shortly afterwards.

The Jacobins then came to power, and the war took a more radical turn. The French government declared war on Britain, Spain, and the Dutch Republic, and began to expand its borders by annexing neighboring territories. The French army, led by generals such as Napoleon Bonaparte and Lazare Carnot, achieved a series of victories, including the Battle of Fleurus in June 1794.

In 1795, the French government signed a peace treaty with Prussia and Spain, but continued to fight against Britain and Austria. In 1796, Napoleon was given command of the French army in Italy and achieved a series of stunning victories against the Austrians. These victories led to the Treaty of Campo Formio, which ended the war with Austria.

The peace did not last long, however, and in 1798, France declared war on the Ottoman Empire and invaded Egypt. This campaign was not successful, and the French were forced to withdraw in 1801. Meanwhile, Britain continued to fight against France, and in 1801, the two sides signed the Treaty of Amiens, which brought a temporary end to the war.

The peace did not last long, however, and in 1803, Britain declared war on France once again. The French responded by invading Britain's ally, Portugal, and by forming an alliance with Spain. This led to a new round of fighting, which continued until 1815.

The Revolutionary Wars had a profound impact on Europe. They resulted in the overthrow of monarchies and the establishment of republics, and they paved the way for the rise of Napoleon Bonaparte. The wars also had a significant impact on military strategy and tactics, as new weapons and technologies were developed and tested on the battlefield.

In summary, the Revolutionary Wars were a period of intense conflict that shaped the political and military landscape of Europe for years to come. They were a direct result of the French Revolution, and they had a profound impact on the course of European history.

Napoleon Bonaparte is a figure that is hard to ignore when discussing the French Revolution and the subsequent history of France. Born in Corsica in 1769, he was educated at a military school in France and graduated at the age of 16. In 1785, he was commissioned as a second lieutenant in the French army, and his career began in earnest.

As a young officer, Napoleon was ambitious and determined to succeed. He quickly rose through the ranks of the French army, and by 1796, he had been appointed commander-in-chief of the Army of Italy. It was in this capacity that he made his mark on history.

Napoleon's early military career was marked by his success in the Italian Campaign. In 1796, he led the French army into Italy, and over the course of the next few years, he won a string of victories against the Austrian forces that were fighting against the French. He also established a reputation for being a brilliant military strategist and tactician.

One of the keys to Napoleon's success in Italy was his use of a new form of warfare that relied heavily on speed and mobility. Rather than engaging in pitched battles with the enemy, Napoleon preferred to use a series of quick strikes and maneuvers to outflank and outmaneuver his opponents. This approach allowed him to win battles with fewer casualties than would have been incurred in a more traditional engagement.

Another important factor in Napoleon's success in Italy was his ability to inspire his troops. He was a charismatic leader who was able to instill in his soldiers a sense of loyalty and devotion that went beyond the normal bonds of military service. He was also a master of propaganda, and he used the press to his advantage in order to build up his own image and discredit his enemies.

As a result of his success in Italy, Napoleon became a national hero in France. He was seen as a brilliant military leader who had restored the honor of the French army after years of defeat and humiliation. His success also helped to consolidate his own power within the French government, and he became a major political figure in his own right.

Napoleon's early military career was not without its controversies, however. He was known for his ruthless tactics, and he was accused of ordering the execution of prisoners and civilians. He was also accused of plundering the cities and towns that he conquered, and of using his position to enrich himself and his family.

Despite these controversies, however, Napoleon's early military career remains one of the most remarkable in history. His victories in Italy established him as a major military leader, and his charisma and political savvy helped to propel him to the pinnacle of power in France. It was a remarkable achievement for a young man from Corsica who had set out to make a name for himself in the world.

In the aftermath of the Reign of Terror and the fall of Robespierre, France found itself in a state of political disarray. The National Convention, which had replaced the Committee of Public Safety, was ineffective and divided. The economic situation was dire, and the country was still at war with a coalition of European powers.

In this context, the Directory was established in 1795 as a new form of government, with a five-man executive council and a bicameral legislature. The Directory aimed to restore order and stability to France, but it faced many challenges from the outset.

One of the main challenges was the continued warfare with the rest of Europe. Despite some early successes, the French army was stretched thin and facing tough opposition from the likes of Austria, Prussia, and Great Britain. The Directory struggled to finance the war effort and to maintain morale among the troops.

At home, the Directory faced opposition from various factions. Royalists and counter-revolutionaries were still active, seeking to restore the monarchy or overturn the gains of the Revolution. Meanwhile, radical republicans and leftists saw the Directory as too conservative and insufficiently committed to revolutionary ideals.

The Directory also faced economic problems. The assignat, the paper currency introduced during the Revolution, had lost its value due to inflation and lack of confidence. The government struggled to finance its operations and maintain the army, leading to widespread corruption and economic hardship.

In the midst of these challenges, Napoleon Bonaparte emerged as a military leader and political figure. After his victories in Italy and Egypt, he returned to France as a hero and was given command of the army in 1799. Seeing the weakness and division of the Directory, Napoleon staged a coup on November 9, 1799 (18 Brumaire in the revolutionary calendar) and established himself as the First Consul of France.

Napoleon's rise to power marked a turning point in French history. He brought stability and order to a country that had been in turmoil for years. He reformed the government and the economy, stabilizing the currency and promoting economic growth. He also reorganized the military and led France to victory against its enemies, establishing the French Empire and expanding its territory across Europe.

However, Napoleon's reign was not without its challenges and controversies. He faced opposition from within France, as well as from other European powers. He also imposed his rule on other countries through military conquest, leading to resentment and resistance.

In the end, Napoleon's ambitions and military campaigns led to his downfall. He was defeated by a coalition of European powers and exiled to the island of Elba. He briefly returned to power in 1815, only to be defeated again at the Battle of Waterloo and exiled to Saint Helena, where he died in 1821.

The Directory and its crisis paved the way for Napoleon's rise to power, but it also highlighted the challenges of governing France in the aftermath of the Revolution. The country was deeply divided, and the government was faced with numerous challenges, including war, economic instability, and political opposition. Despite the Directory's efforts, it was unable to overcome these challenges, leading to the rise of Napoleon and the establishment of the French Empire.

The French Revolution had been a time of great upheaval in France. The old regime, with its hereditary nobility, clerical hierarchy, and absolute monarchy had been overthrown in favor of a new order based on the principles of liberty, equality, and fraternity. But the Revolution had been marked by violence, civil war, and political instability. The Directory, which had been established in 1795, was the fifth government to take power since the fall of the monarchy. The Directory was marked by corruption, scandal, and economic crisis, and was unable to maintain order or secure the loyalty of the military.

It was in this context that Napoleon Bonaparte emerged as a key figure in French politics. Born in Corsica in 1769, he had studied at the Royal Military School in Brienne and had been commissioned as a second lieutenant in the artillery in 1785. He had taken part in the French Revolutionary Wars, rising through the ranks to become a general at the age of 24. In 1796, he was given command of the Army of Italy, and won a series of stunning victories against the Austrians, securing the annexation of Lombardy and the establishment of French client states in northern Italy.

Napoleon's military success, combined with the political instability of the Directory, made him a popular and influential figure in France. In 1799, he returned to Paris, where he was greeted by crowds of cheering supporters. The Directory, meanwhile, was facing a crisis. The economy was in ruins, and the government was deeply unpopular. There were rumors of a royalist coup, and the military was deeply divided.

Napoleon saw an opportunity to seize power. On 18 Brumaire (November 9, 1799), he led a coup against the Directory, with the support of a group of politicians and military leaders. The coup was bloodless, and the Directory was dissolved. Napoleon established a new government, known as the Consulate, and was named First Consul.

The establishment of the Consulate marked the end of the French Revolution and the beginning of Napoleon's rule. The new government was a dictatorship, with Napoleon as its head. But Napoleon was also a visionary leader who brought stability and prosperity to France. He introduced a series of reforms aimed at modernizing the economy, improving public works, and establishing a new legal system. He also consolidated the gains of the Revolution, such as the abolition of feudalism and the establishment of civil liberties.

Napoleon's rule was also marked by military conquest. He embarked on a series of campaigns aimed at establishing a French-dominated Europe. He defeated the Austrians, the Prussians, and the Russians, and established a French client state in Spain. He also conquered Egypt and Syria, although his campaign was ultimately unsuccessful.

Napoleon's military success made him a hero in France, and his reforms made him popular with the people. He was seen as a symbol of the Revolution, and was widely admired for his vision and leadership. But his rule was also marked by authoritarianism and repression. He established a secret police force, and censorship was widespread. His wars led to the deaths of millions of people, and his conquests were often seen as unjust and imperialistic.

Despite these flaws, Napoleon's legacy is a complex one. He is remembered as both a hero and a villain, a visionary and a tyrant. He brought stability and prosperity to France, and his reforms laid the foundation for modern France. He also left a lasting impact on Europe, transforming the political and social order of the continent. But his wars and conquests also brought suffering and death, and his legacy is still debated and contested today.

Chapter 3: The Italian Campaign and the Conquest of Europe

The conquests of Napoleon Bonaparte form a chapter in European history that will ever be remembered with admiration and astonishment. The French general and statesman, born on the island of Corsica in 1769, rose to prominence during the French Revolution and went on to conquer much of Europe during his short but illustrious military career. Among his many campaigns, the Italian Campaign of 1796-1797 stands out as one of his most successful and formative experiences.

After a string of military victories in Italy, Napoleon was appointed as commander-in-chief of the Army of Italy in 1796. At the time, the French army was in a difficult position. They were outnumbered and outmatched by the Austrian forces, who had been successfully pushing them back towards Nice. In order to turn the tide of the war, Napoleon would have to act swiftly and decisively.

The young general quickly proved himself to be a brilliant strategist and a charismatic leader. He quickly reorganized the French forces and developed a new plan of attack. Instead of engaging the Austrians head-on, he decided to move his troops around the enemy's flank and attack their supply lines. In doing so, he was able to cut off their provisions and force them into a defensive position.

The first major engagement of the Italian Campaign was the Battle of Montenotte, which took place on April 12, 1796. Napoleon led a surprise attack against the Austrian forces and was able to break through their lines. He then pressed on towards their main army at Dego, where he won another decisive victory.

Over the next few months, Napoleon continued to win battles and capture territory. He defeated the Austrians at the Battle of Lodi on May 10, 1796, and then pushed on towards the city of Milan. By the end of the month, he had captured the city and was hailed as a hero by the people of Italy.

In June, Napoleon faced his greatest challenge yet when he was confronted by a combined Austrian and Piedmontese army at the Battle of Marengo. The battle was fiercely contested, but Napoleon's troops ultimately emerged victorious. The victory secured his control over Italy and paved the way for further conquests.

One of the keys to Napoleon's success during the Italian Campaign was his ability to win the support of the Italian people. He was a master of propaganda and was able to convince many Italians that he was fighting for their freedom and independence. He also established a number of reforms that were popular with the people, such as the abolition of feudalism and the establishment of a civil code.

The Italian Campaign was a formative experience for Napoleon and would go on to shape his approach to warfare and politics for years to come. It was during this campaign that he developed many of his most innovative military tactics, such as the use of mobile artillery and rapid troop movements. He also learned the importance of winning the support of the local population and establishing a strong civil administration in conquered territories.

In the end, the Italian Campaign was a resounding success for Napoleon and laid the groundwork for his future conquests. It demonstrated his skill as a military commander and his ability to inspire loyalty and support among his troops and the people he conquered. It also revealed his ambitions for territorial expansion and cemented his reputation as a rising star in the French military and political establishments.

In the annals of military history, few battles can claim the strategic and tactical significance of the Battle of Marengo. Fought on the 14th of June, 1800, between the French Army of the Reserve, commanded by General Napoleon Bonaparte, and the Austrian Army under the command of General Michael von Melas, the Battle of Marengo marked a turning point in the French Revolutionary Wars and set the stage for Napoleon's rise to power.

The French Army of the Reserve, numbering around 28,000 troops, was engaged in a campaign to expel the Austrians from Italy. Napoleon had recently assumed command of the army and had embarked on a daring campaign to outflank the Austrians and cut off their lines of communication. His plan was to march his troops through the Alps and into Italy, bypassing the Austrian defenses along the coast.

The Austrians, meanwhile, were divided in their command structure, with General Melas commanding the main army in Italy, and Field Marshal Baron von Kray commanding a separate force in the Tyrol. This division of forces would prove to be a critical weakness in the face of Napoleon's relentless advance.

The French Army of the Reserve marched through the Alps and emerged on the Italian side of the mountains, catching the Austrians off guard. Napoleon quickly seized the initiative, launching a series of lightning-fast attacks that drove the Austrians back towards the town of Alessandria. Melas, realizing the danger he was in, ordered a retreat towards the city of Genoa, where he hoped to regroup and form a new defensive line.

Napoleon, however, had other plans. He knew that the Austrians were weakened and disorganized, and he decided to press his advantage. He ordered his troops to pursue the retreating Austrians and engage them in battle. On the morning of June 14th, the two armies clashed in the fields outside the village of Marengo.

The Battle of Marengo was a fiercely contested engagement, with both sides suffering heavy casualties. The Austrians initially had the upper hand, pushing the French back and threatening to break their lines. But Napoleon remained calm and focused, rallying his troops and launching a counterattack that caught the Austrians off guard. In a daring move, he sent his reserve cavalry charging into the Austrian ranks, breaking their formation and causing chaos and confusion.

As the battle raged on, Napoleon continued to direct his troops with precision and skill. He personally led his grenadiers into the fray, inspiring them with his bravery and charisma. The battle turned decisively in favor of the French, and by midday, the Austrians were in full retreat.

The Battle of Marengo was a stunning victory for the French Army of the Reserve, and it had far-reaching consequences for the course of the war. The Austrians were forced to withdraw from Italy, leaving the French in control of the entire region. Napoleon's reputation as a military genius was cemented, and he became the undisputed leader of France.

The Battle of Marengo also marked the beginning of a new phase in European history. Napoleon would go on to conquer much of Europe, establishing a vast empire that would shape the political landscape of the continent for decades to come. His military tactics and strategies would influence generations of military leaders, and his legacy would endure long after his death.

In summary, the Battle of Marengo was a pivotal moment in the history of the French Revolutionary Wars and a testament to the genius of Napoleon Bonaparte. It demonstrated the power of a skilled military leader to turn the tide of battle and change the course of history. The battle remains a classic example of strategic and tactical excellence, and it continues to inspire military historians and enthusiasts around the world.

In the early days of the 19th century, Napoleon Bonaparte embarked on a bold and audacious campaign in Egypt and the Middle East, seeking to establish a French presence in the region and to challenge British dominance in the Mediterranean. This campaign would ultimately prove to be a mixed success, marked by both triumphs and setbacks, and would leave a lasting impact on the history of the region.

The French expedition to Egypt was launched in the summer of 1798, with an army of around 40,000 men, including soldiers, sailors, and scientists. Napoleon's stated goal was to establish a French colony in

Egypt, to secure control of the Red Sea and the trade routes to India, and to undermine British power in the Mediterranean. The campaign began with a series of victories, as the French army easily defeated the Egyptian Mamluk forces and captured the city of Cairo.

However, the campaign soon encountered numerous challenges and setbacks. The French army was plagued by disease, as well as by the fierce resistance of local Arab and Ottoman forces. Napoleon's plan to disrupt British trade and influence in the region was also thwarted, as the British navy successfully blockaded the French fleet in the Mediterranean and prevented reinforcements and supplies from reaching the French army in Egypt.

Despite these obstacles, the French campaign in Egypt did produce some notable achievements. Napoleon's army brought with them a team of scientists and scholars, who conducted extensive research and exploration in the region, discovering new species, collecting ancient artifacts, and mapping the Nile River. The French also made significant improvements to the infrastructure and economy of Egypt, introducing new technologies and promoting trade and commerce.

The campaign in Egypt also had a significant impact on the military and political career of Napoleon himself. The victories and conquests in Egypt helped to establish his reputation as a military genius and a visionary leader, and propelled him to further success on the European continent. However, the campaign also exposed some of Napoleon's weaknesses and vulnerabilities, as he struggled to maintain control of his army and to adapt to the unfamiliar terrain and culture of the Middle East.

In the end, the French expedition to Egypt would prove to be only a temporary and limited success. The French army was ultimately forced to withdraw from the region, due to the combination of disease, military defeats, and the ongoing British blockade. However, the campaign did leave a lasting impact on the region, both in terms of the scientific discoveries and cultural exchanges that took place, and in the ways in which it shaped the political and military strategies of the French and their European rivals.

In the early years of the 19th century, Napoleon Bonaparte had established himself as the most powerful ruler in Europe. He had successfully conquered much of Western Europe, subduing Austria, Prussia, and Spain, and creating a vast empire that stretched from the Atlantic to the borders of Russia. However, his ambitions continued to grow, and in 1805, he launched the War of the Third Coalition, seeking to expand his control even further.

The war began with Napoleon's invasion of Bavaria, which prompted the Austrian and Russian armies to mobilize against him. The French army quickly swept through Germany, winning several key battles along the way. However, Napoleon faced his most significant challenge when he encountered the Russian army at the Battle of Austerlitz.

The Battle of Austerlitz, fought on December 2, 1805, is considered one of Napoleon's greatest victories. He faced an army twice the size of his own, but his superior tactics and military strategy carried the day. He divided the Allied forces and launched a fierce attack that resulted in the complete collapse of the Russian and Austrian armies. The victory solidified Napoleon's control over much of Central Europe and established him as the most powerful ruler on the continent.

Napoleon's victories did not end with Austerlitz. Over the next few years, he continued to expand his empire, conquering much of Italy and extending his influence into Spain and Portugal. He also established a continental blockade that aimed to cut off British trade and weaken their economy. However, his ambitions proved to be his downfall.

In 1812, Napoleon launched an invasion of Russia, seeking to expand his empire even further. However, the Russian campaign was a disaster. The Russian winter, guerrilla warfare, and disease all took a heavy toll on the French army, and they were forced to retreat, with only a fraction of their troops surviving. The disastrous campaign weakened Napoleon's grip on Europe and emboldened his enemies.

Over the next few years, the tide turned against Napoleon. The coalition of European powers, led by Britain, Prussia, Austria, and Russia, began to gain the upper hand. They defeated Napoleon at the Battle of Leipzig in 1813, forcing him to abdicate and go into exile on the island of Elba. However, he escaped from Elba in 1815 and returned to France, seeking to reclaim his throne.

Napoleon's return, known as the Hundred Days, was short-lived. He was defeated at the Battle of Waterloo on June 18, 1815, and was exiled to the island of Saint Helena, where he spent the rest of his life in confinement. The defeat marked the end of the Napoleonic era and the beginning of a new era of European history.

The War of the Third Coalition and the subsequent events marked a turning point in European history. It marked the end of the Enlightenment and the rise of nationalism and Romanticism. The wars also led to the establishment of new political boundaries, as well as the emergence of new European powers such as Prussia and Russia.

Napoleon's legacy continues to be debated to this day. Some see him as a brilliant military strategist and statesman who brought stability and progress to France and Europe. Others see him as a power-hungry dictator who brought war, destruction, and misery to millions. Regardless of one's opinion, there is no denying that Napoleon's impact on European history was immense and far-reaching.

In the early 19th century, Europe was a continent in turmoil, as various powers vied for supremacy and struggled to maintain their grip on the changing political landscape. Among the many leaders who emerged during this time, none would prove more influential or controversial than Napoleon Bonaparte.

Born on the island of Corsica in 1769, Napoleon rose to prominence as a military leader during the French Revolution. He quickly made a name for himself with his strategic brilliance and charismatic leadership, and by 1799 he was ready to seize power for himself.

On November 9, 1799, Napoleon launched a coup against the existing French government, which had been weakened by years of political instability and military defeats. With the help of his loyal supporters, he overthrew the Directory and established a new government known as the Consulate. This marked the beginning of Napoleon's ascent to power and the start of a new era in French history.

Under the Consulate, Napoleon consolidated his power and worked to restore order to a country that had been torn apart by years of political turmoil. He reorganized the government, strengthened the military, and instituted a series of reforms designed to modernize the French economy and society.

But Napoleon's ambitions extended far beyond France's borders. He was determined to expand his empire and establish French dominance over Europe. His first major conquest came in Italy, where he defeated the Austrians and established a series of puppet states. He then set his sights on Egypt, hoping to disrupt British trade routes to India and establish a French foothold in the Middle East.

The invasion of Egypt proved to be a mixed success for Napoleon. Although he won several early victories, including the capture of Cairo, his army was eventually defeated by a combined British and Ottoman force. Despite this setback, Napoleon returned to France as a hero, and his exploits in Egypt only added to his growing reputation as a military genius.

In 1804, Napoleon was declared Emperor of the French, and the country was transformed into a full-blown empire. Over the next several years, he continued to expand his influence, conquering much of central Europe and establishing puppet states throughout the continent.

But Napoleon's rise to power was not without its challenges. The War of the Third Coalition, which began in 1805, pitted France against an alliance of Austria, Russia, and Britain. Although Napoleon won several early victories, including the famous Battle of Austerlitz, the war ultimately ended in a stalemate.

The Treaty of Tilsit, signed in 1807, marked a turning point for Napoleon's empire. In this treaty, Napoleon forged an alliance with Russia, which had previously been one of his most formidable enemies. This allowed him to consolidate his power and focus his attention on other areas of Europe.

Over the next several years, Napoleon continued to expand his empire, conquering much of Spain and Portugal and establishing puppet states throughout Europe. But his ambitions eventually led to his downfall. In 1812, he launched an ill-fated invasion of Russia, which proved to be a disastrous mistake. His army was decimated by the harsh Russian winter and fierce resistance from Russian forces, and he was forced to retreat back to France with his tail between his legs.

This defeat marked the beginning of the end for Napoleon's empire. Over the next several years, he was gradually pushed back by a coalition of European powers, until he was finally defeated at the Battle of Waterloo in 1815. He was exiled to the remote island of Saint Helena, where he died in 1821.

Despite his ultimate defeat, Napoleon's legacy lived on. His reforms and conquests had a profound impact on Europe, and his military strategies and tactics would continue to influence military leaders for decades to come.

Chapter 4: Napoleon's Military Tactics and Strategies

The French Revolution and the subsequent rise of Napoleon Bonaparte marked a dramatic turning point in the history of France and Europe. One of the key factors that contributed to Napoleon's military success was his innovative military organization known as the "Corps System". This system revolutionized the way armies were organized and operated, and it played a crucial role in Napoleon's victories on the battlefield.

Under the Corps System, Napoleon divided his army into self-contained units or corps, each with its own infantry, cavalry, and artillery components. Each corps was composed of between 10,000 and 30,000 soldiers, and was led by a Marshal or General. This structure allowed Napoleon to rapidly deploy and concentrate his forces, as well as to coordinate multiple attacks across the battlefield.

One of the key advantages of the Corps System was its flexibility. The self-contained nature of each corps allowed them to operate independently or in coordination with other corps, depending on the situation. This made it easier for Napoleon to adapt his strategy to the changing conditions of the battlefield. Additionally, the corps structure allowed for greater efficiency in the supply and logistics chain, which was critical in a time when armies often suffered from disease and starvation due to poor management.

Another important aspect of the Corps System was the emphasis on the use of artillery. Napoleon recognized the potential of artillery as a decisive force on the battlefield, and he made it a priority to develop and train his artillery units. The Corps System allowed Napoleon to coordinate and concentrate his artillery more effectively, which proved to be a major advantage in battle.

The Corps System was also instrumental in Napoleon's ability to fight wars on multiple fronts simultaneously. By dividing his army into self-contained corps, he was able to engage in battles on different fronts without leaving his other fronts vulnerable. This allowed him to pursue a more aggressive and expansionist foreign policy, ultimately leading to the establishment of the French Empire.

In addition to its military advantages, the Corps System also had important political implications. By entrusting his Marshals and Generals with significant autonomy, Napoleon was able to cultivate a sense of loyalty and obedience among his subordinates. This helped to solidify his grip on power and maintain the stability of his regime.

Despite its numerous advantages, the Corps System was not without its drawbacks. The autonomy of each corps could sometimes lead to confusion and miscommunication, particularly during larger battles. Additionally, the system was resource-intensive, requiring a large number of trained officers and support personnel to effectively operate. However, these limitations were outweighed by the system's overall effectiveness, and it remained a key component of Napoleon's military strategy throughout his reign.

In summary, the Corps System was a key factor in Napoleon's military success and played a significant role in shaping the course of European history. Its innovative structure and flexibility allowed Napoleon to rapidly deploy and concentrate his forces, coordinate multiple attacks, and fight wars on multiple fronts. By dividing his army into self-contained corps, Napoleon revolutionized the way armies were organized and operated, ultimately leading to the establishment of the French Empire.

Throughout his career, Napoleon Bonaparte proved himself to be a master of military tactics and strategy. One of the most important innovations that he introduced to the battlefield was the use of the grand battery, a tactic that relied on massed artillery to create a devastating barrage of firepower against enemy positions.

The grand battery was a natural evolution of the artillery tactics of the time. In the 18th century, most armies used artillery as a supporting element for their infantry and cavalry. Guns were typically deployed in small batteries of six to eight pieces, and were used to soften up enemy positions before the infantry and cavalry moved in for the attack.

Napoleon recognized the potential of artillery to become a decisive factor on the battlefield. He began to experiment with massed batteries of artillery during his campaigns in Italy in the late 1790s. By the time of the Battle of Marengo in 1800, he had refined the technique to a fine art.

At Marengo, Napoleon deployed 60 guns in a single battery, a concentration of firepower that was unheard of at the time. He positioned the battery in the center of his line, where it could enfilade the entire length of the Austrian position. When the order to fire was given, the battery unleashed a withering barrage of cannon fire that shredded the Austrian ranks and shattered their morale. The French infantry was then able to advance behind the curtain of fire and carry the day.

The success of the grand battery at Marengo convinced Napoleon of its value, and he began to use the tactic in all of his subsequent battles. At Austerlitz in 1805, he deployed a battery of 120 guns, which proved to be the decisive factor in his victory over the combined armies of Russia and Austria. At Wagram in 1809, he used a battery of 100 guns to devastating effect against the Austrians.

The grand battery was not without its drawbacks, however. Massing so many guns in one place made them vulnerable to counter-battery fire, and it could take hours to move them into position. It also required a significant investment in resources, both in terms of the number of guns and the amount of ammunition required to sustain a prolonged barrage.

Despite these challenges, the grand battery remained a cornerstone of Napoleon's tactical arsenal. It allowed him to concentrate overwhelming firepower on a single point, creating a breach in the enemy line that his infantry could exploit. It also enabled him to dictate the pace of battle, forcing his opponents to react to his moves rather than vice versa.

The legacy of the grand battery extended well beyond Napoleon's time. Military commanders in the 19th and early 20th centuries continued to use massed artillery as a way to soften up enemy positions before launching attacks. The tactic reached its apogee during World War I, when both sides deployed vast batteries of artillery to devastating effect.

Today, the grand battery is seen as a historical curiosity rather than a viable military tactic. The development of precision-guided munitions and other advanced technologies has made the massed use of artillery largely obsolete. Nevertheless, the legacy of Napoleon's innovation remains an important part of the history of military tactics and strategy.

In the annals of military history, few commanders have made such an indelible mark as Napoleon Bonaparte. The French general's career spanned two decades, during which he fought in numerous campaigns and left his mark on the world. One of the hallmarks of Napoleon's style of warfare was his use of flanking maneuvers, which allowed him to take his opponents by surprise and gain the upper hand. Among these maneuvers, one of the most significant was the "Manoeuvre sur les Derrières," or the "Maneuver on the Rear."

The Manoeuvre sur les Derrières was a flanking maneuver used by Napoleon in several of his battles, including Marengo and Austerlitz. The purpose of the maneuver was to surprise the enemy by attacking their rear while their attention was focused on the main battle. The maneuver was often used in conjunction with a frontal assault, which would keep the enemy occupied while the flanking force moved into position. Once the enemy's rear was exposed, the flanking force would attack, causing confusion and panic in the enemy ranks.

The success of the Manoeuvre sur les Derrières depended on several factors. First, it required a well-trained and disciplined force that could move quickly and silently into position. Second, it required a commander who could accurately judge the enemy's movements and anticipate their reactions. Finally, it required favorable terrain, such as hills or forests, that could provide cover for the flanking force and conceal their movements from the enemy.

One of the most notable uses of the Manoeuvre sur les Derrières was at the Battle of Marengo in 1800. In this battle, Napoleon faced an Austrian army that was positioned on the other side of the Bormida River. Napoleon launched a frontal assault across the river, which drew the bulk of the Austrian army to the front line. At the same time, Napoleon sent a flanking force under the command of General Desaix to cross the river further downstream and attack the Austrian rear.

Desaix's force marched through the countryside undetected and arrived behind the Austrian lines just as the main battle was reaching its climax. The Austrians, who had been confident of victory, suddenly found themselves under attack from two sides. The confusion and panic that ensued allowed Napoleon's forces to gain the upper hand, and the Austrians were forced to retreat.

The success of the Manoeuvre sur les Derrières at Marengo was not unique. Napoleon would go on to use similar tactics in other battles, including Austerlitz and Wagram. The maneuver proved to be a key element of Napoleon's military strategy, allowing him to outmaneuver and defeat much larger armies.

Despite its success, the Manoeuvre sur les Derrières was not without its risks. The flanking force was often isolated and vulnerable to attack, and if the main force was unable to hold the enemy's attention, the flanking force could be easily overwhelmed. In addition, the maneuver required a significant amount of coordination and communication, which could be difficult to achieve on a chaotic battlefield.

Despite these challenges, the Manoeuvre sur les Derrières remains one of the most iconic and effective flanking maneuvers in military history. Its success in numerous battles is a testament to Napoleon's strategic genius and the effectiveness of his corps system. Today, the maneuver continues to be studied and analyzed by military historians and strategists around the world, as a testament to the enduring legacy of Napoleon Bonaparte.

The French Emperor Napoleon Bonaparte is renowned for his military prowess, and one of the most important aspects of his success was his use of cavalry. In Napoleon's time, cavalry was an essential part of any army, but the way that Napoleon utilized his cavalry was revolutionary, and became one of the hallmarks of his military strategy.

Napoleon's cavalry consisted of light cavalry and heavy cavalry, each with a specific role on the battlefield. The light cavalry was used for scouting and reconnaissance, and to harry the enemy's flanks and rear. The heavy cavalry, on the other hand, was used for shock attacks, charging into the enemy's lines and breaking them apart. These charges were devastating to the enemy, both physically and psychologically, and often caused them to break and flee.

One of the most famous examples of Napoleon's use of cavalry was at the Battle of Austerlitz in 1805. The battle was fought between the French and the combined armies of Austria and Russia, and was one of the most decisive victories of Napoleon's career. The French army was outnumbered, but Napoleon's tactical genius and the bravery of his soldiers, especially his cavalry, carried the day.

At Austerlitz, Napoleon ordered his cavalry to attack the enemy's left flank. The cavalry charged forward, and the enemy's infantry, unable to withstand the impact, broke and fled. The cavalry then turned on the enemy's right flank, which was similarly crushed. The battle was won, and Napoleon's cavalry had played a key role in the victory.

Napoleon's use of cavalry was not limited to battlefields alone. In his campaigns, his cavalry was often used to harass and disrupt enemy supply lines, weakening their ability to fight. The cavalry was also used for reconnaissance, providing valuable information on the enemy's movements and intentions. This information was essential for Napoleon's strategy, as it allowed him to make informed decisions about where and when to attack.

One of the most famous units in Napoleon's cavalry was the Imperial Guard. The Guard was made up of elite soldiers who were handpicked by Napoleon himself, and they were known for their bravery and loyalty. The Guard was often used as a reserve force, ready to step in and turn the tide of battle if needed.

Napoleon's use of cavalry was not without its drawbacks, however. Cavalry charges were often risky, and if they failed, the cavalry could be vulnerable to counterattacks. Furthermore, the use of cavalry required extensive training and discipline, and many armies of the time did not have the resources to train and maintain a large and effective cavalry force.

Despite these challenges, Napoleon's use of cavalry was a key element of his military strategy, and it helped him win many of his most famous battles. The impact of his cavalry charges, especially against infantry, was devastating, and it helped to create a sense of fear and panic among the enemy. Today, Napoleon's use of cavalry is still studied and admired by military historians and strategists around the world.

The history of warfare is full of tales of generals who transformed the art of war through their tactical innovations and strategic brilliance. In the 19th century, there was perhaps no greater military innovator than Napoleon Bonaparte, whose campaigns and conquests transformed Europe and the world. From his early victories in Italy to his final defeat at Waterloo, Napoleon's military career was characterized by boldness, adaptability, and an unrelenting focus on victory.

One of Napoleon's greatest contributions to military strategy was his emphasis on the importance of speed and mobility. He understood that in order to win battles, it was essential to be able to move troops quickly across the battlefield and strike at the enemy's weak points before they could react. To achieve this, he developed a number of innovative tactics and techniques that allowed his armies to move with remarkable speed and flexibility.

Perhaps the most famous of these tactics was the use of the "Manoeuvre sur les Derrières," or "maneuver on the rear." This was a flanking maneuver in which Napoleon would launch an attack on the enemy's flank, forcing them to either turn and face the new threat or risk being cut off from their supply lines and reinforcements. By constantly threatening the enemy's flanks,

Napoleon was able to keep them off-balance and force them to constantly adjust their positions, which in turn made them vulnerable to attack from other directions.

Another important innovation of Napoleon's was his use of cavalry. He understood that cavalry could be used not only for reconnaissance and harassment of the enemy, but also as a powerful striking force that could break through enemy lines and disrupt their formations. To make the most of his cavalry, Napoleon developed a number of new tactics, such as the use of the "charge en masse," in which a large number of cavalry units would charge at once, overwhelming the enemy with their sheer numbers and momentum.

Napoleon also placed great emphasis on the use of artillery, recognizing that a well-placed battery of cannons could wreak havoc on enemy formations and create openings for his infantry and cavalry to exploit. He developed a number of new techniques for using artillery, such as the "Grand Battery," in which multiple batteries of cannons would be concentrated in a single location and unleashed on a specific target. This could cause devastating damage to the enemy and create openings for his troops to exploit.

Perhaps most importantly, Napoleon revolutionized the way armies were organized and deployed. He developed the concept of the "corps system," in which armies were organized into smaller, more mobile units that could be quickly deployed to different parts of the battlefield as needed. This allowed him to move troops quickly and respond to changing circumstances, giving him a decisive advantage over his enemies.

Overall, Napoleon's military innovations had a profound impact on the conduct of war and helped him achieve some of the greatest military victories in history. His focus on speed, mobility, and adaptability allowed him to outmaneuver and outfight much larger and better-equipped armies, and his tactical innovations continue to influence military strategy to this day. While his legacy is certainly mixed and his methods often brutal, there can be no denying the impact that Napoleon had on the art of war and the history of Europe and the world.

Chapter 5: The Egyptian Campaign and the Battle of the Pyramids

The invasion of Egypt is a curious episode in the military career of Napoleon Bonaparte, and one that has been the subject of much speculation and debate. For many historians, it remains a mystery why Napoleon chose to launch an expedition to Egypt in 1798, and what his ultimate objectives were.

One theory is that Napoleon saw Egypt as a stepping stone to the East, and hoped to use the country as a base from which to launch an assault on the British colonies in India. This view is supported by the fact that Napoleon brought with him a team of scholars and scientists who were tasked with exploring and documenting the country, its people, and its history. However, while it is clear that Napoleon had a keen interest in Egyptology and archaeology, it is less clear how this related to his military strategy.

Another theory is that Napoleon was seeking to establish a French presence in the Middle East in order to disrupt British trade routes to India, and to counter the influence of the British in the region. This view is supported by the fact that Napoleon brought with him a large army and navy, which were tasked with securing the country and ensuring that French interests were protected.

Yet another theory is that Napoleon was simply seeking to assert his dominance over the European powers by launching a spectacular military campaign that would capture the imagination of the public and cement his reputation as a military genius. This view is supported by the fact that Napoleon's campaign in Egypt was widely celebrated in France and throughout Europe, and helped to boost his popularity and prestige.

Whatever the reasons behind Napoleon's invasion of Egypt, it is clear that the campaign was marked by both successes and failures. On the one hand, Napoleon's forces were able to achieve a number of impressive military victories, including the capture of Alexandria and the defeat of the Mamelukes at the Battle of the Pyramids. On the other hand, the French army was beset by disease, desertion, and supply shortages, which severely hampered their ability to maintain control over the country.

In the end, Napoleon's campaign in Egypt was ultimately doomed to failure. Despite his initial successes, he was unable to establish a lasting French presence in the country, and was forced to abandon his ambitions in the Middle East in order to return to France and deal with the growing threat of the Third Coalition. Nonetheless, the invasion of

Egypt remains an intriguing chapter in the history of Napoleon and the French Empire, and one that has continued to fascinate historians and the public alike.

The year was 1798, and Napoleon Bonaparte was at the height of his power. Having risen to prominence in the French Revolution, he was now leading an ambitious expedition to Egypt. The goal was to establish a French presence in the Middle East, disrupt British trade with India, and uncover the mysteries of ancient Egypt. The French force, consisting of nearly 40,000 soldiers, landed in Alexandria in July 1798 and quickly moved inland towards Cairo.

The first major battle of the campaign took place on July 21, 1798, near the village of Embabeh, a few miles south of Cairo. There, the French army encountered a large Mamluk force, consisting of as many as 20,000 cavalry and infantry. The Mamluks were a powerful group of Turkish slave-soldiers who had ruled Egypt for centuries, and were feared throughout the region for their martial prowess.

The Mamluk forces were led by Murad Bey and Ibrahim Bey, two of the most skilled and experienced military leaders in Egypt. They had spent years honing their tactics and strategy, and had amassed a formidable force of cavalry and infantry. The French, on the other hand, were relatively inexperienced in desert warfare, and their soldiers were unaccustomed to the harsh conditions of Egypt.

Despite these disadvantages, Napoleon was confident of victory. He had carefully planned his strategy, and had deployed his troops in a manner that would allow them to withstand the Mamluk charge. He also had a secret weapon - a powerful artillery force, consisting of over 50 cannons, which he had brought with him from France.

The battle began with a ferocious Mamluk charge, as the Turkish cavalry swept down upon the French lines. The French infantry held their ground, forming a square formation that allowed them to repel the Mamluk attack. The French artillery, meanwhile, unleashed a devastating barrage of cannon fire, decimating the Mamluk ranks.

Despite their initial success, the Mamluks regrouped and launched a second charge, this time targeting the French flanks. But Napoleon had anticipated this move, and had stationed his cavalry and infantry in such a way as to prevent the Mamluks from gaining the upper hand. The French cavalry, led by General Jean-Baptiste Kléber, launched a fierce counter-attack, driving the Mamluks back and securing a French victory.

The Battle of the Pyramids, as it came to be known, was a stunning victory for Napoleon and his army. The French suffered only a few hundred casualties, while the Mamluks lost thousands of men, including both of their commanders. The victory also had wider implications, as it gave Napoleon control of Egypt and allowed him to establish a French presence in the Middle East.

But the battle also had its downsides. The French troops, many of whom were suffering from disease and malnutrition, plundered the nearby village of Embabeh, killing and looting indiscriminately. The incident tarnished the reputation of the French army, and gave ammunition to those who opposed Napoleon's campaign in Egypt.

Nevertheless, the Battle of the Pyramids remains a key moment in the history of Napoleon's conquests. It showcased his tactical brilliance and military innovations, and demonstrated his ability to defeat even the most feared and formidable opponents. It also paved the way for further French expansion in the Middle East, and laid the foundations for the modernization of Egypt.

The late 18th and early 19th century saw the emergence of one of the greatest military commanders in history: Napoleon Bonaparte. This French general and statesman rose to prominence during the French Revolution and went on to conquer much of Europe, establishing the French Empire and shaping the course of world history. One of the lesser-known episodes of his career is his invasion of Egypt, a campaign that was as audacious as it was ambitious.

In the spring of 1798, Napoleon embarked on a military expedition to Egypt, then a province of the Ottoman Empire. The reasons for this campaign were complex and multi-faceted. Napoleon had long harbored dreams of military glory and empire-building, and Egypt offered the opportunity for both. He also sought to undermine Britain's strategic position in the Mediterranean by cutting off its access to the Suez Canal and the Red Sea. In addition, the campaign was seen as a way to spread revolutionary ideas and establish French influence in the Middle East and North Africa.

The invasion force consisted of over 35,000 troops, including infantry, cavalry, and artillery, as well as a large contingent of scientists, scholars, and artists. The French were initially welcomed by the local population, who saw them as liberators from Ottoman rule. However, this support quickly eroded as the French began to requisition supplies and impose heavy taxes on the population.

Napoleon's first major engagement in Egypt was the Battle of the Pyramids, fought on July 21, 1798, against the Mamluk forces led by Murad Bey. The battle was a resounding victory for the French, who deployed their artillery and infantry to devastating effect. Murad Bey's forces were routed, and the French took control of Cairo, the capital of Egypt.

The French victory at the Battle of the Pyramids was followed by the Siege of Jaffa, a coastal city in Palestine that was held by the Ottomans. The siege lasted for several weeks, during which the French faced fierce resistance from the defenders. Despite the odds, the French eventually breached the city's walls and stormed the fortress, resulting in a bloody hand-to-hand combat. In the aftermath of the siege, Napoleon ordered the execution of several thousand Ottoman prisoners, a decision that has been widely criticized by historians.

Despite these early victories, Napoleon's campaign in Egypt would ultimately prove to be a failure. The French forces were beset by disease, desertion, and supply shortages, and were unable to hold on to their gains. In addition, a British naval blockade prevented reinforcements and supplies from reaching the French, further weakening their position. In 1801, the French were forced to abandon their positions in Egypt and return to France.

Despite its ultimate failure, Napoleon's invasion of Egypt was a significant episode in his career and in world history. The campaign demonstrated his military prowess and strategic acumen, as well as his ambition and willingness to take risks. It also marked the beginning of France's involvement in the Middle East, a region that would become a source of conflict and competition in the years to come.

The Egyptian Campaign of 1798-1801 marked a turning point in Napoleon Bonaparte's career and had far-reaching consequences for both France and Egypt. While the campaign was ultimately a military failure, it had several significant achievements, one of which was the discovery of the Rosetta Stone, a key artifact in the decipherment of hieroglyphs.

In the course of the campaign, Napoleon brought with him a team of scholars and scientists who were tasked with studying Egypt's history, culture, and society. They were given the ambitious goal of producing a comprehensive study of Egypt, including its geography, history, religion, and economy. As part of this effort, the team began excavating and surveying ancient Egyptian sites, recording their findings in detailed reports and drawings.

One of the most important discoveries made by the team was the Rosetta Stone, a large inscribed stele that had been uncovered by French soldiers during the siege of the port city of Rosetta. The stone, which is now housed in the British Museum in London, bears an inscription in three different scripts: hieroglyphs, demotic (a cursive script used for everyday purposes), and Greek. The Greek text was easily readable, but the other two were still a mystery.

The significance of the Rosetta Stone lay in the fact that it provided the key to deciphering hieroglyphs, the ancient Egyptian writing system that had been lost for over a thousand years. Scholars had long been fascinated by hieroglyphs, but their meanings had remained a mystery until the discovery of the Rosetta Stone. With its inscription in both hieroglyphs and Greek, scholars were able to compare the two texts and slowly begin to piece together the meanings of individual hieroglyphic symbols.

The task of deciphering hieroglyphs fell to Jean-Francois Champollion, a French scholar who was only a teenager when the Rosetta Stone was discovered. Champollion devoted his life to studying hieroglyphs, and eventually succeeded in cracking the code. His work was a major breakthrough in the field of Egyptology and allowed scholars to gain a much deeper understanding of ancient Egyptian civilization.

The discovery of the Rosetta Stone also had wider cultural significance. It sparked a wave of interest in ancient Egypt and fueled a fashion for Egyptian-style art and design. It was also a key factor in the development of the science of archaeology, as scholars began to see the importance of careful excavation and recording of artifacts.

The Rosetta Stone continues to fascinate scholars and the public alike, and its legacy can be seen in the many popular books, films, and exhibitions devoted to ancient Egypt. Its discovery during Napoleon's Egyptian Campaign was one of the most significant achievements of the expedition, and had a profound impact on the study of history and archaeology.

The expedition to Egypt marked a turning point in Napoleon's military career and the history of France. After the successful conquest of Italy and the establishment of the Cisalpine Republic, Napoleon was eager to embark on new conquests and expand his empire. The Egyptian campaign was initially intended to disrupt British trade routes to India and establish French influence in the Middle East. However, it quickly turned into a protracted struggle against the Ottomans and the Mamluks, and ultimately ended in failure.

Napoleon arrived in Egypt in July 1798 with a force of nearly 40,000 men, including soldiers, scholars, and scientists. He saw the campaign as an opportunity to assert France's cultural and intellectual superiority over the region, and established a commission of scholars and experts to study and document Egypt's ancient history and culture. This commission included mathematicians, astronomers, engineers, and artists, and produced a wealth of valuable knowledge and discoveries.

Despite initial victories at the Battle of the Pyramids and the capture of Cairo, the French soon faced resistance from the Mamluks and the Ottomans, who were determined to expel the foreign invaders from their lands. Napoleon's forces were also plagued by disease, lack of supplies, and harsh desert conditions, which further weakened their position.

One of the most infamous episodes of the campaign was the siege of Jaffa, a coastal city in Palestine. After a failed attempt to capture the city, Napoleon ordered his troops to storm the walls and take it by force. The defenders, consisting of local Arab and Ottoman soldiers, put up fierce resistance, but were eventually overwhelmed by the French assault. In the aftermath of the battle, Napoleon allegedly ordered the execution of over 2,000 Ottoman prisoners of war, an act that was later used as a propaganda tool by his enemies to discredit him.

The discovery of the Rosetta Stone, a slab of inscribed stone that contained three versions of a decree issued at Memphis in 196 BC, was one of the most significant finds of the expedition. The stone was discovered by a French officer near the town of Rosetta, and was later taken to Cairo and eventually to the British Museum in London. The stone proved to be a key to deciphering ancient Egyptian hieroglyphs, and was instrumental in unlocking the secrets of the ancient world.

By the end of 1799, with the situation in Egypt deteriorating and the French army facing increasing challenges from local resistance and Ottoman armies, Napoleon decided to abandon the campaign and return to France. He left General Jean-Baptiste Kléber in charge of the remaining troops, but Kléber was assassinated in 1800 and the French forces were ultimately forced to withdraw from Egypt.

The failure of the Egyptian campaign was a major blow to Napoleon's reputation and ambitions. It revealed the limits of French power and exposed the vulnerabilities of the army to disease and external threats. However, the expedition also resulted in important discoveries and advancements in the fields of archaeology, science, and culture. The expedition also demonstrated the potential of the French army and its ability to project power beyond Europe, foreshadowing Napoleon's future conquests in Europe and beyond.

Chapter 6: The Rise to Emperor and Consolidation of Power

The French Revolution, which had begun in 1789, had radically transformed France's political and social landscape. The monarchy had been overthrown, and the First Republic established in 1792. The period that followed was marked by a series of political upheavals, as various factions vied for power and the revolution descended into a reign of terror.

By the end of the 1790s, France was exhausted and in need of stability. This was the context in which Napoleon Bonaparte came to prominence. Born in Corsica in 1769, Napoleon was a talented military officer who had risen to fame through his victories in Italy and Egypt. In 1799, he led a coup against the Directory, the government that had been established after the fall of the monarchy, and established himself as First Consul, effectively the ruler of France.

The coup of 18 Brumaire (November 9, 1799) was the culmination of a series of political crises that had engulfed France in the late 1790s. The Directory, which had been established in 1795 as a five-man executive body, had proved to be ineffective and unpopular. It was plagued by corruption and factionalism, and the French people had grown weary of its constant political instability.

Napoleon's rise to power was not a foregone conclusion. The coup of 18 Brumaire was a risky undertaking, and Napoleon faced significant opposition from both within and outside the government. His success was due in part to his military prowess and reputation, but also to his political skill and ability to negotiate with key power-brokers.

The coup itself was a carefully orchestrated affair. Napoleon had been planning it for some time, and he had assembled a group of loyal military officers and politicians to help him carry it out. On the morning of 18 Brumaire, he arrived at the Tuileries Palace, where the Directory was meeting, accompanied by a contingent of troops. The Directory was quickly dispersed, and the Council of Ancients, a legislative body, was convened to formalize the coup.

Over the course of the following weeks, Napoleon consolidated his power and established himself as First Consul. He introduced a new constitution, which gave him sweeping powers, and set about reforming the government and the military. He also worked to restore stability to France, which had been wracked by years of political turmoil and war.

The coup of 18 Brumaire marked the end of the French Revolution and the beginning of Napoleon's rule. It was a turning point in French history, and had significant implications for the rest of Europe. Napoleon's rise to power would lead to years of military conquest and political intrigue, as he sought to establish a French-dominated Europe. The legacy of the coup of 18 Brumaire is still felt today, as it marked the beginning of a new era in French and European history.

The French Revolution of 1789 had brought about radical political, social, and economic changes in France. However, the period of the Revolution was characterized by political instability and turmoil, which left the country in a state of chaos. In 1799, a military coup put an end to the instability and marked the rise of a new government under Napoleon Bonaparte.

The coup of 18 Brumaire, as it was known, took place on November 9 and 10, 1799 (according to the French revolutionary calendar). The coup was the result of the growing dissatisfaction among the French people with the government of the Directory, which had been in power since 1795. The Directory was seen as corrupt and ineffective, and its leaders had lost the support of the people.

Napoleon, who was then a successful general in the French army, saw an opportunity to seize power. With the support of his fellow generals, including Emmanuel-Joseph Sieyès, he launched a coup against the Directory. The coup was successful, and the Directory was dissolved.

Napoleon then established a new government, called the Consulate. Under the Consulate, the executive power was vested in three consuls, of which Napoleon was the first consul. The Consulate marked the beginning of Napoleon's rise to power, and it paved the way for the establishment of the First French Empire in 1804.

The establishment of the Consulate was significant for several reasons. Firstly, it marked the end of the turbulent period of the French Revolution and the beginning of a new era of stability and order. The Consulate was a more efficient and effective form of government than the Directory, and it was able to restore law and order in France.

Secondly, the Consulate was significant because it marked the beginning of Napoleon's rise to power. Napoleon was the dominant figure in the new government, and he quickly consolidated his power. He was able to use the military victories he had achieved in Italy and Egypt to gain the support of the people, and he was able to establish himself as the most powerful figure in France.

Thirdly, the Consulate was significant because it represented a break with the ideals of the French Revolution. The Revolution had been characterized by the principles of liberty, equality, and fraternity, and it had sought to establish a democratic form of government. However, the

Consulate was a more authoritarian form of government, and it represented a departure from the democratic ideals of the Revolution.

In summary, the coup of 18 Brumaire and the establishment of the Consulate marked a significant turning point in French history. It brought an end to the instability of the French Revolution and paved the way for Napoleon's rise to power. The Consulate represented a more stable and efficient form of government than the Directory, but it also represented a departure from the democratic ideals of the Revolution.

The Concordat of 1801 was a significant event in the history of France, as it marked the end of the long-standing conflict between the state and the church that had characterized the country's history since the French Revolution. The Concordat was an agreement between the government of the First Consul, Napoleon Bonaparte, and Pope Pius VII, which established a new relationship between the French state and the Catholic Church.

The French Revolution had brought about significant changes in the relationship between the state and the church. The Revolution had sought to reduce the power of the church, which had long been a significant political and social force in France. The French Revolutionaries had declared the separation of church and state, and the state had confiscated the church's property and abolished the monasteries and convents.

These measures had led to significant tensions between the state and the church. Many Catholics had resisted the changes brought about by the Revolution, and the church had become a center of opposition to the new government. This opposition had led to a period of persecution of the church, which had included the execution of many Catholic priests and the closing of many churches.

The Concordat of 1801 was an attempt to resolve the conflict between the state and the church. The agreement was negotiated by the First Consul, Napoleon Bonaparte, and the papal legate, Cardinal Ercole Consalvi. The Concordat recognized the Catholic Church as the religion of the majority of French citizens, but it also established the state's right to regulate the church's affairs.

The Concordat abolished the revolutionary government's system of electing bishops and replaced it with a new system in which the pope appointed bishops, who were then approved by the French government. The agreement also established a new system of state support for the church, which included the payment of salaries to priests and the restoration of many of the church's properties.

The Concordat was a significant achievement for both the French state and the Catholic Church. It allowed the state to re-establish control over the church while also recognizing the importance of religion in French society. The agreement also allowed the church to regain some of its lost property and to re-establish its presence in French society.

However, the Concordat was not without its critics. Many French citizens, particularly those who had supported the Revolution, saw the agreement as a betrayal of the principles of the Revolution. They saw the Concordat as an attempt to restore the power of the church and to undo the progress made during the Revolution.

Despite these criticisms, the Concordat of 1801 remained in force until 1905, when the French government passed a law separating church and state. The law abolished state support for the church and made the church's property the property of the state.

In summary, the Concordat of 1801 was a significant event in French history. The agreement marked the end of the conflict between the state and the church that had characterized French society since the French Revolution. The Concordat allowed the state to re-establish control over the church while also recognizing the importance of religion in French society. Although the Concordat was not without its critics, it remained in force for over a century and played an important role in shaping the relationship between the state and the church in France.

In the aftermath of the French Revolution, France was in dire need of a new legal system that would serve as the basis for the new republic. In response to this need, Napoleon Bonaparte introduced the Napoleonic Code, also known as the French Civil Code, in 1804. This monumental legal document played a crucial role in shaping the modern legal systems of Europe and other parts of the world.

The Napoleonic Code represented a radical departure from the patchwork of laws that existed in France prior to its introduction. Prior to the French Revolution, France was divided into a patchwork of legal jurisdictions, each with its own distinct set of laws and customs. This made it difficult for citizens to navigate the legal system, and often resulted in a lack of justice for those who could not afford to hire expensive lawyers to represent them.

The Napoleonic Code was designed to rectify this problem by creating a unified legal system for all of France. It was based on the principles of equality before the law, legal certainty, and the protection of property rights. The code also abolished feudalism and serfdom, and gave French citizens the right to choose their own profession.

Perhaps the most revolutionary aspect of the Napoleonic Code was its emphasis on legal certainty. Prior to its introduction, French law was notoriously vague and uncertain. The Napoleonic Code introduced clear, concise language that was designed to be easily understood by ordinary citizens. This made the legal system more accessible and ensured that justice was more readily available to those who needed it.

Another important feature of the Napoleonic Code was its emphasis on property rights. Under the code, property rights were protected and individuals were free to buy, sell, and trade property as they saw fit. This helped to spur economic growth and laid the foundation for the modern capitalist system.

Despite its many benefits, the Napoleonic Code was not without its critics. Some argued that it was too rigid and did not allow for enough flexibility in the legal system. Others complained that it was overly focused on individual rights at the expense of the greater good.

Despite these criticisms, the Napoleonic Code has had a lasting impact on legal systems around the world. It served as the basis for legal reform in many European countries in the 19th century, and was even adopted by some countries outside of Europe, including Egypt and Japan.

In summary, the Napoleonic Code represented a radical departure from the legal systems that existed in France prior to its introduction. It was based on the principles of equality before the law, legal certainty, and the protection of property rights. The code has had a lasting impact on legal systems around the world, and has helped to shape the modern legal systems of Europe and other parts of the world.

The coronation of Napoleon as Emperor of the French on December 2, 1804, marked the pinnacle of his power and the establishment of the French Empire. The event, which took place in the Notre-Dame Cathedral in Paris, was an elaborate and meticulously planned ceremony that aimed to cement Napoleon's status as the ruler of France and symbolize the continuity of French power after the turbulent years of the Revolution.

The coronation ceremony was steeped in symbolism and spectacle, drawing on the traditions and rituals of the ancient Roman Empire and the French monarchy. Napoleon, dressed in a richly embroidered robe and a laurel wreath, was anointed with holy oil by Pope Pius VII, who had traveled from Rome to preside over the ceremony. As the pope crowned him with a golden crown, Napoleon took the crown from his head and placed it on his own head, proclaiming himself Emperor of the French.

The coronation of Napoleon was a carefully staged event that aimed to convey a sense of legitimacy and continuity, as well as to reinforce the idea of Napoleon as a ruler chosen by destiny. The ceremony was designed to create a sense of grandeur and spectacle, with thousands of soldiers, dignitaries, and spectators in attendance. The cathedral was decorated with elaborate tapestries, sculptures, and paintings, and the ceremony was accompanied by music and prayers.

The coronation of Napoleon was also significant for its political implications. It marked the end of the French Republic and the establishment of the French Empire, with Napoleon as its absolute ruler. The ceremony was a powerful statement of Napoleon's ambitions and his determination to create a new order in Europe, one in which France would be the dominant power. The creation of the empire was seen by many as a return to the traditions of the Old Regime, with Napoleon as the new king.

However, the coronation was also controversial, with many critics seeing it as a symbol of Napoleon's excessive ambition and his disregard for the principles of the Revolution. Some saw it as a betrayal of the ideals of liberty, equality, and fraternity that had inspired the Revolution, and as a step towards dictatorship and despotism.

The coronation of Napoleon was not just a significant event in French history, but also in European history. It marked the rise of a new power in Europe and signaled a shift in the balance of power. Napoleon's empire would go on to shape the political and military landscape of Europe for the next decade, as he pursued a policy of expansion and conquest, and sought to create a new order in Europe.

In summary, the coronation of Napoleon was a highly significant event in French and European history. It marked the establishment of the French Empire and the rise of Napoleon as its absolute ruler. The ceremony was a carefully staged event that aimed to convey a sense of legitimacy and continuity, as well as to reinforce the idea of Napoleon as a ruler chosen by destiny. However, the coronation was also controversial, with many critics seeing it as a betrayal of the ideals of the Revolution. The event would have profound political and military implications, shaping the course of European history for the next decade.

Chapter 7: The Administration and Governance of the Empire

In the history of the French Empire, few measures were as crucial to its success as the creation of the centralized bureaucracy. This system, established by Napoleon Bonaparte in the early years of his rule, allowed for a level of governance and control over the far-flung territories of the empire that was unprecedented in European history.

At its core, the centralized bureaucracy was a system of government that placed power in the hands of trained administrators rather than the traditional ruling classes of aristocrats and monarchs. The new officials were appointed on merit, based on their skills and knowledge, rather than their social rank or family connections. In this way, Napoleon was able to tap into the talents of the middle class, and harness their abilities for the good of the empire.

The new bureaucracy was created by a series of administrative reforms that began with the establishment of the Consulate in 1799. One of the first acts of the new government was the creation of the Council of State, which acted as a supreme court and also advised the First Consul on matters of policy. The Council was made up of trained jurists, who were appointed based on their legal knowledge and experience.

Another key aspect of the new system was the division of France into administrative departments, each of which was governed by a prefect. These prefects were responsible for maintaining order, enforcing the law, and collecting taxes. They were also responsible for overseeing local elections, and ensuring that the government's policies were being implemented at the grassroots level.

Perhaps most importantly, the centralized bureaucracy allowed for a level of economic and social planning that was unprecedented in European history. The government was able to collect vast amounts of data about the population, including birth and death rates, marriage statistics, and information about property ownership and trade. This information was then used to create policies that were tailored to the needs of specific regions and populations.

The centralized bureaucracy also played a key role in the administration of the empire's territories beyond France itself. Officials were appointed to govern the annexed territories, and these administrators were given wide-ranging powers to ensure that the laws and policies of the empire were being implemented. This allowed for a level of control over the conquered territories that had not been seen since the days of the Roman Empire.

Despite its many benefits, the centralized bureaucracy was not without its critics. Some argued that the system was too rigid and inflexible, and that it stifled creativity and innovation. Others saw it as an example of the overweening power of the state, and as an infringement on individual rights and freedoms.

Nevertheless, there can be little doubt that the centralized bureaucracy played a key role in the success of the French Empire, both at home and abroad. It allowed for a level of governance and control that was unparalleled in European history, and paved the way for the modern administrative state that we know today.

In the early years of the French Empire, Napoleon Bonaparte undertook a series of administrative reforms aimed at creating a centralized and efficient government. Among the key innovations was the creation of the prefects, officials appointed by the central government to oversee the administration of France's departments, or administrative regions.

Prior to Napoleon's reforms, the departments had been administered by locally elected officials who often lacked the resources and authority to effectively govern their regions. This decentralized system had contributed to inefficiencies and corruption, and had hindered the government's ability to enforce its policies and maintain order.

To address these problems, Napoleon created the office of the prefect in 1800. The prefects were appointed by the central government and given wide-ranging powers to oversee the administration of their respective departments. They were responsible for enforcing the law, collecting taxes, maintaining public order, and overseeing public works projects.

The prefects were also tasked with implementing the policies of the central government, and were required to report regularly to the minister of the interior. This system ensured that the government's policies were enforced consistently and efficiently across all of France's departments.

One of the key features of the prefects' role was their ability to appoint and dismiss local officials within their departments. This gave them significant control over the administration of their regions, and allowed them to ensure that local officials were loyal to the central government and committed to enforcing its policies.

The prefects were also responsible for maintaining public order, and had the power to call upon the military to assist them in this task. They could also suspend local officials who were deemed to be hindering the government's efforts to maintain order.

Overall, the creation of the prefects represented a significant shift in the way that France was governed. By creating a centralized administrative system that was overseen by loyal officials appointed by the central government, Napoleon was able to ensure that his policies were enforced effectively and efficiently across the entire country.

The system of prefects that Napoleon introduced in France proved to be highly influential, and was adopted by many other countries in Europe and around the world. Today, many countries continue to use a similar system of central government-appointed officials to oversee their administrative regions.

In addition to their practical role in governing France, the prefects also played an important symbolic role in the construction of the French Empire. By creating a system of loyal officials who answered directly to him, Napoleon was able to reinforce his own status as the ultimate authority in France. The prefects embodied his vision of a centralized, efficient, and powerful state, and helped to create the image of the French Empire as a modern, forward-looking nation.

The French Revolution brought many changes to French society and government. Among these changes was the introduction of a new award system that recognized achievements in various fields. However, it was Napoleon Bonaparte who truly revolutionized the award system with the creation of the Legion of Honor.

The Legion of Honor was established in 1802 by Napoleon Bonaparte, who saw the need to honor those who had served France and the Empire. The award was designed to recognize the contributions of military and civilian individuals who had served the country with distinction. The Legion of Honor was intended to be the highest honor that could be bestowed upon an individual in France.

The Legion of Honor was created as an order of merit, and it was awarded to those who had shown exceptional service and achievement in various fields. The Legion was divided into five classes, and the highest class was reserved for the most distinguished individuals. In order to receive the Legion of Honor, one had to be nominated by someone in a high position of government or by a current member of the Legion.

The award ceremony for the Legion of Honor was a grand affair. Recipients were invited to the Palace of the Legion of Honor, where they were presented with a medal and a certificate. The medal was made of gold and silver, and it featured an image of Napoleon on one side and a wreath of laurels on the other. The certificate was signed by Napoleon himself, and it recognized the individual's achievements and service to France.

The Legion of Honor was not just an award, but it was also a way for Napoleon to create a new social class in France. The members of the Legion were known as "legionnaires," and they were given certain privileges and benefits. Legionnaires were exempt from certain taxes, and they were given priority for government positions and promotions. Membership in the Legion of Honor was seen as a sign of prestige and influence, and it was highly sought after.

The creation of the Legion of Honor was a major achievement for Napoleon. It was a way for him to recognize and reward those who had served the Empire, and it was also a way for him to create a new social class that was loyal to him and his regime. The Legion of Honor was an important part of

Napoleon's propaganda machine, and it helped to boost his popularity and support among the French people.

The legacy of the Legion of Honor lives on today. The award is still given out by the French government to recognize exceptional service and achievement in various fields. The medal has undergone some changes over the years, but it still features an image of Napoleon and a wreath of laurels. The Legion of Honor remains one of the highest honors that can be bestowed upon an individual in France.

In summary, the creation of the Legion of Honor was a major achievement for Napoleon Bonaparte. It was a way for him to recognize and reward those who had served France and the Empire, and it was also a way for him to create a new social class that was loyal to him and his regime. The award ceremony was a grand affair, and membership in the Legion of Honor was seen as a sign of prestige and influence. The legacy of the Legion of Honor lives on today, and it remains one of the highest honors that can be bestowed upon an individual in France.

The expansion of Napoleon's empire did not end with the borders of France. In fact, one of the most notable aspects of his reign was the annexation of numerous satellite states throughout Europe. These annexations came about through a combination of military conquest and diplomatic maneuvering, as Napoleon sought to establish a French-dominated hegemony over the continent.

One of the earliest examples of this expansionist policy was the annexation of the Republic of Genoa in 1805. This state, which had been a longstanding rival of France, was quickly overrun by French forces during the War of the Third Coalition. Rather than simply occupying the city and withdrawing, however, Napoleon chose to annex Genoa outright, incorporating it into France as the Department of Genoa.

This move was followed by the annexation of the Kingdom of Etruria in 1808. This state had been established as a French client state in 1801, but was dissolved by Napoleon in 1807 due to political instability. In 1808, however, Napoleon revived the Kingdom, renaming it the Grand Duchy of Tuscany and installing his sister, Elisa Bonaparte, as its ruler. This move was made possible by the fact that the previous Grand Duke of Tuscany had been forced to abdicate due to the collapse of the Kingdom of Naples, which had been one of its major supporters.

The annexation of other Italian states followed in quick succession. In 1808, Napoleon established the Kingdom of Italy, which incorporated the former Republic of Venice, the Duchy of Milan, and other territories under French control. This new state was ruled by Napoleon himself, who took on the title of King of Italy. The Kingdom of Naples was also annexed in 1808, and was merged with the Kingdom of Sicily to form the Kingdom of the Two Sicilies.

Napoleon's expansionist policy also extended beyond Italy. In 1810, he annexed the Kingdom of Holland, which had been established as a French client state in 1806. The King of Holland, Napoleon's brother Louis, had been unwilling to support French policy in Europe, leading to his forced abdication and the incorporation of the Kingdom into France.

The annexation of satellite states was not without its critics. Some saw it as a violation of national sovereignty, while others feared that it would lead to French domination of the entire continent. Nevertheless, Napoleon saw the creation of a French-dominated empire as the key to establishing his legacy as a great leader. He sought to create a system of government and administration that would endure long after his death, and viewed the annexation of new territories as an essential step in achieving this goal.

Despite the controversy surrounding his annexations, it cannot be denied that Napoleon's expansionist policy had a profound impact on European history. The establishment of the Kingdom of Italy, for example, paved the way for the eventual unification of the Italian peninsula, while the annexation of Holland helped to establish Dutch independence from French influence. Similarly, the creation of the Kingdom of the Two Sicilies helped to solidify French control over the Mediterranean, while the annexation of Genoa gave France control over important trade routes and access to the Ligurian Sea.

In the end, however, Napoleon's efforts to establish a lasting empire proved unsuccessful. The collapse of his regime following the disastrous Russian campaign of 1812 and the subsequent defeat at the Battle of Leipzig marked the end of his reign, and led to the restoration of the Bourbon monarchy in France. Nevertheless, his legacy as an empire-builder and conqueror remains a significant chapter in the history of Europe, and his annexation of satellite states played a key role in shaping the political landscape of the continent for decades to come.

The story of Napoleon Bonaparte, the French Emperor, is one that has captured the imagination of many historians and scholars over the years. He is known for his military conquests and political achievements, as well as his eventual downfall and exile. The events of his life and rule have been the subject of much debate and analysis, and his legacy still remains a topic of discussion today.

Napoleon's exile is one of the most intriguing aspects of his life. It is a tale of a man who was once the most powerful ruler in Europe, brought down by his own ambition and the opposition of other European powers. It is a story of defeat and triumph, of sadness and hope, and of the enduring legacy of one of history's greatest figures.

The exile of Napoleon began in 1814, after his defeat in the War of the Sixth Coalition. He was forced to abdicate his throne and was exiled to the island of Elba, off the coast of Italy. Despite the setback, Napoleon remained determined to regain his power and was soon planning his return to France.

In 1815, Napoleon escaped from Elba and returned to France, where he was welcomed by the people and quickly regained his position as Emperor. However, his victory was short-lived, as he was soon defeated by the Allied Powers at the Battle of Waterloo. This defeat led to his second and final exile, this time to the remote island of Saint Helena in the South Atlantic.

Napoleon's exile on Saint Helena was a far cry from his previous life as Emperor of France. He was confined to a small house on the island, where he was closely watched by British guards. Despite this, Napoleon remained active and engaged, dictating his memoirs and engaging in intellectual discussions with those around him.

During his exile, Napoleon's health began to deteriorate. He suffered from various ailments, including stomach problems and a persistent cough, which eventually led to his death on May 5, 1821. His body was returned to France in 1840 and is now buried in a tomb at Les Invalides in Paris.

The exile of Napoleon had significant consequences for the French Empire and for Europe as a whole. In the years following his downfall, France underwent a period of political instability, with several changes in government and a series of unsuccessful military campaigns.

The exile of Napoleon also marked the end of an era in European history. It was the final act in the long struggle for power and influence that had characterized the continent for centuries. With his defeat, the balance of power shifted in Europe, leading to a new period of peace and stability.

Despite his defeat and exile, Napoleon's legacy continues to be felt today. He is remembered as one of the most innovative and successful military commanders in history, and his political achievements, such as the introduction of the Napoleonic Code, have had a lasting impact on French and European society.

In summary, the exile of Napoleon was a defining moment in European history. It marked the end of an era of conflict and the beginning of a new era of peace and stability. It also marked the end of the reign of one of history's greatest figures, whose legacy continues to be felt today.

Chapter 8: The Continental System and the War of 1812

The French Revolution brought about significant changes in the political, social, and economic landscape of France. But it was Napoleon Bonaparte who transformed France into a formidable empire that rivaled the great powers of Europe. One of the key policies that Napoleon introduced to challenge Britain's naval supremacy was the Continental System, which aimed to isolate the British economy from the rest of Europe.

The Continental System was announced by Napoleon in the Berlin Decree of 1806, which stated that no European country was allowed to trade with Britain or any of its colonies. The goal was to strangle the British economy, which heavily relied on overseas trade, and weaken its military power. To enforce the Continental System, Napoleon established a network of allies and satellite states throughout Europe that would cut off all trade routes to Britain.

At first, the Continental System appeared to be a success, as many countries in Europe joined the alliance and stopped trading with Britain. The French economy also benefited from the system, as it created a captive market for French goods and boosted French industry. However, the policy soon ran into difficulties, as Britain responded with its own blockade of European ports and started to smuggle goods into the continent.

The Continental System also had negative consequences for Napoleon's allies and satellite states, as it caused economic disruption and led to shortages of essential goods. Russia, in particular, was hard hit by the system, as it relied heavily on exports of grain and other commodities to Britain. In retaliation, Russia withdrew from the alliance and resumed trade with Britain, a move that eventually led to the disastrous French invasion of Russia in 1812.

The Continental System ultimately failed to achieve its goals, as Britain's economy remained resilient, and the system caused economic hardship for Napoleon's allies and satellite states. The policy also created resentment towards France and contributed to the eventual downfall of Napoleon's empire.

Despite its shortcomings, the Continental System had a lasting impact on European trade and economic relations. It set the stage for the development of a modern system of international trade and finance and influenced the growth of nationalism in Europe. The system also paved the way for future economic warfare tactics and had a profound impact on the subsequent history of Europe.

In summary, the Continental System was one of Napoleon's most significant policies, aimed at challenging Britain's naval supremacy and isolating its economy from the rest of Europe. Although it initially appeared to be successful, the policy ultimately failed to achieve its goals and caused economic hardship for Napoleon's allies and satellite states. However, the system had a lasting impact on European trade and economic relations and paved the way for future economic warfare tactics.

The early 19th century was a period of immense political upheaval in Europe, with Napoleon Bonaparte, the French Emperor, at the center of it all. As the most powerful man in Europe, Napoleon sought to extend his power beyond the confines of France, and he believed that one of the keys to doing so lay in crippling Great Britain economically. Thus, he devised the Continental System, an economic blockade against British trade in Continental Europe. This system was enforced through a series of decrees, the most important of which was the Berlin Decree, issued in November 1806.

The Berlin Decree marked a turning point in the history of Europe, as it signaled Napoleon's determination to take on Britain's naval dominance with economic warfare. It declared that British trade was prohibited in all the territories under French control, and all merchandise that had come from Great Britain or its colonies was to be seized and destroyed. This was to be enforced through the imposition of heavy fines on anyone found to be trading with the British. Furthermore, all ships that had sailed from British ports, or that had been visited by British warships, were to be prevented from entering any French port.

The Berlin Decree was a clear indication of Napoleon's intentions to challenge Britain's economic power. He believed that by cutting off British trade with Continental Europe, he could not only weaken the British economy, but also create a united European front against the British. This would ultimately lead to his own domination of the continent. However, the implementation of the Continental System was not without challenges.

The Berlin Decree was initially met with widespread compliance from the various countries under French control. The French had successfully created a vast continental market for their goods, and the British found themselves cut off from this lucrative market. However, the success of the Continental System was short-lived. The British responded by imposing their own economic blockade against Continental Europe, and this led to a decline in European trade. The French attempted to enforce the system through a series of increasingly harsh measures, but this only led to resentment and opposition from the populations of the countries under French control.

The Berlin Decree was also instrumental in causing the downfall of Napoleon's empire. The economic blockade had a devastating impact on the economies of the countries under French control, and this led to widespread unrest and rebellion. The Continental System ultimately proved to be a failure, as the British were able to circumvent the blockade by trading with other countries. It also led to a significant decline in French trade, and this contributed to the collapse of Napoleon's empire.

In summary, the Berlin Decree was an important moment in the history of Europe, as it marked Napoleon's attempt to challenge British naval dominance through economic warfare. The Continental System had far-reaching implications for the economies of the countries under French control, and it ultimately contributed to the downfall of Napoleon's empire. Despite its failure, the Berlin Decree was an important development in the evolution of economic warfare, and it served as a model for future efforts to use economic means to achieve political ends.

The Napoleonic Wars are among the most significant events in modern history. The scale and scope of these conflicts, which engulfed most of Europe for over a decade, have made them a subject of intense study and fascination. Among the many campaigns of this era, the Peninsular War stands out as one of the most complex and protracted. This conflict, which lasted from 1808 to 1814, involved multiple armies, alliances, and political factions, and had far-reaching consequences for the future of Europe.

At the heart of the Peninsular War was the French emperor Napoleon Bonaparte's attempt to establish his continental system, an economic blockade that aimed to isolate Britain and force it to sue for peace. This system, which prohibited European countries from trading with Britain, was intended to weaken the British economy and reduce its military power. However, its implementation had unintended consequences, particularly in Spain and Portugal.

The Iberian Peninsula was a crucial link in the global trade network that Britain relied on. The British had long-standing economic and political ties with Portugal, which was one of its oldest allies. In 1807, the French invaded Portugal, prompting the Portuguese royal family to flee to Brazil. This event effectively made Portugal a British protectorate and led to the deployment of British troops to the region.

In 1808, Napoleon ordered the invasion of Spain, which had become a key ally of France in the continental system. However, the Spanish population rose up in revolt against the French, and this sparked a wider conflict that soon engulfed the entire peninsula. The British saw an opportunity to strike a blow against Napoleon's ambitions, and they launched a campaign to support the Spanish resistance.

The Peninsular War was characterized by a series of fierce battles, sieges, and guerrilla warfare. The Spanish and Portuguese forces, supported by the British, fought a series of campaigns against the French. These conflicts often involved complex alliances and shifting loyalties. In some cases, Spanish forces fought against Portuguese forces, while British forces found themselves battling against Spanish forces that had sided with the French.

One of the most notable campaigns of the war was the siege of Ciudad Rodrigo. This fortress town was one of the key strongholds held by the French, and its capture was seen as crucial to breaking the French hold on the region. The siege lasted for several weeks, and it was marked by intense fighting and brutal tactics. The British ultimately emerged victorious, but the siege had taken a heavy toll on both sides.

The Peninsular War also saw the emergence of new military tactics and innovations. The Spanish guerrilla fighters, in particular, became known for their hit-and-run tactics and their ability to operate in difficult terrain. The British, meanwhile, introduced new forms of artillery and made use of the latest military technology.

Despite the challenges faced by the Spanish and Portuguese forces, they were ultimately able to hold off the French and force them to retreat. The Peninsular War played a crucial role in the eventual defeat of Napoleon, and it helped to establish the British as a major military power in Europe. The conflict also had significant cultural and political consequences. The war inspired a new sense of national identity among the Spanish and Portuguese people, and it led to the creation of new political institutions and alliances.

In summary, the Peninsular War was a complex and multifaceted conflict that had far-reaching consequences for the future of Europe. The war was driven by the French emperor Napoleon's attempt to establish his continental system and isolate Britain. However, the conflict quickly grew into a wider struggle for control of the Iberian Peninsula, and it saw the emergence of new military tactics and alliances.

The invasion of Russia by Napoleon Bonaparte in 1812 is considered one of the most disastrous campaigns in military history. The campaign was launched with the aim of expanding the French Empire and consolidating

Napoleon's power in Europe, but it ultimately led to the downfall of his regime. Next, we will examine the reasons behind the invasion of Russia, the course of the campaign, and its consequences.

The Continental System, which was introduced by Napoleon in 1806, aimed to block British trade with the European continent in order to weaken the British economy and force them to negotiate a peace treaty. The system consisted of a series of trade restrictions and tariffs that were enforced by France and its allies. However, the system was not very successful and only served to hurt the economies of the countries that enforced it. Russia was one of the countries that suffered the most from the system, as they relied heavily on trade with Britain.

In 1810, Russia withdrew from the Continental System and resumed trade with Britain. This act was seen as a direct challenge to Napoleon's authority and his efforts to control Europe. In response, Napoleon decided to launch a military campaign against Russia to force them to rejoin the Continental System and submit to his authority.

The invasion of Russia began in June 1812, with the French army of about 600,000 men crossing the Niemen River and entering Russia. The campaign started off well for Napoleon, with his army winning several battles and capturing several Russian cities, including Smolensk and Moscow. However, the Russian army retreated and avoided direct engagement with the French, instead using scorched earth tactics to deny the French army food and shelter. This strategy, combined with the brutal Russian winter and the lack of supplies and reinforcements for the French army, led to the eventual collapse of the campaign.

By the end of the campaign, the French army had suffered massive losses, with only about 100,000 men returning to France. The invasion of Russia had cost Napoleon the majority of his troops, and he was forced to abdicate his throne and go into exile on the island of Elba. This campaign is often cited as one of the major factors in Napoleon's downfall, as it weakened his military power and undermined his reputation as an invincible conqueror.

The consequences of the invasion of Russia were far-reaching, both for France and for Europe as a whole. The defeat of Napoleon's army led to the weakening of the French Empire and the eventual restoration of the Bourbon monarchy. The campaign also weakened the Russian Empire and contributed to the spread of nationalist movements throughout Europe. The invasion of Russia is often cited as one of the turning points in European history, as it marked the beginning of the end of the Napoleonic era and the emergence of a new balance of power in Europe.

In summary, the invasion of Russia by Napoleon in 1812 was a pivotal event in European history. The campaign was launched with the aim of expanding the French Empire and consolidating Napoleon's power, but it ultimately led to his downfall and the weakening of the French Empire. The consequences of the campaign were far-reaching, as it marked the beginning of a new era in European history and contributed to the emergence of a new balance of power in the region.

In the year 1812, the world was plunged into a series of conflicts that would shape the course of history for years to come. Among them was the War of 1812, a conflict between the United States and Great Britain that is often overshadowed by the much larger and more well-known Napoleonic Wars. Yet, the War of 1812 was intimately tied to the events unfolding in Europe, particularly the Continental System established by Napoleon Bonaparte.

The Continental System was a policy enacted by Napoleon to cut off trade between Great Britain and continental Europe, with the aim of weakening Britain's economy and military power. In response, the British government implemented its own policy of economic warfare, including blockades of French ports and efforts to disrupt French trade.

These economic policies had significant consequences for the United States, which was caught in the middle of the conflict. American merchants were heavily involved in trade with both Europe and Britain, and the policies of both sides put pressure on the American economy. Britain's blockades, in particular, led to the seizure of American ships and goods, and sparked a series of confrontations between American and British forces.

The situation was further complicated by the presence of Native American tribes in the western territories, who had long-standing grievances with the United States government over land rights and other issues. The British government saw an opportunity to use these tensions to their advantage, and began supporting Native American forces in the hopes of destabilizing the American frontier.

In the summer of 1812, the United States declared war on Great Britain, citing a variety of grievances including British interference with American trade, the impressment of American sailors into British service, and British support for Native American forces. The war quickly became a brutal and bloody conflict, with battles raging across the Great Lakes region, the Atlantic coast, and the Gulf of Mexico.

Although the war had a number of significant battles and tactical victories on both sides, it ultimately ended in a stalemate. The Treaty of

Ghent, signed in December 1814, restored the pre-war status quo, with no major territorial or economic concessions made by either side.

Despite the lack of any clear winner, the War of 1812 had significant consequences for the United States and the broader world. The conflict marked a turning point in American history, cementing the country's status as a rising global power and leading to a renewed sense of national identity. It also set the stage for future conflicts between the United States and Great Britain, including the Mexican-American War and the Civil War.

From a broader perspective, the War of 1812 was also intimately connected to the Napoleonic Wars and the Continental System. Although the conflict was fought primarily in North America, its roots lay in the economic and political tensions of Europe, and its outcome had significant implications for the balance of power on the continent.

In many ways, the War of 1812 can be seen as a microcosm of the larger conflicts of the early 19th century, and a reminder of the interconnectedness of global events. As such, it deserves a place alongside the Napoleonic Wars and other major conflicts of the period, as a key moment in the history of the world.

Chapter 9: The Downfall of Napoleon and the Congress of Vienna

It was in the year 1812 that Napoleon Bonaparte, Emperor of the French, embarked on one of the greatest military campaigns in history, the invasion of Russia. The reasons for this military expedition were many, but the primary one was the desire to force Tsar Alexander I to comply with the Continental System, an economic blockade that Napoleon had imposed against Great Britain. In addition, Napoleon wanted to extend his empire into the east, and the vastness of Russia offered the perfect opportunity to do so. However, despite Napoleon's military prowess, the campaign would ultimately prove to be a costly failure, with disastrous consequences for his empire.

The initial phase of the campaign was marked by several military successes, including the capture of Smolensk and the Battle of Borodino, which was the largest and bloodiest single-day battle of the Napoleonic Wars. However, these successes came at great cost to the French army, which suffered heavy casualties, and by the time they reached Moscow, the army was exhausted and demoralized.

Upon arriving in Moscow, Napoleon hoped to find the Tsar willing to negotiate a peace settlement. However, the city had been abandoned by the Russian authorities, and a devastating fire broke out, leaving the French army stranded in a burned-out city without supplies or shelter. Despite this setback, Napoleon refused to give up, and he attempted to negotiate a peace settlement with the Russians, but his terms were too harsh, and the Tsar refused to accept them.

With winter approaching and his army already weakened, Napoleon was faced with a difficult decision: to continue the campaign or to retreat. He chose to retreat, but the Russian army, now reinvigorated and reinforced, pursued the retreating French, harrying them at every turn. The retreat quickly turned into a disaster, with the harsh Russian winter taking its toll on the already weakened and demoralized French army.

The retreat was marked by hunger, cold, disease, and the constant threat of attack from the Russian army. The Grand Army, which had entered Russia with over 600,000 men, was reduced to just 100,000 by the time it crossed the border into Poland. The campaign had been a costly failure, and it marked the beginning of the end for Napoleon's empire.

The reasons for the failure of the Russian campaign are many, but one of the primary factors was Napoleon's overconfidence in his abilities and the effectiveness of his army. He had underestimated the vastness of Russia and the difficulty of fighting a war in such a vast and inhospitable country. In addition, the failure of the Continental System meant that the campaign was no longer economically viable, and the loss of men and resources proved to be too great a burden for the French economy to bear. The Russian campaign also had wider implications for the Napoleonic Wars and for Europe as a whole. The failure of the campaign weakened Napoleon's position, and it emboldened his enemies, who saw an opportunity to defeat him. The Battle of Leipzig, which took place the following year, marked the beginning of the end for Napoleon's empire, as it signaled the start of a series of defeats that would lead to his ultimate downfall. In summary, the Russian campaign was a critical event in the history of Napoleon's empire, and it had far-reaching consequences for Europe as a whole. It was a costly failure that exposed the weaknesses of the French army and marked the beginning of the end for Napoleon's empire. The reasons for its failure were many, but ultimately, it was a combination of factors, including overconfidence, poor planning, and the harsh Russian winter, that led to the campaign's downfall. In the annals of military history, few battles are as significant as the Battle of Leipzig, fought between the forces of Napoleon Bonaparte and the allied armies of Russia, Austria, and Prussia in October of 1813. The battle, which took place near the city of Leipzig in Saxony, Germany, is often referred to as the "Battle of Nations" due to the large number of troops involved on both sides, with estimates ranging from 500,000 to 600,000 soldiers. The Battle of Leipzig marked a turning point in the Napoleonic Wars, and ultimately led to the downfall of Napoleon's empire. After several years of military successes, Napoleon's fortunes began to decline in the early 1800s, as his empire became embroiled in a series of wars and conflicts that drained its resources and strained its military forces.

The Battle of Leipzig was the culmination of these conflicts, and was fought over the course of three days, from October 16 to October 19, 1813. The battle was preceded by a series of smaller skirmishes and engagements between the two sides, as the allied forces attempted to force Napoleon's troops out of Germany and push them back into France.

The allied forces were led by a coalition of commanders, including Prince Karl Philipp of Schwarzenberg, General Gebhard Leberecht von Blücher, and Tsar Alexander I of Russia. Their troops were drawn from a variety of different countries, including Russia, Prussia, Austria, and Sweden, and were united in their determination to defeat Napoleon and restore order to Europe.

Napoleon's forces, by contrast, were composed primarily of soldiers from France, as well as other countries that had been incorporated into the French Empire. Although Napoleon was widely regarded as one of the greatest military commanders of his time, his forces were outnumbered by the allied armies and were at a disadvantage in terms of resources and supplies. Despite these challenges, Napoleon's troops fought valiantly during the Battle of Leipzig, launching several successful attacks against the allied forces and inflicting heavy casualties. However, as the battle wore on, the allied armies began to gain the upper hand, and Napoleon was eventually forced to retreat.

The Battle of Leipzig was a significant turning point in the Napoleonic Wars, and marked the beginning of the end for Napoleon's empire. After his defeat, Napoleon was forced to abdicate his throne and go into exile on the island of Elba, while the allied forces occupied Paris and began the process of restoring order to Europe.

The Battle of Leipzig also had far-reaching consequences for the world at large, and helped to shape the political and military landscape of Europe for decades to come. The defeat of Napoleon's forces paved the way for the Congress of Vienna, a series of meetings and negotiations that sought to establish a new balance of power in Europe and prevent future conflicts. Despite the significance of the Battle of Leipzig, however, its legacy has been somewhat overshadowed by other events in the Napoleonic Wars, such as the Battle of Waterloo and Napoleon's eventual exile to Saint Helena. Nevertheless, the Battle of Leipzig remains an important moment in the history of Europe, and a testament to the bravery and sacrifice of the soldiers who fought and died on both sides of the conflict. The events that led to the First Abdication of Napoleon, the most powerful ruler in Europe at the time, were complex and multifaceted. As a consequence of the disastrous Russian campaign, the French Empire was in disarray, and the armies of the Allied forces were closing in on Paris. In March 1814, Napoleon was forced to abdicate and was exiled to the island of Elba, a small Mediterranean island off the coast of Italy. The reasons for Napoleon's abdication are many and varied. The most immediate cause was the military situation. The Russian campaign had been a catastrophic failure, resulting in the loss of an entire army and severely weakening the French military. The allied forces of Russia, Austria, Prussia, and Great Britain took advantage of the situation, launching an invasion of France that threatened to topple the French Empire. With his armies scattered and weakened, Napoleon was unable to hold back the Allied advance and was forced to retreat towards Paris.

However, the causes of the French defeat were not solely military. Napoleon's Continental System, a blockade against British trade in continental Europe, had resulted in a series of economic and political repercussions that had weakened France's economy and its relationships with its allies. The system, intended to isolate Britain and weaken its economy, had failed to achieve its objectives and had instead created a series of trade imbalances and political tensions that had undermined the French position in Europe. The political situation in France was also a factor in Napoleon's abdication. The revolution of 1789 had left a legacy of political instability and social unrest that continued to plague France throughout the Napoleonic era. The restoration of the Bourbon monarchy was a goal shared by many Frenchmen, and Napoleon's rule had been marked by repeated attempts to suppress opposition and maintain his grip on power. With his position increasingly untenable, Napoleon was forced to abdicate on April 6, 1814. He was exiled to the island of Elba, where he was allowed to rule as a sovereign prince with a small army and some limited control over the island's affairs.

Despite his exile, Napoleon remained a figure of great interest and fascination in Europe. His campaigns, his military tactics, and his sweeping ambitions had left an indelible mark on the continent, and his legend only grew during his exile. In 1815, he escaped from Elba and returned to France, leading his famous Hundred Days campaign in an attempt to reclaim his empire. Though he was ultimately defeated at the Battle of Waterloo, his legacy continued to inspire generations of soldiers and leaders.

In many ways, the First Abdication marked the end of an era. The Napoleonic era had been one of immense change and transformation in Europe, marked by sweeping political and social reforms, vast military campaigns, and the rise of nationalism and the nation-state. Napoleon had been at the center of all of these developments, and his abdication marked a turning point in European history.

The First Abdication also marked the beginning of a new era, as the Allied powers struggled to create a new order in Europe in the wake of Napoleon's defeat. The Congress of Vienna, held in 1815, was intended to create a new balance of power in Europe and prevent any one nation from becoming too dominant. The principles of the Congress, including the principle of the balance of power, would shape European politics for decades to come.

In summary, the First Abdication of Napoleon was a complex and multifaceted event that marked the end of an era and the beginning of a new one. It was the result of a combination of military, economic, and political factors, and it set in motion a series of events that would shape European history for years to come.

The Hundred Days was a period of tumultuous change in French history. It marked the return of Napoleon Bonaparte to power after his exile on the island of Elba, and the brief resurgence of his Empire in France. The Hundred Days were characterized by rapid military and political developments that culminated in Napoleon's final defeat at the Battle of Waterloo.

Napoleon's return to France was greeted with mixed feelings. Some saw him as a savior who could restore order and stability to a nation that had been in chaos since his abdication in 1814, while others saw him as a power-hungry tyrant who would plunge France back into war and destruction.

Regardless of public opinion, Napoleon quickly set about reorganizing his army and reestablishing his control over the French government. He was able to rally much of the French population to his cause, and his army grew rapidly in size and strength.

Napoleon's reign was not without its challenges, however. The Allied powers had united against him, and the Congress of Vienna had redrawn the map of Europe in a way that weakened France and strengthened its neighbors. The British Navy had blockaded French ports, and the continental system was no longer effective. The economic situation was dire, and the French people were suffering.

Despite these challenges, Napoleon was determined to reclaim his former glory. He embarked on a series of military campaigns, hoping to expand his empire and reestablish French dominance in Europe. But his ambitions were thwarted at every turn. The Battle of Waterloo, fought on June 18, 1815, marked the end of his hopes for a military victory. He was finally defeated by a coalition of British, Dutch, and Prussian forces, led by the Duke of Wellington.

Napoleon was subsequently exiled once again, this time to the remote island of Saint Helena in the South Atlantic. There he lived out the remainder of his days, dictating his memoirs and reflecting on his life and career.

The Hundred Days were a time of great turmoil and upheaval in French history. They marked the end of the Napoleonic era, and the beginning of a new period of French history characterized by political instability and economic hardship. Despite the challenges he faced, Napoleon's legacy remains an enduring symbol of French power and glory.

In the aftermath of Napoleon's defeat, the powers of Europe gathered together in the Congress of Vienna to reorganize and reestablish the balance of power on the continent. The Congress of Vienna, which lasted from September 1814 to June 1815, was one of the most significant diplomatic gatherings in European history.

The Congress was attended by representatives from all of the major European powers, including Austria, Britain, France, Prussia, and Russia, as well as smaller states such as Denmark and Sweden. The Congress was intended to be a forum for the negotiation of peace treaties and the redrawing of national borders, but it quickly became a forum for the discussion of broader political and social issues.

One of the major concerns of the Congress was the reestablishment of the European balance of power, which had been upset by Napoleon's conquests. The delegates sought to create a system of checks and balances that would prevent any one state from becoming too powerful and threatening the stability of Europe. To this end, they established a number of alliances and coalitions that would allow the major powers to work together to maintain the balance of power.

Another major concern of the Congress was the issue of territorial boundaries. The Congress sought to create a stable and permanent system of national boundaries that would be respected by all of the major powers. This was a difficult task, given the numerous changes that had occurred as a result of Napoleon's conquests. However, by the end of the Congress, most of the major powers had agreed to a new system of national boundaries that would remain largely unchanged for decades to come.

The Congress also addressed the issue of political and social reform. Many of the delegates were concerned about the rising tide of nationalism and liberalism, which they saw as a threat to the established order. To address these concerns, they established a number of institutions and policies designed to promote stability and order, including the Holy Alliance, which was created to promote Christian values and conservative politics.

Despite its successes, the Congress of Vienna was not without its critics. Some believed that the Congress had not gone far enough in promoting political and social reform, while others argued that it had failed to address the fundamental causes of the problems that had led to Napoleon's rise in the first place. Nonetheless, the Congress of Vienna remains a landmark event in European history, and its legacy can still be felt today in the political and social systems of many of the countries that participated in it.

Chapter 10: Napoleon's Legacy and Influence on World History

The Napoleonic Code, also known as the French Civil Code, was introduced by Napoleon Bonaparte in 1804. This set of laws was intended to replace the patchwork of laws and customs that existed in France before the Revolution, and establish a uniform legal system throughout the country. The Code was based on the Roman legal tradition, and was designed to be a concise, clear, and easily understood body of law.

The Code was an important reform for France, and had a profound impact on the legal systems of other countries, particularly in Europe and Latin America. It was seen as a model for modern legal systems, and was adopted, in whole or in part, by many other countries.

The Code consisted of five books, covering civil law, commercial law, maritime law, and the law of civil procedure. The civil law section established principles of property law, contract law, family law, and inheritance law. The commercial law section covered topics such as bankruptcy, commercial contracts, and negotiable instruments. The maritime law section dealt with maritime commerce and shipping, while the law of civil procedure set out the rules for litigation and court procedure.

One of the key principles of the Code was the idea of legal equality. The Code abolished feudalism and established a system of equal rights and duties for all citizens. It also abolished privileges based on birth or social status, and established the principle of meritocracy. This was a major step forward in the development of modern legal systems, and helped to promote social mobility and economic development.

The Code was also notable for its emphasis on individual rights and freedoms. It enshrined the right to property, the freedom of contract, and the freedom of religion. It also recognized the right to a fair trial, the right to privacy, and the right to freedom from arbitrary arrest and detention. These principles were revolutionary at the time, and continue to be important in modern legal systems.

The Napoleonic Code was not without its critics, however. Some argued that it was too rigid and inflexible, and that it did not allow for the evolution of the law in response to changing social and economic conditions. Others criticized its emphasis on individual rights, arguing that it ignored the social responsibilities that accompany those rights.

Despite these criticisms, the Napoleonic Code had a profound impact on the development of modern legal systems. It helped to establish the idea of legal equality, individual rights and freedoms, and a uniform system of law throughout a country. It influenced the legal systems of many other countries, and is still seen as a model for modern legal codes.

In summary, the Napoleonic Code was a significant reform in French law, and had a far-reaching impact on legal systems throughout the world. Its emphasis on legal equality, individual rights and freedoms, and a uniform system of law helped to promote social mobility and economic development, and established a model for modern legal codes. While it was not perfect, and faced criticism for its rigidity and inflexibility, its enduring legacy is a testament to its importance in the development of modern legal systems.

In the wake of Napoleon Bonaparte's conquests and reforms, a new sense of national identity began to emerge in Europe. Napoleon's empire sought to break down the barriers between regions and create a more cohesive, centralized state, but in doing so, he inadvertently helped to foster a sense of national pride and loyalty that would shape Europe for centuries to come.

Before Napoleon, most people in Europe identified more closely with their local region or city than with a broader national identity. In France, for example, people saw themselves as Bretons or Normans or Parisians, rather than as "French" in the modern sense of the word. Napoleon's military conquests and political reforms helped to change that. By creating a centralized government and standardizing laws and administrative procedures across his empire, he helped to create a sense of unity among the people he ruled.

At the same time, Napoleon's policies also created resentment among those who felt that their regional identities were being suppressed. In Spain, for example, Napoleon's attempts to impose French-style laws and institutions led to a rebellion that eventually drove the French out of the country. In other parts of Europe, such as Italy and Germany, Napoleon's rule helped to foster a sense of national identity by providing a common enemy and a shared struggle against foreign domination.

After Napoleon's defeat and the Congress of Vienna in 1815, many of the old borders and political structures were restored, but the sense of national identity that had been awakened by Napoleon's empire could not be easily extinguished. In many parts of Europe, people continued to identify more closely with their nation than with their local region or city. This sense of nationalism would play a major role in the events of the 19th and 20th centuries, including the unification of Italy and Germany, the rise of nationalist movements in Eastern Europe, and the two world wars.

One of the lasting legacies of Napoleon's empire was the Napoleonic Code, also known as the French Civil Code. This legal system, which was introduced in 1804, helped to standardize laws and legal procedures across France and other parts of Europe that were under French control. It was based on the principles of equality before the law, the right to private property, and the sanctity of contracts, and it served as a model for legal reform throughout the world.

The Napoleonic Code was notable for its emphasis on individual rights and freedoms, and it helped to shape modern legal systems in many countries, including Germany, Italy, and Japan. It also influenced the development of civil law systems in Latin America and other parts of the world. Today, the principles of the Napoleonic Code continue to underpin the legal systems of many countries, and they are recognized as an important milestone in the development of modern law.

In addition to its influence on legal systems, Napoleon's empire also had a significant impact on the development of modern nationalism. By creating a centralized government and breaking down regional barriers, Napoleon helped to create a sense of unity among the people he ruled. This sense of national identity was strengthened by the shared struggle against foreign domination and by the creation of new symbols and traditions that emphasized national pride and loyalty.

Today, the legacy of Napoleon's empire can still be seen in the political and cultural landscape of Europe. The sense of national identity that was fostered by Napoleon's conquests and reforms continues to shape the way that people think about themselves and their place in the world. The Napoleonic Code and other legal reforms introduced by Napoleon helped to lay the foundation for modern legal systems, while his military innovations and strategic genius continue to influence the conduct of warfare to this day. Overall, Napoleon's impact on Europe and the world was immense, and his legacy continues to be felt in countless ways.

The impact of Napoleon's Empire on the evolution of European cooperation and integration cannot be overstated. During his reign, Napoleon introduced numerous reforms, military campaigns, and political changes that would set the stage for a united Europe in the future. His vision of a continental system, where national borders were less significant and a more integrated economic system would promote prosperity, served as a model for the development of the modern European Union.

Napoleon's empire was built on the principles of rationality, efficiency, and modernization. His reforms were aimed at creating a more centralized and efficient government, promoting economic growth, and spreading the benefits of education and enlightenment to all. The Napoleonic Code, which he introduced in 1804, became a model for civil law systems around the world, and his educational reforms laid the groundwork for modern public education systems.

The continental system was a key component of Napoleon's vision for Europe. It aimed to create a single economic area that would promote trade, commerce, and prosperity. By imposing a blockade on British goods, Napoleon hoped to force Britain to negotiate a peace treaty and recognize the French Empire's dominance over the continent. While the continental system ultimately failed to achieve its goals, it laid the groundwork for modern European economic integration, which has been a driving force for European prosperity in the post-war era.

Napoleon's military campaigns also played a significant role in shaping Europe's modern borders. His conquests and annexations created new territories, redrawn borders, and established new states, many of which still exist today. These territorial changes, in turn, created new economic, social, and cultural opportunities and challenges that helped shape the course of modern European history.

Furthermore, Napoleon's empire provided a model for centralized government and modernization that influenced other European countries in the decades that followed. The need to compete with France and keep up with its rapid modernization led other European nations to adopt similar reforms in areas such as education, transportation, and industry.

In addition to his impact on European politics and governance, Napoleon also contributed to the development of European culture and identity. His campaigns and conquests helped spread French language and culture across Europe, while his patronage of the arts and literature supported the development of new cultural movements and styles. The French Empire under Napoleon was seen as a beacon of modernity and enlightenment, inspiring other European nations to embrace similar values and ideals.

In summary, Napoleon's empire was a significant force in shaping the evolution of European cooperation and integration. His reforms, military campaigns, and political changes created new opportunities and challenges, laying the groundwork for a more integrated and prosperous Europe in the future. The continental system, the Napoleonic Code, and his military campaigns continue to influence modern European politics, economics, and culture, highlighting the enduring impact of Napoleon's legacy on the continent.

In the annals of military history, few names are as prominent as Napoleon Bonaparte. The French Emperor's campaigns and tactics have been studied and emulated for centuries, and his legacy as a military leader remains unmatched. Even in the modern era, military strategists still analyze and employ Napoleon's tactics and innovations on the battlefield. This essay will examine the continued relevance of Napoleon's military strategies in modern warfare.

Napoleon's military genius was evident in his innovative use of tactics, including the Corps system, massed artillery, and flanking maneuvers. These innovations allowed him to overcome superior forces, as demonstrated by his early victories in Italy and Egypt. Moreover, his introduction of the Grande Armée, a massive and highly trained fighting force, enabled him to conduct sustained campaigns against multiple opponents simultaneously.

One of Napoleon's most significant contributions to modern warfare was his use of the Corps system. By dividing his armies into smaller units, he could move quickly and flexibly across the battlefield, allowing him to exploit weaknesses in his enemies' defenses. Today, modern militaries have adapted and refined this concept, incorporating it into their own structures. The U.S. Army, for example, has employed the modular force structure, which allows for more efficient and flexible deployment of troops and resources.

Napoleon's use of massed artillery also continues to influence modern warfare. He recognized the power of artillery in breaking down fortifications and disrupting enemy formations, and he employed it to great effect. Today, artillery remains a key component of modern armies, providing long-range fire support and precision strikes against enemy positions.

Perhaps Napoleon's most famous tactic was the flanking maneuver, or the "manoeuvre sur les derrières." By outflanking his opponents, Napoleon could disrupt their lines and force them to retreat or surrender. Today, flanking maneuvers remain an essential component of modern military strategy. The U.S. military, for example, often employs flanking maneuvers in its operations, seeking to gain positional advantages and surprise the enemy.

In addition to his tactical innovations, Napoleon also revolutionized logistics, intelligence gathering, and communications. He recognized the importance of supply lines, depots, and hospitals, ensuring that his armies were well-fed, equipped, and cared for. He also established a vast network of spies and informants, providing him with valuable intelligence on enemy movements and intentions. Finally, he pioneered the use of semaphore, a system of visual signaling, to communicate with his commanders across great distances.

Napoleon's legacy in military strategy extends beyond his tactical innovations and organizational reforms. His campaigns also exemplify the importance of strategic thinking and adaptability. Napoleon was a master of both offensive and defensive warfare, and he demonstrated a remarkable ability to adjust his tactics to suit changing circumstances. His strategic vision allowed him to identify and exploit the weaknesses of his enemies, while his tactical flexibility enabled him to seize and hold the initiative on the battlefield.

In summary, Napoleon Bonaparte's military strategies and innovations continue to influence modern warfare. His use of the Corps system, massed artillery, flanking maneuvers, logistics, intelligence gathering, and communications all continue to shape the way modern militaries operate. His strategic thinking, adaptability, and tactical flexibility also serve as models for modern military leaders. Though his reign as Emperor ended over 200 years ago, his legacy as a military genius remains relevant and enduring.

The figure of Napoleon Bonaparte is one of the most complex and debated in the annals of history. Some view him as a military genius and revolutionary hero, while others consider him a tyrant and a warmonger. The debate over Napoleon's legacy has persisted for two centuries and continues to fascinate scholars and the general public alike.

One of the main reasons for the ongoing fascination with Napoleon is his enduring impact on the course of European history. His conquests and reforms transformed the political, social, and economic landscape of the continent and ushered in a new era of modernity. Napoleon's Code Civil, for example, became the basis for legal systems throughout Europe and Latin America, while his campaigns helped to spread the ideas of nationalism and democracy.

Despite his accomplishments, however, Napoleon's legacy remains contested. On the one hand, he is admired for his military prowess and his efforts to modernize Europe. On the other hand, he is criticized for his aggressive expansionism, his autocratic tendencies, and his role in the deaths of millions of people.

Napoleon's image has also been shaped by the changing political and cultural landscape of Europe over the past two centuries. During the Romantic era, he was celebrated as a heroic figure who embodied the ideals of individualism, passion, and glory. In the 20th century, however, he was often depicted as a symbol of totalitarianism and imperialism, particularly in the aftermath of World War II.

Today, Napoleon's legacy continues to be debated and reinterpreted in various ways. Some see him as a model of military leadership, while others view him as a cautionary tale about the dangers of unchecked ambition and power. His life and achievements have inspired countless works of art, literature, and film, as well as numerous academic studies and public debates.

In recent years, there has been renewed interest in Napoleon's legacy, particularly in light of contemporary debates over nationalism, globalization, and the role of the state. Some have argued that Napoleon's vision of a united Europe, based on the principles of equality, liberty, and fraternity, is more relevant than ever in today's world. Others have criticized his methods and goals as inherently authoritarian and imperialistic.

Ultimately, the debate over Napoleon's legacy reflects the complex and multifaceted nature of history itself. The impact of his actions and ideas can be seen in everything from modern legal systems to political ideologies, from military strategy to cultural identity. Yet, at the same time, his legacy is shaped by the perspectives and biases of those who interpret it, and by the ever-changing forces of history and culture.

In the end, the enduring fascination with Napoleon is a testament to the power of history to shape our understanding of ourselves and the world around us. Whether we view him as a hero or a villain, a genius or a tyrant, his life and legacy continue to inspire and challenge us, and to offer new insights into the complexities and contradictions of the human experience.

Conclusion

In Conquerors: From Steppe to Empire, readers embark on a journey through the lives and legacies of some of history's greatest conquerors. From Genghis Khan's unification of the Mongol tribes to Napoleon Bonaparte's rise to power in post-revolutionary France, each of the four books in this bundle explores the unique circumstances that led to the creation and expansion of an empire.

In Genghis Khan: The Rise of a Conqueror, we see how a young boy named Temujin rose from obscurity to become one of the most feared and respected leaders in history. Attila the Hun: From Barbarian to Legend reveals the true story behind the man who terrorized the Roman Empire, and explores the cultural and societal factors that contributed to his reign of terror.

Alexander the Great: From Macedonia to the Indus takes readers on a journey through the life of the young king who conquered much of the known world before his untimely death at the age of 33. Finally, in Napoleon Bonaparte: From Revolution to Empire, readers witness the rise and fall of one of history's most enigmatic and ambitious leaders, from his humble beginnings as a Corsican soldier to his ultimate defeat at the Battle of Waterloo.

Through these four books, readers gain a deep understanding of the factors that led to the creation and expansion of empires, as well as the cultural and societal factors that shaped the lives of these four legendary conquerors. Conquerors: From Steppe to Empire is a must-read for anyone interested in history, leadership, and the enduring legacy of some of the world's greatest conquerors.

About A. J. Kingston

A. J. Kingston is a writer, historian, and lover of all things historical. Born and raised in a small town in the United States, A. J. developed a deep appreciation for the past from an early age. She studied history at the university, earning her degree with honors, and went on to write a series of acclaimed books about different periods and topics in history.

A. J.'s writing is characterized by its clarity, evocative language, and meticulous research. She has a particular talent for bringing the lives of ordinary people in the past to life, drawing on diaries, letters, and other documents to create rich and nuanced portraits of people from all walks of life. Her work has been praised for its deep empathy, its attention to detail, and its ability to make history come alive for readers.

In addition to her writing, A. J. is a sought-after speaker and commentator on historical topics. She has given talks and presentations at universities, museums, and other venues, sharing her passion for history with audiences around the world. Her ability to connect with people and make history relevant to their lives has earned her a devoted following and a reputation as one of the most engaging and insightful historical writers of her generation.

A. J.'s writing has been recognized with numerous awards and honors. She lives in California with her family, and continues to write and speak on historical topics.

Milton Keynes UK
Ingram Content Group UK Ltd.
UKHW021836031123
431812UK00015B/536